T0329851

Market Threads

Market Threads

HOW COTTON FARMERS AND TRADERS
CREATE A GLOBAL COMMODITY

Koray Çalışkan

PRINCETON UNIVERSITY PRESS

PRINCETON AND OXFORD

Library of Congress Cataloging-in-Publication Data
Çalışkan, Koray, 1972–
Market threads : how cotton farmers and traders create a global commodity / Koray
Çalışkan
p. cm.
Includes bibliographical references and index.
ISBN 978-0-691-14241-8 (hardcover : alk. paper) 1. Cotton trade. 2. Markets. I. Title.
HD9070.5.C35 2010
382'.41351—dc22
2009054355

British Library Cataloging-in-Publication Data is available

This book has been composed in Sabon

Printed on acid-free paper ∞

Printed in the United States of America

10 9 8 7 6 5 4 3 2 1

FOR ZEYNEP

Contents

Preface

WE LIVE IN THE AGE of the market without knowing how and whether it works. *Market Threads* addresses this puzzle at a time when new crises in world markets cannot be managed with old ideas. At the beginning of the twenty-first century, two hegemonic approaches govern our consideration of markets. The neoclassical hegemony insists that the market is a mechanism that draws on universal economic rationality. The free market reforms of the last quarter-century were inspired by this observation. On the other hand, the institutionalist hegemony argues that the market is embedded in society and calls for the study of the conditions making markets possible. This book argues that neither can fully grasp how markets work on the ground.

Since the 1980s, an increasing number of market studies has challenged the terms of the neoclassical and institutionalist debate, giving birth to a novel theoretical and empirical approach. By drawing on new directions of research on the market, *Market Threads* explores a simple question: What is a global market? Drawing on the production and trading of cotton, a global commodity that connects the three major economic activities in the world—industry, services, and agriculture—I examine how the world cotton market is produced and maintained on the ground. This book presents a detailed analysis of the arrangements, institutions, calculative devices, power relations, and forces on which the production and circulation of cotton depend. It starts by examining the mechanisms that make it possible to produce global, regional, and local spot, options, and futures prices. It then traces the circulation of cotton, exploring how it crosses various borders. Lastly, it examines how cotton is grown, studying the struggles of humans and nonhumans to control it in the countryside.

Market Threads deviates from the understanding of markets prevailing in both political economy and economic sociology. Markets do not just emerge as a relationship among self-interested buyers and sellers, governed by appropriate economic institutions. Nor are they to be understood as networks embedded in wider social structures. They are relations of power maintained every day by constant interventions; the production of mercantile tools such as prosthetic, associate, and rehearsal prices; and the waging of various forms of struggle among market actors. This book shows that researchers and policy-makers must focus on the specific practices of price realization and market-making and maintenance in order to understand the conditions of the vast majority of the global population whose survival is pegged to the working of world markets. Drawing on methods from the social study of science and technology, as well as new studies of markets developed in political science, sociology, economics, and economic sociology and anthropology, the book presents an analysis of how a multitude of market agents with different capacities to shape each others' possible fields of action negotiate, accept, reject, resist, and reproduce a global market that connects social positions to power.

Acknowledgments

As I CARRIED OUT THE RESEARCH and writing of the present book, I relied on the energy, inspiration, support, and friendship of many, without whose help the story I tell here would be shorter and incomplete. The Wenner-Gren Foundation for Anthropological Research, the American Research Center in Turkey (ARIT), and the Population Council Meawards Dissertation Grant funded most of the research. I am grateful to these three institutions. ARIT and Boğaziçi University (Scientific Research Grant BAP 07C302) also extended their support by funding various visits to the fieldwork sites in 2003 and between 2006 and 2009, allowing me fill in some of the gaps that appeared only as I began to envision this book.

Many people assisted me during the fieldwork and welcomed me into their lives. In Turkey, without the help of the following persons, I might still be carrying out the research: Cennet Uyanık, Durmuş Nizam, Fatma Nizam, Hasan Gök, Hayri Özmeriç, Hulusi Özbaşatak, Hüseyin Oymaz, Kerim Uyanık, Metin Budak, Murat Nizam, Nükhet Sirman, Pınar Nacak, Beyza Balpazarı, Turcan Uyanık, and Veli Yavaş. In Egypt, I received help from Abdel Aziz Mohammed Eesheey, Abdelmawla Ismail, Abubakr Ghoneim, Albert Gierend, Galal Al-Rifai, Hamdy Zidane, Hanaa Baddar, Madhet Al-Alfi, Mahmoud Abdel Aal, Mohammed Bishara, Moushira Elgeziri, Nawal Omran, Nicholas Hopkins, Rabie Wahba, Reem Saad, Sherene Hamdy, and Wagdy Hendy. Without the company and support of Laura Bier and Nawga Hassan Ali, neither my research nor the time I spent in Egypt would have been enjoyable. I am most indebted to the children, women, and men of the villages of Pamukköy, 'Izbet Sabri, and Kafr Gaffar, all of whom invited me to share their lives. I learned from their wisdom. I am especially grateful to the late Ahmet Uyanık of Pamukköy, whose friendship, support, and encouragement helped me become a better researcher. Without Mahmoud and Mohammed's help, I would not have been able to find my way around the Egyptian villages. In the United States, I am indebted to the following persons for helping me better appreciate the intricate details of cotton markets: Brijest Sampat, Dan Watts, Gerard Estur, Gerardo Garcia, Loukas Louktodis, Marco Varini, Mustafa Kocabaş, Pierre Viscolo, and Woodson Dunavant. William Griffin trained me in spot, futures, and options cotton markets. Without Bill's help, it would have been very difficult to comprehend the complex world of trading.

I would also like to acknowledge the following organizations for providing me invaluable institutional support during the research: the Land Center for Human Rights (Cairo), the Izmir Mercantile Exchange, the Alexandria Cotton Exporters' Association, Cotlook Ltd. (Liverpool), the International Cotton Advisory Council (Washington DC), the Agricultural Economics Research Institute (Ankara), and the Unions of Agricultural Cooperatives for the Sales of Figs, Raisins, Cotton, Olives, and Olive Oil (Izmir).

Many colleagues and friends helped me in thinking and rewriting this book. Without the editing help and wonderful critique of Hanan Kholoussy, Tiare Rath, Danielle Vinocur, Rania Jawad, Jacquelyn Mourad, Laura Kaehler, Julia Elyachar, Özlem Altan, and Sherene Seikaly, it would have been very difficult for me to navigate the rich alleys of the English language. Nina Ergin and Jennifer Slater read and edited the entire manuscript with great care in order to ensure that I express my ideas clearly. Special thanks go to Judy Warren for helping me develop new ways of making sense of the world. For their various forms of contribution to the book, I am also grateful to Andrew Barry, David Stark, Peter Lindner, Christian Berndt, Marc Boeckler, Peter Karnoe, Ceren Özselçuk, Donald MacKenzie, Fabian Muniesa, Deniz Yükseker, George Marcus, Hiro Miyazaki, James Ferguson, Janet Roitman, Javier Lezaun, Bruno Latour, Ethel Brooks, Jean-François Bayart, John Willis, Julie Graham, Karin Knorr Cetina, Katherine Fleming, Yuval Millo, Lila Abu-Lughod, Michael Gasper, Murat Yüksel, Olga Sezneva, Molly Nolan, Neil Brenner, Nejat Dinç, Petter Holm, Bill Carrick, Khaled Fahmy, Shiva Balaghi, Zachary Lockman, Sherene Seikaly, Verena Paravel, Phillip Mirowski, Ray Bush, Richard Swedberg, Sharon Zukin, Vincent A. Lepinay, Viviana Zelizer, Wilson Jacob, and Yahya Madra.

While I lived in New York City, I had the privilege of working with Talal Asad, Partha Chatterjee, Michael Gilsenan, Bertell Ollman, Tim Mitchell, and Elisabeth J. Wood. Among the many things I learned from them, a few were especially precious: the courage to ask questions, the patience to address them, and the humility to admit that a good answer is usually too good to be true. I believe that I have learned the first two fairly well. I would also like to express my appreciation to my Modern Standard Arabic teacher, Ahmad Farhadi, and also to Munir Fakher Eldin, who never let me give up, although I tried many times after realizing the great difficulty of mastering Arabic. Thanks are also due to Russel Sayyed, Hamdy Zidane, and Rafat Amin, without whom I would never have grasped colloquial Egyptian Arabic.

I received my undergraduate degree from Boğaziçi University, whose faculty was the first to help me appreciate the rich life of academia, without hiding its financial shortcomings. I owe to them a great debt for allowing me to envision an exciting life in research and teaching. I would like to thank Gürol Irzık and Ferda Keskin for helping me find my way. Like many others, I benefited greatly from the mentorship of Taha Parla. Thanks to his support, his superb teaching, and his many seminars that taught me to read for the second time, a whole new generation of scholars, including myself, has emerged, and I am honored to have them as my colleagues today. Also thanks to the students who have taken my course on Political Anthropology of Markets and Capitalism at Boğaziçi University. Their superb comments made this book a better one.

Having returned to Boğaziçi University as a professor, I could not have written this book in its present form without the continuous support of the Department of Political Science and International Relations. Many friends, professors, and colleagues helped me. Taha Parla, Mine Eder, Nükhet Sirman, Murat Akan, Özlem Öz, Zühre Aksoy, Binnaz Toprak, Yeşim Arat, and Fikret Adaman supported me immensely, and I thank them all.

Richard Baggaley from Princeton University Press encouraged and helped me write this book. Without his innovative editing, the present work would be much poorer. Of course, any mistakes that remain are my own.

İlker Bıçakçı, Alev Dumanoğlu, and Senem Saner were always around, even though geographically they lived far away. Nejat O. Dinç introduced me to the world of anthropology. Without his friendship, support, and influence, not only this book, but also my life, would be less enjoyable.

Michel Callon has been a careful reader of my work since I began to scribble strange ideas about markets. His own work has influenced my writing and thinking immeasurably. I am honored to now call Julia Elyachar a good friend. She has been my staunchest critic since she started to advise me. Michael Gilsenan never lost faith in me as I tried to use the tools of anthropology, of which he is a master.

My mentor, Tim Mitchell, could have written one more book if he had not spent so much of his spare time on me. His never-ending encouragement, generosity, intellectual brilliance, and unparalleled personality will continue to make him one of the richest sources of inspiration in my life. With him, during countless conversations and correspondence, I developed the questions asked in this book and arrived at ways to address them.

I would like to thank my immediate and extended family for their love. Without the unconditional support of my parents, Ruhsar and Süleyman Çalışkan, life would be much less enjoyable, as they have always been close by to help. Sezer Çalışkan and Sezin Okkan have been excellent friends, ready to do anything in their capacity in order to make my life better. Over the years, Ekrem and Nedret Çatay have become second parents, making it at times difficult to remember that I am actually not their son.

Elif Nare joined us as I began planning the book. Since then, she has been the richest source of happiness in my life. I hope that one day she forgives me for the time I took away from her to put into this book and other projects of mine.

My partner Zeynep Çatay's understanding attitude toward my long absence as I studied Arabic and carried out research, her patience and love that never ceased to make me feel privileged, her encouragement as I pursued my endless questions, and her contribution to my personal maturation have been the single largest support ever extended to me. Without Zeynep's love, both this work and my life would be incomplete, and for this, I dedicate the book to her.

Chapter 1 has been published in an earlier version as "The Meaning of Price in World Markets" in the *Journal of Cultural Economy* 2 (2009): 239–68. An earlier version of chapter 3 has been published as "Price as a Market Device: Cotton Trading in Izmir Mercantile Exchange" in *Market Devices, Sociological Review Monographs*, ed. M. Callon, Y. Millo, and F. Muniesa (Oxford: Blackwell Publishing), 241–60. Chapter 5 has appeared in *New Perspectives on Turkey* 37 (2007): 115–46. I would like to thank the publishers and editors for permitting me to use the material in this book.

Market Threads

How to Study a Global Market

WHAT IS A GLOBAL MARKET? *Market Threads* addresses this question by empirically analyzing the world cotton market and bringing together insights from the social sciences and new directions in the study of markets. For more than a quarter of a century, a social experiment unprecedented in world history has been in progress: neoliberal market reform on a global scale. This experiment has revealed a remarkable fact: we do not know how markets work, let alone what the term "global market" means in practice. This book presents a study of the making and maintenance of a global commodity market, drawing on twenty-four months of fieldwork on four continents. The research was carried out in seven market places that cover the rural and urban sites of the world cotton market: three cotton-growing villages—'Izbet Sabry and Kafr Gaffar (Lower Egypt), and Pamukköy (Western Turkey)—and four merchant cities—Izmir (Turkey), Alexandria (Egypt), Memphis (TN), and New York City.[1]

Markets are elusive. Disciplines have been established to study their nature; entire libraries are filled with accounts of how they work; and global institutions have been formed to facilitate their expansion. Nevertheless, a quick look at ambitious projects aiming to analyze markets reveals the striking and complete absence of an answer to the question "what is a market?"[2] Douglass North, the 1993 Nobel laureate in economics, has stated this point better than anyone else: "It is a peculiar fact that the literature on economics [. . .] contains so little discussion of the central institution that underlies neoclassical economics—the market."[3] More arresting still, this curious silence about the market is shared by competing social research paradigms that ostensibly represent different political aspirations. Hayek is considered the ultimate ideologue of market expansion. His oeuvre does not offer concrete insights into how markets work, but rather a set of theoretical assumptions about how markets disseminate subjective information by converting knowledge into prices and serve as a mechanism of resource distribution.

---

[1] All the names of villages, hamlets, their neighboring towns, and informants are pseudonyms, unless otherwise stated.

[2] For a review of this gap in market literature, see Lie (1997).

[3] Cited in Callon (1998).

For Marx, too, markets are elusive. *Capital* opens with a discussion of commodity markets, drawing on a hypothetical trading example of cotton. In his famous discussion, in which he discloses the "general formula for capital," perhaps one of the most important arguments in the history of political economic thinking, Marx presents the following statement: "If I purchase 2,000 lbs. of cotton for £100, and resell the 2,000 lbs. of cotton for £110, I have, in fact, exchanged £100 for £110, money for money" (Marx 1995). Because another trader could appear and take the very profit one makes during a market exchange, Marx concludes that one can make money, but not create value in markets.

A REVIEW OF LITERATURE ON THE MARKET

The study of the market was a formative research engagement during the period when all social science disciplines emerged. Anthropology began with studies of the human condition with a focus on various market and nonmarket exchange relations. The discipline of economics presents a variety of means to understand the market; one of its main branches, microeconomics, is entirely based on market analysis. Both sociology and political science have subdisciplines that study the market and the way markets relate to social and political worlds. Yet, we still do not know how markets work on the ground. How is it possible to address this puzzle within the existing literature on markets and their agents?

All sciences studying forms of the human condition have a subdiscipline studying economic phenomena. This vast literature falls into three broad categories, which only partially address the problem of the market: (1) the neoclassical approach, (2) institutionalism, and (3) social studies of the market. According to neoclassical researchers, the market refers to any domain of economic interaction, where prices are responsive to supply and demand. Unless impeded by nonmarket forces, all markets have a natural and spontaneous inclination to evolve into a perfectly self-regulating one, where resources are distributed efficiently, if not justly (Becker 1976; Marshall 1982; Balassa 1986; De Soto 1989). To ensure both the evolution of markets toward a perfect version and the market setting its prices freely, neoclassical researchers argue that nonmarket forces should not intervene in the delicate balance of supply and demand.

The neoclassical approach has been extremely influential, not necessarily in understanding markets, but in making them. These researchers' perception of the market as a natural balance of the forces of supply and demand has contributed to the making of markets by informing the construction of various options markets, ranging from agricultural commodities to securities (MacKenzie 2006). The neoclassical approach supplies options markets with a standard method for pricing the interaction of risk and time, thus exerting an effect on the price movements in futures and spot markets. One mirroring the other, the distinction between the theory of markets and the reality of exchange has become blurred. As I will argue in chapter 1, the Black and Scholes formula, the fundamental building block of all options markets, draws on the main assumptions of the neoclassical approach to the market.

Furthermore, most of the early experiments in neoliberal market reform took their inspiration from neoclassical research. The primary assumption was that, once the state was rolled back from intervening in market affairs, the rules of the market would ensure growth and development. As the early results proved disastrous, policy and academic circles gradually replaced market universalism with a hybrid approach located somewhere along the continuum between market universalism and institutionalism.[4] As many critics have noted, the neoclassical perspective is analytically weak; it cannot account for the conditions that sustain the very self-regulating market it prescribes. Critiques of neoclassical research have chronicled the empirical shortcomings of the approach and its neglect of the historical and social conditions that sustain even the market it imagines.[5] One of the strongest arguments has come from institutionalism.

Institutionalists have diverged from neoclassical researchers by arguing that all free markets require an institutional structure to mediate the convergence of market forces. Moreover, spontaneous development of markets could be stalled by nonmarket factors such as the state. From this perspective, institutions directly affect economic outcomes, and the agents of markets use them to reach their individual ends (Coase 1937; Williamson 1975; North 1977; Bates 1981; Wade 1988; Thompson 1991; Ensminger 1992).

Social Studies of the Market

Anthropological and sociological approaches, at times drawing on institutionalism, have contributed to a better understanding of markets in a variety of ways. The study of exchange and production relations has formed anthropology as a discipline. Although Barton and Seligman had

---

[4] Many differences within these approaches exist, such as an emphasis on transaction cost reduction in markets (Working 1949; Telser 1958; Williams 1986), or a stress on the idea of insurance (Keynes 1936; Hicks 1939; Johnson 1960; Williams 1986). For a review of this literature, see Goldberg (1988).

[5] For comprehensive reviews of this literature and its critiques, see Chaudhry (1993); Leys (1996).

touched on economic relations, it was the work of Malinowski (1922) and Mauss (1925) that contributed the most important theoretical building blocks to the incipient discipline of economic anthropology (Seligman et al. 1910; Malinowski 1922; Mauss 1954 [1925]).

Anthropological approaches to the market have created one of the discipline's longest debates between formalists and substantivists. Polanyi's *Great Transformation*, drawing on the work of early anthropologists such as Malinowski, prefigured the emergence of the substantivist approach to markets (Polanyi 1944). Substantivists derived inspiration and many central concepts from Polanyi; they argued that the study of markets in non-Western contexts requires the study of local relations of exchange, which are embedded in various sociocultural settings, whereas in the West the market has become mostly "disembedded" (Arensberg 1957; Chayanov et al. 1966; Kaplan 1968; Dalton 1971; Sahlins 1972; Halperin and Dow 1977). Echoing some of the institutionalist arguments, substantivists saw the emergence of markets as dependent economic encounters, always made and embedded in society or culture.

Formalists, on the other hand, while accepting the institutional power of the cultural contexts of markets, have argued that, regardless of the specifics of market or exchange contexts, the long-term economic rationality of individuals is universal. A student of Malinowski himself, Firth formulated the earliest formalist position and paved the way for methodological individualism in the social study of markets (Firth 1929, 1939). Formalist anthropologists, mostly following Firth's footsteps, borrowed their framework from neoclassical economics. They applied these assumptions to the non-West and held the view that, when it comes to economics, individuals in all social contexts behave in similar, universally recognizable ways (Bohannan and Dalton 1962; Salisbury 1962; Belshaw 1965; Bohannan and Dalton 1965; Burling 1968; Cancian 1968; Cook 1968; Epstein 1968; LeClair et al. 1968; Swetnam 1973; Schneider 1974).

Although formalists seem to have lost the debate to a variety of substantivist and institutionalist approaches, one strong point they have sustained is to resist essentializing a categorical difference in the logics of economic encounters in the West and the rest. Ironically, they achieved this by imposing a universal rationality across the board. Ethnographic research became synonymous with locating the emergence of these assumptions in fieldwork and recording an increasing number of empirical findings to show the validity of a few universalist assumptions.

Despite the fierce struggle between formalists and substantivists, there was still an important agreement between them.[6] They disagreed on the roles and importance of institutions, on the one hand, and individual

---

[6] For a more detailed discussion of this point, see Çalışkan and Callon (2009).

agencies, on the other hand. However, both the universal rationality of the individual and the embedded nature of institutional settings—the cornerstones of the difference between substantivists and formalists—are located in a universally accepted ground, defined by "the economy," drawing on the unquestioned distinction between production, consumption, and exchange. Wherever researchers go, whether their goal is to locate the rational individual or the embedded institution, they are certain to find a universalized understanding of a "society" and an "economy" that operate by producing things and exchanging them to finally consume the produced and exchanged goods (Çalışkan and Callon 2005, 2009) Formalists and substantivists were allies in pursing a specific anthropology of "the economy" as the making of either a universal individual or a deified society.

Another dimension of the silent peace between substantivists and formalists is their mutual construction of each others' explanatory space. Formalists have carved out an independent economic space of market rationality and located a universal individual in it as the agent of change. Substantivists, however, have located a different logic for nonmarket conditions, by building the very boundary between the market and its exterior. Finally, substantivists have problematized formalist theses on the workings of "the economy" as we know it in the West. The problem area here is the economy of the other. This, perhaps more than anything else, sealed the peace between the seemingly different strands of thought in economic anthropology.

It was a curious coincidence that in the late 1970s the entire debate between substantivists and formalists vanished at a time when the study of markets constituted the most urgent research program. The world entered an age of neoliberal reforms aimed at allowing domestic national markets to set their prices freely and then connecting them to an all-encompassing global market. A reconstruction of anthropology's curiosity and an internal critique of functionalist and/or structuralist tendencies in the discipline made the tacit peace visible (Clifford and Marcus 1986). As the debate waned, anthropologists realized that it narrowed research options, rather than opening them.

In the 1980s and 1990s, however, a number of new interdisciplinary approaches challenged both the terms of the formalist-substantivist debate and the main arguments of neoclassical and institutionalist research. These developments also provided revolutionary theoretical possibilities for field research (Mintz 1985; Thomas 1991; Gibson-Graham 1996; Wells 1996; Callon 1998; Elyachar 1999; Koptiuch 1999). Opening the black box of markets revealed that it was no more than a blank space, occupied by a diversity of struggles in both the West and the non-West (Tribe 1981). It was argued that the assumed characteristics of markets that facilitated economic analysis—such as information or rationality—were highly relative and contextual, and that, for instance, it was very difficult not only for the market agents but also for social scientists to acquire information (Dilley 1992). Hence, Gudeman has argued that many existing analyses drawing on formal economic models continually reproduce and discover their own assumptions in actual market relations (Gudeman 1986).

In 1985, with the publication of Granovetter's essay on the problem of embeddedness, the main arguments of substantivism reemerged in economic sociology (Granovetter 1985). A renewed interest in Polanyi's work in economic sociology prefigured the shaping of the debate, the development of which is reminiscent of the emergence of substantivism itself. Polanyi's statement that "human economy [. . .] is embedded and enmeshed in institutions, economic and noneconomic" became the point of entry to the neosubstantivism of embeddedness literature (Polanyi 1957). According to this approach, economic processes take place within social networks. In a move reminiscent of Durkheim's precaution concerning the noncontractual universe of every contract, this approach underscores the noneconomic universe of economic markets.

Without changing the theoretical cartography of the substantivist argument, sociologists have dragged the explanatory frame from the exotic non-West to the West. The critical potential of this operation is immense, for it shows in multiple ways the potential flaws of the formalist description of economic processes. However, the neosubstantivist approach has pursued a new objective with an old theory, which led its proponents to theorize the blurred boundary between the society and the economy and make the case for the embeddedness of the economic in the social.

Neosubstantivism provides for social theory a precaution against the universalizing tendencies of neoclassical logics.[7] Research has shown that the making of market prices and the organization of market places take place in socially embedded institutional forms and that due to their embedded nature markets connect social positions to power (Fligstein 1996; Uzzi 1996; Swedberg 1997; Carruthers and Stinchcombe 1999; Podolny 2001; Le Velly 2002; Velthuis 2003; Duina 2004; Uzzi and Lancaster 2004; Aspers 2005). It has also shown that markets and their prices are produced in settings embedded in cultures or systems of meaning (Velthuis 2003).

New Directions in the Social Study of Markets

Implicitly informed by a Foucauldian agenda of making visible the relationship between modern forms of scientific knowledge and power, and

---

[7] For a review of this literature, see Friedland and Robertson (1990); Lie (1997); Swedberg (1997).

explicitly drawing on Austin (1962), a group of researchers has revealed that modern economics and modern economic markets are mutually constructive. Bringing the insights of social studies of science and technology to the study of markets, these researchers have demonstrated that modern markets are not only represented but also manufactured by the institutionalization of neoclassical assumptions in market architectures (Callon 1998; Desrosieres 2001; Maurer 2002; Callon and Muniesa 2003; Lepinay 2003; Muniesa 2003; MacKenzie 2004; MacKenzie et al. 2007). *Market Threads* contributes to this literature in that it shows how global market prices of cotton are realized through the ways in which neoclassical assumptions have been deployed in futures and options markets.

Another related issue that has emerged in recent anthropological research is the increasing importance of research conducted by nonscientists and the ways in which it informs market agency (Callon 2003). *Research in the wild*, as Callon calls it, seems to be a central activity conducted every day by market agents; yet the everyday research of these subjects of research has not made it into sociological analyses so far (Callon et al. 2001). Especially in the working of markets, this insight seems to be central, because the very market work of traders starts with market research and continues with trying to make sense of the market in which it operates (Zaloom 2003; Levin 2004). The ways in which traders and all other market agents carry out research in the wild seems to be a crucial market activity that has yet to be researched extensively. Moreover, in combining nonprofessional and professional research in the university, market agents also contribute to the making of markets by imagining novel market designs.

A new strand of market research problematizes the ontological distinction that causes the gap between objects and subjects, between things and their circulation. According to this body of research, the anthropological terrain of markets is not a world of anthropogenic agents only. This research has two concentrations; the first shows that market agents and their tools interact in multiple and heterogeneous ways. The tools of market agents contribute to the making of the universe of possibilities, which make the economic action itself. The argument here is reminiscent of the difference between the lobby of the National Rifle Association (NRA) and their critics. The NRA argues that it is not guns that kill, but people. Their critics, being aware that guns are not just tools, argue that controlling them would have a direct effect on limiting their use.

Market tools are not just tools. As shown in the work of Knorr Cetina, and Brugger (2002), computers that are used to screen the markets can be the very market locations that make the terrain of trading possible. Similarly, the formulas used by traders to put together calculative capacities can further make and perform markets (Çalışkan 2003; Lepinay 2003; Muniesa

2003; Beunza and Stark 2004; Callon et al. 2007). This book contributes to this literature by arguing that even the market price itself is a mercantile tool produced to make traders trade cotton in international markets.

Social studies of science and technology, the second concentration of research that problematizes agency in markets, bring into focus the contribution of nonhumans to the making of markets and economic phenomena. Written from an ethnographic viewpoint, this literature underscores the inherent contingencies of social phenomena and how they take shape in the interaction of humans and nonhumans—such as insects, viruses, animals, or other incipient agencies (Latour 1999; Callon et al. 2001; Mitchell 2002). The contribution of nonhumans to the world in which humans live seems to be more visible in the making of world markets. As we will see in the last three chapters of the book, the fields where cotton and markets are produced are locations of a struggle between many actors, ranging from merchants and farmers to worms and weeds.

The concrete practices of everyday market maintenance represent another research site that has gained attention in the new directions in market research. Granovetter's work has shown that it requires endless everyday work of investing in relations and networks in order to make a market function (Granovetter and McGuire 1998). Similarly, Smith and Swedberg's work in securities has pointed toward a similar conclusion: it is crucial for markets to draw on a universe of everyday market work, from networking to research (Smith 1981; Swedberg 1990).

Social studies of finance have further created problems for the distinction between the seemingly different forms of capital—the productive and the financial. By focusing on the materiality of financial products and the sites of their creation, ethnographic work has demonstrated that what was taken to be a representation of the industrial has become a building block of an economic composition made up of cascading derivations. If this is the case, as Lepinay has argued, the question we should pursue is not the accuracy of representations assumed to be categorically separate from the realities they represent, as in the case of asymmetrical price information arguments. The main question for Lepinay is to understand how the economic arrangements that take place in indexical fields are made stable and maintained anew (Lepinay 2003). This book's findings on how the realities of world commodity markets derive from their representations complement Lepinay's work.

Even in situations where the actual workings of markets come close to their depiction in formal models of market behavior, the very correspondence between model and reality can be sustained only by continuous market maintenance work, carried out by market boards, regulatory bodies, and formulary formatting of market exchange (Lepinay 2003; Muniesa 2003; Zajac and Westphal 2004). This is why Callon has argued that *homo economicus* may be alive, but that one has to carry out ethnographic research on the very conditions that produce the context that makes it possible to proclaim *ecco homo economicus*! (Callon 1998) This work, however, does not indicate the need to simply register the inherently social character of the instances of economic encounters. Callon shows the emergence of a field in which agents, nonhumans, and the tools they use interact in a field of power that transcends the mere topography of the embeddedness of the social and the economic.

COMMODITY CHAINS, SYSTEMS OF PROVISION, AND THE SOCIAL LIVES OF THINGS

Although rich and exciting, the new directions in the social study of markets still lack a case study of a global market that simultaneously connects and disconnects millions of market agents from different locations in the world. It is not a coincidence that new research began with financial markets. These markets are defined by organized and neoclassically disciplined exchanges, such as the Chicago Board of Trade, the Paris Bourse, New York City's trading houses, or London banks.

The commodity chain approach aims to address this missing link (Gereffi and Korzeniewicz 1994 [1986]; Wallerstein and Hopkins 2000; Daviron and Gibbon 2002). Mostly by drawing on the work of world systems and dependency theories, researchers advancing this approach have located three main forms of commodity chain: buyer-driven chains, producer-driven chains, and trader-driven chains (Gereffi and Korzeniewicz 1994). According to this approach, commodities circulate in the world to reach their consumers through their chains of production and distribution. This strand of research is one of the best examples of how the normalized distribution of the economy among the three spheres of action—exchange, production, and consumption—can have a direct effect on the ways in which world trade is imagined.

The commodity chain approach has yet to present a convincing account of the workings of markets and trading in the world. Its most serious weakness is its exaggeration of the power of commodity chains. Research has shown that capitalists strive to create a chain of the type theorized in the commodity chain perspective; however, the chain makers of capitalism have yet to create such a commodity chain in the world (Cox 2002). Moreover, in the commodity chain perspective one does not see the everyday work of chain making. Interestingly, the theory is silent on the very construction of the chain whose name it carries.

The commodity chain perspective also lacks an analysis of the nature of the commodity, the routes of its exchange and sustenance, and the agents who incessantly negotiate a space of encounter in order to make a living from the commodity assumed to flow through the chain. Finally, actors in these chains perform roles with a set of fixed, stable preferences assigned by the theory. These actors cannot move away from the functional and structural unity of the global chain of a certain commodity (Raikes et al. 2000; Pietrobelli and Sverrisson 2003; Skov 2005). The workings of the world market of the underlying commodity are completely invisible in this approach. Furthermore, those sociologically informed approaches that focus on trade networks in a global context, like that of Gereffi and Korzeniewicz (1994), neither present an account of these networks from the vantage point of their agents, nor describe the nature of local power struggles carried out within and outside the chains of production and exchange.

The rigidity of the commodity chain approach has been softened by Fine and Leopold's systems of provision approach (Fine and Leopold 1993; Fine 2002). Their research focuses on the world of consumption and studies the relations of production and exchange in specific systems of provision, such as those of food and garments. Although corrective of the oversimplifications of the commodity chain approach and taking into consideration that economic agents do not necessarily follow the disciplinary taxonomy of the social sciences, this approach still limits itself in registering the material limits defining the world of the system in individual sectors. What happens in the sector itself, how its markets are organized, how its prices are set, networks built, and research carried out—these questions still do not figure in the systems of provision approach.[8]

There is another possibility that seems to offer a more convincing perspective than the commodity chain and systems of provision approaches: the theoretically sophisticated (but ethnographically still unsupported) account of the *social life of things*. Appadurai's edited volume presents the idea that operating on analytical distinctions between consumption, production, and exchange is problematic. Instead, he proposes that ethnographers should follow the social lives of things as they circulate. He argues that "from a *theoretical* point of view human actors encode things with significance, [while] from a *methodological* point of view it is the things-in-motion that illuminate their human and social context" (Appadurai 1986).

However, the argument remains theoretical. Ironically, as Ferguson has shown, the ethnographic material following Appadurai's introductory essay presents contradictory evidence (Ferguson 1988).[9] The theory

---

[8] For an internal critique of this approach, see Skov (2005).

[9] One good example is Kopytoff's problematic acceptance of money and its destructive force, which dissolves a multicentric economy into "the" economy. However, less than a decade later Zelizer's ethnography has shown exactly the reverse to be true (Zelizer 1994).

seems to be suffering from a kind of formalism surprising to observe in an account that critiques formalism. Appadurai problematizes the approach of locating the creation of value in the relations of production, because, as he suggests at the beginning of his introductory essay, "economic exchange creates value" (Appadurai 1986). For Appadurai, it is not the idea of a universally normalized conception of value, but the location of its emergence that is problematic.[10] This replacement of a hierarchy of determination between production and exchange not only deifies their analytical separability, but also obscures what really happens in a relationship of exchange.[11] Analysts following in Appadurai's footsteps have located the same dynamic in finance (Lee and LiPuma 2002), and their general conclusions have been shown to be empirically problematic in ethnographies of financial production (Lepinay 2003).

WHY COTTON?

My choice of cotton is deliberate. No other commodity gives us a better vantage point to study the making of global markets in all of their main production fields. Cotton is located at the intersection of industrial, financial, and agricultural relations of exchange and production, connecting more than a billion people to each other through routes that span agriculture, trade, and textile manufacturing.

Every year, more than fifty million farmers from eighty-one countries produce around ninety million bales of cotton, a nonperishable cash crop whose only usage is to exchange it for money. This amount of cotton is more than enough to produce eighteen T-shirts for every person in the world.[12] The total surface of the agricultural land used for cotton farming is slightly larger than Britain and Switzerland combined. Compared to other cash crops that farmers all over the world rely on—excluding those that farmers can consume directly, such as wheat—cotton has the largest area of production in the world, followed by sugar cane, sunflowers, coffee, and tobacco.

---

[10] Ferguson rightly criticizes Appadurai's problematic and to a certain extent his selective reading of Simmel (1978) (Ferguson 1988).

[11] Appadurai's account has also been critiqued for its inability to bring together the larger picture that it seeks to paint by looking at three locations or vantage points, belonging to traders, consumers, and producers, respectively. Skov has shown that "each scenario is analyzed as a world unto itself which can only be understood from within, and at the expense of its relation with other nodes on the chain" (Skov 2005).

[12] 480 pounds of cotton can make approximately 1,217 men's T-shirts, 3,085 diapers, 1,256 pillowcases, 4,321 women's socks, and 3,557 men's socks. Source: www.econcentral.com.

In terms of trade volume, no other agricultural commodity can come close to the circulation of cotton in the world. Every year, one-third of the cotton produced globally crosses the boundaries of nation-states and is consumed in a country other than its original location of production. This is the largest share in the world of any agricultural market. Historically, too, the cotton trade has put its mark on world trade, with its total value twice that of gold and silver combined in the late nineteenth century (Farnie 2004). Thus, the global cotton trade and the technologies of its marketing offer a unique site for studying a global phenomenon in one of its most obvious manifestations.

In addition, cotton has other qualities that make it an ideal subject for the study of markets. Raw cotton is at the same time a fiber, food, and feed crop. Approximately two-thirds of the harvested crop is composed of the seeds, which are processed to separate their three components: oil, meal, and hulls. Cottonseed oil is a major component of cooking oil. For example, in Turkey cottonseed oil composes twenty percent of the total vegetable oil used, while in Egypt it is almost eighty percent. In the United States, cottonseed oil is used extensively in the production of snack foods: almost all junk food is cooked in cottonseed oil. Furthermore, most farm fish is fed with cottonseed hulls. Cotton meal and hulls are also used as animal fodder and fertilizer. The remaining part of raw cotton is called lint. After it is ginned, the plant's fiber, or lint cotton, is processed for different uses, as in yarn. We dress ourselves in cotton textiles. The plant's fibers cover the most personal parts of our bodies, the most vital sectors of our economies, and the busiest intersections of our social relations. Even money is made out of cotton. Seventy percent of the U.S. dollar bill, effectively the currency of the world, is made of cotton.

The historical importance of the plant's commercial growth and trade also played a role in my choice. Cotton was frequently referred to as the source of power that made the modern world. Because the plant was located at the heart of the making of the Industrial Revolution, no other commodity has contributed to the emergence of capitalism and colonialism more than cotton. Its production fueled colonial struggles to secure the main input product for the textile factories. The institutions of its trading contributed the earliest financial instruments to the workings of capitalism. Trademarks were developed to locate the specificity of cotton bales, and in 1875 forty-five percent of all marks in Britain were registered as cotton marks. Cotton merchants were the first market actors in the world to imagine a world of markets. The Atlantic cable was laid by a merchant who owed his wealth to cotton. Cotton merchants were the first to use the telegraph to exchange quotes. John Jones's *Annual Cotton Handbook* was the first publication that made visible a global commodity market.

In 1880, the world's major cotton exchanges—Alexandria, Le Havre, New Orleans, New York, and Liverpool—were created as sites of a global market, exchanging spot and futures contracts by cross quotations with the help of specialized cotton trade codes sent via telegraph (Garside 1935). As we shall see in chapter 4, the expansion and globalization of markets were a direct result of colonialism and its imperial technologies; this was the only time in world trade when more than half of the bales produced in the world crossed national borders to be opened in a different location. After decades of neoliberal reforms and regimes of exchange imposed by the World Trade Organization, only about thirty percent of cotton is now being exported.

The unmatched importance of cotton is also evident in the emergence of political economy and its critique. From Adam Smith to Karl Marx, analyses of commodities began with agricultural products and never ceased to mention cotton or textiles. When Adam Smith was a customs official, his main task was to observe cotton's circulation and production in the world. Karl Marx's famous argument on the impossibility of producing value by exchange drew on a trading example of 2,000 lbs of cotton. Marx's most important research entailed visiting Manchester's mills at least twenty-four times between 1845 and 1880 (Farnie and Jeremy 2004).

Finally, the global growth and circulation of cotton contributed to the imagination of various paradigms of the global economy. Hobsbawm has proposed that the most telling visual image of the world economic order is Edgar Degas's famous painting of cotton merchants in New Orleans, *Un bureau de coton à Nouvelle-Orléans, 1873* (Hobsbawm 1975).

How to Follow Cotton?

In order to study a global market, one first has to locate the "global." As will become clear in the first two chapters, the location is not geographical, although it is produced in geographically bounded fields of encounter. I argue that the global market is an indexical possibility. We see this by following cotton's growth and circulation which map the multisited fields of a global market. The research on which I draw in order to follow cotton is informed by recent theoretical contributions of multisited ethnographies, as discussed in Marcus (1998). On a methodological basis, my research relates to emergent multisited fieldwork studies that connect various research locations through which the ethnographer passes (Mintz 1985; Haraway 1991; Myers 1992; Martin 1994; Latour 1999).

Rather than seeing the global market as an external entity imposed on various articulations of the local, I approach each point of this nexus—whether nominally "global," like Memphis-based global merchant houses, or "local," like farming villages of some two hundred house-holds—as sites in which the global and the local are mutually constitutive. I began conducting my research with the assumption that the global is integral to and embedded in the practices of the agents who themselves actually make the market (Marcus 1998). Yet, like so many fertile grounds, this one is also somewhat muddy. Where should one begin to follow cotton? What exactly does it mean to follow a thing? Which locations of the plant's growth and trade would provide the analysis with the best ethnographic engagement? Study of the making of global markets in one country can only partly address these questions, because such a study cannot incorporate the varying experiences of cotton farmers and traders in a transnational field of trade relations. On the other hand, enlarging the scale of comparison too much would hinder an in-depth analysis of particular market practices.

WHERE TO FOLLOW COTTON?

Egypt, Turkey, and the United States present an excellent context in which to study a world commodity market, for a number of reasons. First, they cover all main geographic regions of economic encounter at various levels of development in the world. As the largest national economy, the United States is a test case of the developed West. Contrary to many theorists' expectations, this industrial giant is the main agricultural export country that fulfills the cotton requirements of less developed and less industrial Turkey. Turkey represents an ideal case for a middle-income country, wedged between the developed West and the underdeveloped East. As a candidate for the European Union, one of the largest producers and consumers of cotton in the world, and the largest buyer of U.S. cotton, Turkey presents an ideal case to study the making of a world market.

Finally, Egypt—once the host of the first cotton futures market and the second commodity futures market in the world—is now struggling to continue the production of the world's best cottons. Moreover, the country has been a test case for almost all major global social experiments of modernity. It was during the colonization of Egypt that modern technologies of governing populations and their political economy were developed. Following decolonization, the country again became the center of global attention, making it an exemplary forerunner of planned development projects in the era of import-substitution industrialization. Egypt's first president, Nasser, was the beacon of Third World development. The policies of Sadat and those of his successor Mubarak prepared the ground for making Egypt a test case of the last major global transformation, neoliberal reforms. A study of the lives of Egyptian traders and cotton farmers, therefore, also adds to the analysis a perspective that takes into account the geography of all the major market and development experiments of world history.

Furthermore, Egypt and Turkey were among the first states to initiate market reforms in the late 1970s; United States–based international financial institutions have since described the results as a "remarkable success" in the case of Egypt and an "undoubted success" in Turkey (Bank 1988; IMF 1998). Turkey in particular has been the recipient of one of the two largest World Bank Structural Adjustment Loans, receiving over one-third of the World Bank's policy-based lending in the 1980s (Öniş 1998). For many scholars, Turkey's success presents a model for Arab states (Richards 1995). Egypt, on the other hand, as the largest Arab economy, has been considered a pioneer of free market reforms. As the second largest recipient of American foreign aid in the world and ranked as the world's fourth most successful case of privatization (IMF 1998), Egypt's encounters with a world market present an interesting comparison to Turkey and the United States.[13]

The book focuses on the experiences of cotton farmers in three villages in Egypt and Turkey. There are two main reasons for my choice of Pamukköy in Turkey, and Kafr Gaffar and 'Izbet Sabry in Egypt. First, they were among the first cotton-producing villages in the two countries when cotton was introduced to the Ottoman Empire, of which both were formally a part at the time. Second, their population is close to the average size of Lower Egyptian and Aegean villages in Turkey, which make them representative of the rural conditions of production and exchange. I carried out the urban component of the field work in the two busiest cotton trading hubs of the respective countries, in Izmir and Alexandria.

In the summer of 2000, I spent a total of three months in the field and completed my final preparations for the following year's fieldwork. While in the countryside, I worked in the fields with several farmers and became better acquainted with the practicalities of growing cotton. My discussions with cotton farmers and a few local traders convinced me to incorporate port cities into the research framework, because these villages are well connected to closer and more distant market fields via polymorphous links. Following these links brought me to Izmir in Turkey and Alexandria in Egypt. I spent a total of forty days in these cities and met various cotton traders and international merchants. Their views on

---

[13] In a book on the world cotton market, it would be better to incorporate local and regional markets in large producers such as India and China. Yet, practically it would not be possible for me to pursue further research if I had taken that route. Moreover, lack of empirical data on other geographies of cotton markets would not change the theoretical approach the book proposes to understand world markets and their prices.

the idea of the market, coupled with those of the farmers, made me seriously question my own ideas. I was particularly struck by one "global broker," as he called himself, who told me during the open cry-out cotton trading session in the Izmir Mercantile Exchange that "I could never understand cotton markets because they operate on invisible networks and the statistics did not speak about the market, they were part of it." This important comment further convinced me to focus not only on practices of production and exchange, but also on how such practices take shape on the ground.

I started fieldwork in April of 2001 and completed it in October of 2002. I lived for six months in Pamukköy and spent my days observing cotton farmers' everyday lives, from the time they broke the ground to sow cotton until they sold their crop. Following the cotton, I moved to Izmir and observed cotton trading in the Izmir Mercantile Exchange and the trading houses of Izmir merchants and traders. Finishing my research in Izmir in December of 2001, I moved to Alexandria to work with Egyptian cotton traders whom I had met previously. At the end of March of 2002, just before the beginning of the new cotton season in Lower Egypt, I moved to the Egyptian countryside and began studying the fields of global markets from the vantage point of Egyptian farmers. I had to take a break to move to Memphis, Tennessee, to be trained as a spot, futures, and options trader for two months in the professional degree program of the American Cotton Shippers Association. This experience effectively put me in contact with all the major cotton trading houses in the global market and provided me with an important experience of the way in which global traders relate to other sites of trade in the world. I also found time to observe trading and even traded myself in one trading house based in Memphis. In July of 2002, I went back to the Egyptian countryside and completed my fieldwork as the crop of the two villages was sold on the market. I returned to New York in October of 2002 and continued my research on the New York Board of Trade, while organizing the data. Based on this research, I wrote a Ph.D. dissertation with a focus on the everyday practices of merchants and peasants. Between 2005 and 2008, I made various short-term visits to all the main fieldwork sites except Memphis and revised the data. I wrote the book between September 2008 and March 2009 in Istanbul.

Summary of Arguments

The six chapters of the book each focus on one general question and one specific site of production and exchange. Chapter 1 discusses the process of price realization in the world cotton market. It argues that the market is made in multiple fields that produce not only its commodities, but also their prices. The market price is a *prosthetic device* realized by world traders and market analysts to trade cotton on the ground. Yet this price form is not used as an actual price of a transaction. Based on the shaky ground of indices, on a bridge of encounter between the realities and their representations in world markets, the chapter shows that the realities of world commodity markets derive from their representations. It concludes by showing that markets are neither embedded in social relations, nor disembedded from them. They are fields of power operating on dynamic and heterogeneous platforms of power/knowledge relations. The making of prices is carried out through constant interventions in the markets by different forms of perception, standardization of the object of exchange, prostheses, rumors, indices, research in the wild, scientific statements (such as neoclassical assumptions), and their rejection. Market fields are also at times formatted by the direct intervention of market boards and formulas, utilizing assumptions about the neoclassical economy of things. The chapter demonstrates that markets are constantly intervened in and maintained, even when there are no government regulations.

Chapter 2 furthers this argument by changing the vantage point from market price realization to commodity circulation. As the chapter follows two thousand bales of cotton from the United States to Turkey, it documents how two parallel routes of circulation are forged in world trade by various agents of global markets. It shows that the very circulation of commodities requires everyday maintenance work. This work also makes possible the stabilization of price realization processes, for without execution no market exchange takes place. Taking a price is a promissory act only. For the exchange to take place, traders forge a documentary circulation that informs promissory trade itself and either maintains and concludes the making of the price, or challenges and revises it, depending on what happens during different rounds of renegotiation and arbitration. The execution cannot be seen as a function or determination of the trading decisions only, for the ways in which trades are executed, revised, or dissolved after the prices are made inform future rounds of exchange. In other words, all trading decisions incorporate different effects of previous contract executions.

Redefinition of the market action to cover the very execution of buying and selling decisions opens an entirely new avenue for understanding world commodity markets. The agents of these world markets, as chapter 2 shows, build a platform from the interaction of capital, knowledge, and networks in order to relate to and profit from the market. On these platforms of trading, human and nonhuman agents are simultaneously constructed, such as "human bridges," by means of networks ensuring that traders concurrently know and make the market. On this platform, gift and commodity exchange do not exclude each other. Gift exchange is a technology of power for those who exchange commodities and who need to network to be able to know and make the market. However, these global traders need thousands of other agents to maintain the world market and continue working on bridges of commodities, gifts, and documents.

To understand the world markets of cotton better, one has to write the story of global market-making from the vantage point of the other side of the bridge constructed by global merchants. Following the trading bridge of chapter 2, chapter 3 reaches Izmir, Turkey, to discuss how market prices are made in locations such as the Izmir Mercantile Exchange (IME), which inform and are informed by the realization of global prices of cotton. It is only by bringing together all building blocks of this globality that one can see the larger picture. The chapter on Izmir begins to draw a more complete depiction of a world commodity market, by showing how the practices of global price- and market-making are articulated in locations where the global and the local interact, such as the IME.

The nature of this interaction between Izmir and its external world, however, is not merely a trade relationship between a global and a local site. The relationship is between different agents who have asymmetrical mercantile platforms in terms of capital, knowledge, and network; yet, global and regional merchants are still local agents. The interaction between global and local markets is a relationship of derivation, not of encounter. Chapter 3 shows that global things are derivatives of their local articulations. In that sense, the global can be seen more vividly as a universe of indexical possibilities from/in Izmir. The location of the global market is not geographical, but graphical. It is made up of documentary, technological, and indexical tools. The global market and its prices are made in indices, reports, and market pictures. Such a site of globality is deployed every day by traders in order to govern local acts of trade. These individual acts of trade are then used by market experts, researchers, and traders, ensuring the further maintenance of global markets. The market fields of the world are produced not only by bringing together dyadic encounters of exchange, but also through the making of the very prices of distant yet related local markets. The IME's realization of a unique price form—*the rehearsal price*, made in a limbo between indexicality and actuality—presents the empirical framework of the discussion.

Moreover, chapter 3 demonstrates that, similar to other fields of market encounter, the market in Izmir has multiple boundaries, drawn according to specific negotiations in the production of exchange relations. In this sense, the market and the nonmarket are strange bedfellows that together inform the realization of market prices. The theoretical consequences of this conclusion are vast, for they make the outcomes of and political stake in locating the boundaries of markets visible. Setting the boundary becomes the very power that makes the market. Moreover, showing that a boundary is not a line demarcating two worlds, but a field of the market itself, reveals the weakness of theoretical attempts to construct different forms of embeddedness of markets in their nonmarket externalities, be they cultures or societies. The market is a power field in itself.

Chapter 4 examines how cotton trade is carried out in Alexandria, Egypt, by locating this new market field in relation to the previously analyzed sites of exchange. Unlike Izmir or New York City, Alexandria seems to lack a mercantile architecture that contains scattered instances of trade and brings merchants together under one roof. There is no "organized market" in the city. However, the city was home to the first cotton futures market of the world, which no longer exists. By historically locating this interesting trajectory of market development in Egypt, chapter 4 shows the colonial background of the rise of market orders. Then, the chapter analyzes the making of market prices in Alexandria and their contribution to the realization of prices in the world market. The city contributes another price form to the rich universe of prosthetic prices, the *associate price*.

Alexandria's price is categorically different from both the prosthetic prices of cotton and the IME's rehearsal price. The associate price is not produced as an index; yet, like an indexical price, it does not refer to the actual worth of a bale of cotton. It is not a rehearsal price either, for it is not produced in a pit where traders exchange cotton by rehearsing the crop's price. However, similar to prosthetic and rehearsal prices, the associate price of Alexandria draws on everyday politics of market-making in associated practices of trade. The discussion of the price realization and market-making technologies of Alexandria's merchants helps to break up the naturalized world of prices which creates an effect of a nonpolitical, almost natural characteristic of the market price. It is misleading to assume that markets or prices are things that we can know without carrying out concrete research on their making on the ground. Any a priori assumption about how markets work or prices are made necessarily becomes a condition of market-making. As chapter 4 will demonstrate, the market price is not realized in the geographical coming together of the two lines of supply and demand. The making and realization of market prices—whether they are associate, rehearsal, or strictly global prosthetic—reflect the rich platforms of power relations that manufacture the prices in their multiple forms.

However, when the neoclassical political interventions of economists, such as those of the World Bank and the IMF, are taken too seriously by policy circles, as was the case in Egypt, the markets are made in ways totally alien to their functioning as assumed in scientific statements.

Egypt lost its world market share to the United States, precisely because U.S. growers and merchants could afford not to take the economists too seriously; Egyptian public companies and farmers did not have such a choice.

Chapters 5 and 6 analyze the universe of cotton markets from the vantage point of cotton farmers in Western Turkey and Lower Egypt. The everyday engagement of cotton growers in their fields of production and exchange does not confirm assumptions about sites of life as being analytically distinct between market or nonmarket, capitalist or non-capitalist, exchange or production. Neither farmers nor traders in these multisited fields of work engage in only either exchange or production. The very growing of cotton, its "production," entails a simultaneous engagement of relations that consists not only of exchange and production, but also of a series of activities that make up a rich and undertheorized world of encounters and struggles among pests, children, merchants, migrant workers, women, *khoulis*, farmers, cotton, cows, *gamusas*, economists, ginners, *elchis*, and so on.

Chapters 5 and 6 also show how cotton is grown and its global market made on the ground in Pamukköy, Kafr Gaffar, and 'Izbet Sabry, by many forms of cooperative living among farmers, animals, plants, and their environment. By following cotton's growth, the chapters discuss the struggles in which farmers are engaged in order to continue growing cotton in the context of the political economy of life and death based on neoliberal reforms in the countryside.

Furthermore, the chapters discuss the making of the global bridges of trade from the vantage point of farmers. How does the market, as traders see it, look from the vantage point of farmers? How does cotton change hands in the fields of growth and exchange? What forms of struggle inform the marketing of cotton? The answers that these chapters offer depict a world of market-making whose every moment of realization is informed by power contests that defy a priori logic of calculation. It is in these relations of power that markets are made in the simultaneous processes of exchange and production of commodities, their translations, research results, and struggles between farmers, children, overseers, graders, traders, pests, and all other agents who want to use the cotton for satisfying their own needs. Cotton as a living organism is a part of this power field, too.

Chapters 5 and 6 also describe the effect of neoliberal reforms in Egypt and Turkey. They show that structural adjustment programs have affected configurations of power in the countryside and paradoxically violated even neoliberal objectives of formalizing the rules of the markets. These reforms manufacture and foster a number of informalities, from illegal trading to increased violence in the countryside. The chapters argue that it is misleading to see these reforms as projects of letting the market work by itself, for they are making the object of their reformation. As they empower traders, these reforms create regimes of exchange/production that may lead to the disappearance of cotton as the most important agricultural market commodity in Turkey and Egypt.

Finally, chapters 5 and 6 ethnographically map a market universe from the viewpoint of Turkish and Egyptian farmers. This universe cannot be analytically located by imposing boundaries that attach categorically separate logics of economic, scientific, social, or political encounter. In the fields of growth and exchange that dot the global sites of cotton markets, almost all forces—such as those of supply, demand, yield, and growing area—are negotiated on unequal platforms.

The market, perceived to be operating as a balancing act of supply and demand, seems to be overflowing with various calculative dynamics of power. The market idea of neoclassical logic is itself a tool that frames exchange relations and their production on the ground. Thus, the market is not the name of the location where exchange takes place, but rather the very tool of engagement used by market participants, almost without exception nonfarmer participants—whether they are economists like Black and Scholes, factory owners like the J. R.'s of the Turkish Söke Plain, merchants on trading platforms like Mr. White, or representatives of the merchants of Alexandria like Khaled.

The market exchange in the countryside takes place in locations where farmers feel very uncomfortable. "Things" happen there, as we will see in chapters 5 and 6. It is a field of power where even the knowledge of what will happen does not help. Years of experience coupled with an expressed use of power meet the low level of experience of indebted farmers in the traders' exchange theaters. Furthermore, farmers enter mercantile sites after spending all of their available time growing cotton, killing insects and cows, hiring or pooling labor in cooperatives, hoeing their fields, or picking their cotton. Farmers do not have the time and energy to produce two things simultaneously: they cannot maintain market platforms and grow cotton at the same time, for both the market exchange and cotton-growing draw on concrete forms of production, performance, and maintenance. Finally, the conclusion will present the theoretical consequences of seeing a world market as I have summarized it here. *Market Threads* ends with an elaboration of the practical consequences of framing the market as a field of power and the policy options that follow from these consequences.

CHAPTER 1

What Is a World Price?

THE PROSTHETIC AND ACTUAL WORTH OF COTTON

PRICE SHAPES OUR ECONOMIC life in late capitalist modernity. On opening the economics section of any major newspaper, one will encounter columns of commodity prices. Taken-for-granted facts of modern life, prices are accepted as signals of the world economy. It is with reference to prices that economic processes are made visible, discussed, and intercepted, and that markets are made and understood. However, strikingly enough, world market prices do not correspond to the actual worth of commodities. One cannot buy a single bale of cotton by paying the world price of the commodity. To what, then, do these prices refer? What effect do these prices have on the setting of the *actual* monetary worth of commodities traded on the ground? How are prices made in world markets?

The relevant literature answers these questions in three ways, but it does not convincingly address the mystery of the price. Microeconomists describe markets as price-making contexts and explain prices as things that are made in the market. Although this approach accepts the sociological determinants of changing supply and demand, it limits itself to describing the change itself, by shifting the curves representing supply and demand without describing how various market price forms are made on the ground, even in the small universe of a single market.

This circularity has in many ways been corrected by institutionalist researchers who underline the social and cultural nature of markets and prices (North 1977; Zelizer 1981; Robinson 1980; Alexander and Alexander 1991; Zafirovski 2000; Geismar 2001; Zajac and Westphal 2004; Velthuis 2005). Inspired by Polanyi's work and frequently drawing on his central concept of "embeddedness," researchers have argued that prices are culturally constructed within relations of power in socially and politically embedded markets (White 1981; Granovetter 1985; Fligstein 1996; DiMaggio and Louch 1998; Dobbin 2004; Duina 2004; Lapavitsas 2004; Uzzi and Lancaster 2004). It is hard to disagree with this argument; however, a more challenging task awaits us: to better understand the processes through which prices, as well as the types of prices and their forms of realization in the market place, are made. A convincing theory that explains how prices are made on the ground can further reinforce the institutionalist paradigm's strength in explaining what allows markets to function.

Recently, exciting new research in the social studies of the price has focused on markets as sociotechnical universes. Several researchers have even gone further and applied the insights of the social studies of science and technology to the agenda of economic sociology. They have approached processes of economization also from the vantage point of price-making (Callon 1998; Muniesa 2000; Maurer 2002; Çalışkan 2003; Chiffoleau and Laporte 2004; Cochoy 2004; Grandclément 2004; Levin 2004; MacKenzie 2006). Incorporating the insights of institutionalism and drawing on new research in the social studies of the price, this chapter presents an alternative way of understanding price-making, based on the empirical universe of the global cotton market.

I argue that, instead of focusing narrowly on price-setting, policy-makers and researchers should attend to the conditions of price realization. In world and regional markets, prices are realized in multiple forms, each form having gone through a complex, yet identifiable process. Price realization is not price-setting. In cotton markets, complex trading tools help to realize many categorically diverse market prices.

Realization is the most accurate concept to make sense of prices in global trade. The term has multiple meanings, all of which convey the formative processes of price-making in world commodity markets. It means (1) "to bring something into concrete existence." For the prices to be realized in this sense of the concept, they have (2) "to be made to appear real," so that the price can be (3) "conceived vividly as real." This is the way in which parties of exchange relations become (4) "fully aware of" the price and relate to the worth of cotton bales to (5) "convert [them] into actual money" (Merriam-Webster 1998).

Prices are realized in multiple forms and appearances in cotton markets; yet the price for a bale is uniform for the parties of trade in a single exchange. What I call the "actual price of cotton" refers to the amount of money that a seller accepts from the buyer in exchange for the right of ownership over the commodity. The actual price of cotton is the end result of the process of price realization. Price realization does not occur as a natural process, but depends on a set of technical devices and artificial equipment, which is almost never described in economic theory. Following Callon (2002), I call these artificial devices "prostheses." Correspondingly, I will call the price forms that result from the deployment of such equipment "prosthetic prices."

In the price realization process, a rich universe of collective human and nonhuman agents produce prosthetic prices, which inform the making of an actual price of cotton. I define the prosthetic price as a price form produced in the market, but not directly deployed by either buyer or seller in the actual exchange of commodities. Everyday trade in the world cotton market draws on the realization and deployment of a number of key prosthetic prices, such as the World Price of Cotton, the Adjusted World Price, and the A Index. Without understanding how these different prosthetic prices are made, it is impossible to grasp either prices or markets themselves. Without taking into account the specific processes of price realization in world markets, academic accounts of exchange relations and professional reports on market reform remain incomplete at best, wrong-headed at worst.

Without these prostheses, buyers and sellers cannot navigate world markets. The market price as we know it is a product of price realization, and not the end result of unmediated dyadic encounters of exchange. Prices are represented and realized in various frameworks of economization that mediate trading activities and the making of actual prices. These frameworks—such as supply and demand graphs, market reports, futures, and options price tables—are the interfaces of market activity in global trade. Through these frameworks, we can perceive the market, and they contribute to the ways in which market actors carry out calculations and plan their trading practices.

This chapter will show that market prices in their multiple forms are made possible and visible through the tools of price realization and frameworks of economization, and not in the coming together of the two lines of supply and demand as in supply and demand graphs. In the traders' everyday world, the market price as a prosthetic device precedes the making of the actual price accepted for transactions. This is why *Making a Market* begins with a detailed analysis of price realization, for one cannot understand the market without addressing the price.

How Much Does an Actual Bale of Cotton Really Cost?

In order to give an understanding of the making of the world cotton market and its prosthetic prices, this section will begin with a simple question posed daily by cotton traders: "How is the market doing?" When traders ask this question, they want to learn the price of a commodity. The price and the market are synonymous for many cotton traders.

This parallel between the price and the market is also a central tenet of contemporary microeconomics. The introduction of any economics textbook discusses how the market can be represented as price movements, determined by two "universal laws" of human encounter: those of supply and demand.[1] These introductions focus on a hypothetical actor's

[1] See, for instance, Varian (2002).

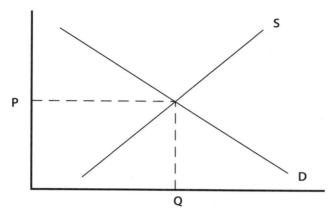

Figure 1   Supply and demand graph

intentions regarding the supply of or demand for a certain quantity of a commodity, for a particular period of time, for a specific price. The construction of a linear relation of causality between quantity and price serves as entry point to a discussion of the market, at least in neoclassical economic logic. Having framed the market in the context of these two forces, textbooks go on to explain how to map the market. They do so by first elaborating on the concept of demand.

According to the universal law of demand, originally conceived by Antoine Augustine Cournot in 1838, when the price of a certain commodity increases, the demand for this same commodity decreases (Cournot 1897). In contrast, the universal law of supply posits that when the price of a certain commodity increases, the quantity supplied of this same commodity increases. It took scholars several decades to bring together these two laws in one visual framework.

Cournout's elaboration has been almost entirely forgotten, and in the late nineteenth and early twentieth centuries Alfred Marshall's name became synonymous with the famous supply and demand curves that college graduates all over the world learn to draw. Marshall worked on these graphs in the 1870s, when the New York Cotton Exchange first traded cotton futures contracts. He improvised novel graphic techniques, mostly invented by physicists, which illustrated the making of the market price (figure 1). Marshall's graphic representation of the market appeared for the first time in 1890 as a footnote in his ground-breaking work *Principles of Political Economy*, commonly held to be the founding text of today's microeconomics; it became one of the best-known scientific images in the following century (Marshall 1982 [1890]).

Like many contemporary economists, Marshall used agricultural markets to explain how the illustration worked: corn farmers would supply a smaller number of bushels of corn per month if the price decreased. Similarly, buyers would want to buy less corn if the price per bushel increased. The price is the point where the two lines representing supply and demand intersect. This meeting point in the graph locates the market price of corn, accepted by the free will of the potential demander and supplier as the monetary worth of a bushel of corn for a specific period of time. This is the point of making the price, and the market, too.

Yet a set of questions lurks behind this seemingly simple graph which claims to represent and explain one of the most complex human encounters. Is it possible to make visible the multiple price forms in supply and demand curves? What kind of market price is P? What effect does it have on the making of actual prices on the ground? How is actual price-making carried out in concrete market settings? Finally, what is the significance of having such a hypothetical price?

One may begin to answer these complex questions with a simple question: how much is cotton? If one were to ask a trader in Memphis, Tennessee, about the price of cotton, he would first want to know what kind of cotton.[2] The first step in determining a price is to locate the object of exchange precisely, the second is to circumscribe the object's rather vague character, which may resist the normalization of its exchange. Since cotton has become a global commodity, traders manage cotton's vagueness by using a measurable and negotiable constant, such as Strict Low Middling (SLM). Thus, one has to replace the vague term "cotton" with a constant and pose a more informed question: "How much is a bale of SLM?"[3]

The trader would then remind the buyer that SLM is sold only by metric ton (MT), not by bale,[4] and ask for further specifications regarding the kind of SLM to be purchased. An acceptable inquiry would include at least a number of primary cotton classification components such as color (cotton is not necessarily white), length, micronaire, and strength. Micronaire (mic.) refers to the coarseness of the fiber. Coarser cotton produces yarn for denim manufacturing, and finer cotton yarn for shirts. The strength of the fiber is measured in grams per Tex (GPT). The stronger the fiber is, the less costly the production of yarn. The color of cotton is measured in reference to its level of brightness and yellow tint. Trash content (T) refers to the amount of noncotton material in a bale,

---

[2] The cotton market is predominantly a men's world. Women are usually excluded from cotton markets, whether in villages in Egypt and Turkey, or in the Cotton Futures and Options Market in New York City.

[3] This observation can be extended to all physical commodities traded in world markets.

[4] 1 metric ton equals 1,000 kilograms, or 2,205 pounds.

such as leaves. The more trash there is in the cotton, the more costly it is to process.

Speaking the language of the market, then, enables the hypothetical buyer to pose a more informed question to the hypothetical trader, representing the will to buy a set quantity of a certain type of cotton: "How much is 1,000 MT of SLM 1 1/16 inches, 3.4–4.9 mic., white, T/4, min GPT of 24?"

At this point, the trader poses his final question: "Do you want a quote or a firm offer?" By doing so, the trader wants to learn whether the buyer is after *his* price of SLM, or whether he is just inquiring about the general prices. If the buyer were to ask for *his* price, then the trader would quote a price representing the range within which he is willing to negotiate. In this case, the trader would then ask two more questions: "When do you want us to deliver?" and "Do you want us to send you a CIF firm offer?" A CIF firm offer means that cost, insurance, and freight are included in the price. The trader's response to the final two questions is very important, because his answer will set the price, and if accepted by the buyer, it will be the last moment of an actual price realization process.

Because the goal here is to locate the *actual* price of cotton, the buyer has to request a firm offer: "Please make us a firm offer for 1,000 MT SLM 1 1/16 inches, 3.4–4.9 mic., white, T/4, min GPT of 24, CIF New York City for November 2003 delivery."[5] In addition to specifying exactly what "cotton" means, the inquiry determines the time and place of delivery. After reading the fax or e-mail request, the cotton supplier makes a firm offer valid only, for example, for the next two hours. His fax or e-mail would probably read: "Basis 515 points on, for the next two hours."

This is the *actual* price of cotton: the trader can supply 1,000 metric tons of SLM for "515 points on for the next two hours." But what does this really mean? In order to understand actual cotton prices, one needs further expertise in the language of the market. Leaving the spot markets where actual bales of cotton are exchanged, we now have to reexamine the price ("515 points on") in the context of the cotton futures market where not cotton itself, but the right to own cotton at a future date is the commodity.

In the futures market, traders buy and sell the claim on the value of cotton at a predetermined future date, by exchanging futures contracts of 100 bales of SLM cotton through intermediary companies, whose orders are executed in the cotton futures trading pit of the New York Board of Trade (NYBOT) in New York City. There is no need to exchange an

---

[5] These standards are usually contested and challenged in almost all rounds of exchange. Buyers and sellers usually hire other agents called controllers to navigate this inherently slippery ground.

actual bale of cotton in the futures market, as long as the contract representing the exchange is bought or sold before the future date. For example, if one cotton futures contract is sold for July 2003, the seller has to deliver a fixed grade and staple U.S. cotton to a specified U.S. warehouse in July of 2003. The seller does not have to own 100 bales of cotton in order to be able to sell the right to own cotton at that date. If he buys back the contract before the closing date of the contract, he does not have to deliver the cotton. As long as one closes a position by selling a previously purchased contract or buying a contract sold in advance, there is no need to exchange an actual bale of cotton. Almost all futures contracts are closed before reaching the date specified. This opportunity to trade cotton without owning it is what makes a functioning futures market possible.

However, if one waits until the date of the contract becomes the present date, the seller has to deliver the cotton, and the buyer has to accept delivery of actual bales. If such a rare instance occurs, the exchange relation in the futures market undergoes a metamorphosis and becomes an exchange relation in the original market from which it derives—that is, the spot market. This is why futures markets are called derivative markets: they derive from relations of actual commodity exchange.

There are two different groups of participants in the futures market: hedgers and speculators. Hedgers demand or supply actual bales of cotton in the spot market in order to make a living. Hedgers limit their risk by reversing their market position in the spot market and reflecting it to the futures market. For example, a trader has to buy actual bales of cotton in order to sell them in the spot market. As soon as a trader buys 100 bales of actual cotton in the spot market, he sells one cotton futures contract in the futures market. The price he pays to the prior cotton owner is the futures market price of cotton, minus trading costs. This offer to the farmer specifies how many points *off the basis* (that is, off the futures market price of cotton) the trader is willing to pay. The trader then offers a price *on the basis* to a possible buyer, adding costs and projected profits.

As a result of the constantly fluctuating futures price of cotton, the trader bears a risk of losing money. If the futures price drops below the price he paid to buy the cotton in the first place, he will end up selling his cotton for less. Thus, in order to hedge his risk, he sells futures contracts as soon as he buys an actual bale of cotton. In this step, the trader buys 100 actual bales of cotton, but sells the *right to own* 100 actual bales of cotton to an anonymous buyer in the futures market. In the second round of exchange, the trader must find a buyer for the bales he has bought. As soon as he sells the cotton he has bought from the farmer, he closes his position in the futures market. In other words, he buys back the futures contract he has previously sold. Now he is even.

In order to illustrate how the trader controls his risk, let us imagine that the futures price decreases as soon as he buys actual bales of cotton from a farmer. He may lose money because he will quote a price based on the futures price. But since he also sold the futures contract as soon as he bought the actual cotton, he will still make money when he buys back the futures contract for less. Therefore, in the spot market he buys for more and sells for less, while in the futures market he sells for more and buys for less. His market position is even, because he has hedged his risk.

This is only one part of the story of how cotton futures markets work. There is also the nonhedging activity of speculators, which makes hedging possible, for if everyone is a hedger, hedging becomes impossible. The speculator's goal is to make monetary gains in the cotton futures market without exchanging a single bale of actual cotton in the spot market, by guessing the future value of cotton. If the speculator thinks that the price will increase, he buys cotton contracts and sells them later. If he thinks that the price will decrease, he sells cotton contracts, buys them back and closes his position as soon as he believes the time is right. He neither needs to own cotton nor be willing to own it.

This explains the term "basis 515 points on, for the next two hours" in the hypothetical trader's contract examined above: he wants the buyer to pay him 5.15 cents more than the futures market price of cotton in November of 2003. In order to locate the futures price, the buyer needs to consult another representation of the market.

The representation of the cotton futures market (figure 2) is essentially similar to the graph of the market in general as a coming together of supply and demand (Like figure 1, figure 2 claims to be "furnished without responsibility for accuracy." It does not have a claim to be *real*, as the note at the end of the table suggests. But an important difference distinguishes figure 2. Instead of spotting the price as a spatial location (P) in the graphic universe of the general market in figure 1, the NYBOT figure locates the price as the monetary indicator of the future worth of one pound of SLM cotton, which has an actual value on a specific day, in this case April 4, 2003.

Similar to locating P in figure 1, one can locate P here again by identifying the intersection of two lines. In figure 2, *time* (contract month) replaces *quantity* (Q). The price remains the second axis in both figures. In order to peruse the NYBOT table to arrive at the price for our hypothetical contract, one needs to start with the "contract month" column on the left-hand side and find December 2003, then follow it horizontally to the right to locate the point where it crosses the vertical price axis. The futures market price of the cotton in question is 60.00 c/lb. The cotton is to be delivered in November, but the table does not include this month. In this situation, traders use as point of reference the month

New York Board of Trade

COTTON NO. 2 (CT)

Friday, April 04, 2003

174 HUDSON STR. 6th FLOOR, New York, NY 10013
TEL. - (212)625-6610 FAX - (212)625-0432

CONTRACT SIZE: 50,000 pounds net weight

CONTRACT MONTH	DAILY PRICE RANGE				SETTLE		VOLUME	***Current Volume Report*** TOTALS AS OF 04/03/2003				CONTRACT	
	OPEN		HIGH	LOW	CLOSE		PRICE	CHANGE		OI	CHANGE	EFP's *	Estimated EFS's *	HIGH	LOW
May 2003	5745	5757	5785	5720	5765	5770	5769	+19	5670	43488	-850	477	0	6055	3870
Jul 2003	5861	5870	5915	5855	5908	5910	5910	+24	3328	23063	+345	0	0	6090	3950
Oct 2003	5900[B]	5930[A]	0	0	5940[B]	5970[A]	5955	+30	43	986	+22	0	0	6010	4360
Dec 2003	5955	5960	6005	5950	6000	0	6000	+30	1720	13399	+392	0	0	6100	4380
Mar 2004	6125[B]	6140[A]	6150	6145	6160[B]	6170[A]	6165	+20	173	2010	+103	0	0	6275	4560
May 2004	6190[B]	6210[A]	0	0	6210[B]	6220[A]	6215	-5	0	433	0	0	0	6350	5150
Jul 2004	6250[B]	6300[A]	0	0	6310[B]	6320[A]	6315	-5	0	541	0	0	0	6350	5675
Oct 2004	6150[B]	6220[A]	0	0	6210[B]	6220[A]	6215	0	0	1	0	0	0	6000	6000
Dec 2004	6150[B]	6220[A]	0	0	6220[B]	6230[A]	6225	0	0	60	0	0	0	6290	6050
Mar 2005	6250[B]	6300[A]	0	0	6300[B]	6320[A]	6310	0	0	0	0	0	0	0	0
Totals									10934	83981	+12	477	0		

Figure 2   The price of futures market.

Source: www.nybot.com. Accessed on April 5, 2003.

Note: The information contained in this report is compiled for the convenience of subscribers and is furnished without responsibility for accuracy and is accepted by the subscriber on the condition that errors or omissions shall not be made the basis for any claim, demand, or cause of action.

closest to the one during which they must deliver in order to calculate the actual price.

Because the hypothetical seller's response is "basis 515 on Nov 03," the buyer needs to add 5.15 to the December 2003 price in order to calculate the price he sent us as firm offer. But when should the buyer do this calculation? Because our temporal vantage point is April 4, 2003, it is impossible for the buyer to know with certainty how much the December 2003 price will be in November 2003. Yet, he does know, in April of 2003, that the December 2003 price is 60.00 c/lb. Thus, the buyer may assume, although with great risk, that he will pay somewhere around 5.15 + 60.00, or a total of 65.15 c/lb, in November of 2003. Because he wants to buy not only one pound, but 1,000 metric tons of cotton, the price he has to pay the trader is USD 1,436,558.[6]

THE PRICE DISAPPEARS AGAIN

Finally, the buyer has found the price. But has he really? Because the trader's offer is valid only for two hours, the actual price has a rather short life. Although the price of the market disappears very quickly, the changing price in the futures market remains constant. Would the buyer actually pay around 65.15 c/lb if he had accepted the offer? On October 16, 2003, the December 2003 contract will be traded at 74.09 c/lb.

It is clear that 74.09 is too high for the buyer, since the seller will add 5.15 c/lb basis to this price, for a total of 79.24 c/lb. The difference between the first actual price and this one is USD 310,684. For a textile mill, this is an enormous margin in one shipment. If repeated frequently, it can even lead to bankruptcy. Such unusual situations rarely emerge, not because the prices are stable, but because the merchants can guarantee a fixed price instead of a dynamic one in the offer, should the mill accept. This will be discussed in further detail later in this chapter.

There is another reason to doubt the answer that the hypothetical buyer obtained concerning the *real* price of cotton. Figure 2 does not help him in locating the actual price quoted. It is only a tool used to locate the trader's price and provides a range of prices around which one can consider buying cotton. The "market price" as posted above is neither the price of an actual pound of cotton, nor its future value. It is only a tool for pricing, not the actual price itself.

In that sense, futures markets serve as bridges between different moments of price realization. The price, as the note in figure 2 reads, is "furnished without responsibility for accuracy." Yet the futures price is

[6] 2,205 (1 metric ton equals 2,205 lbs) × 1,000 (he wants to buy 1,000 MT) × 65.15 cents.

the *basis* for making a price real. The power of the price derives from neither its real nor its fictional nature. It is a creative prosthesis that traders deploy in the middle of the process of price realization. It does not correspond to a real price; however, its fidelity is not contested by market participants during the process of the realization of the price of actual cotton. It is a *prosthetic price*. In the same way in which a cane enables a person with a limp to walk, the prosthetic price enables market actors to negotiate once it is used during trading on the ground.

An interesting set of questions arises when reconsidering the futures market (figure 2) in the framework of the supply and demand graph (figure 1). If we use the language of figure 1, we will have difficulty in understanding the futures market. Indeed, one can still talk about an interaction of supply and demand, but in figure 2 the bearers of supply and demand are not categorically different from each other. In the market in general (figure 1), one agent cannot supply and demand the same commodity at the same time. It would not make sense. However, in the futures market, a speculator can supply 100 bales of cotton for May of 2003 while at the same time demanding 100 bales of cotton for July of 2003. In futures, supply and demand are not entangled in a search for a marginal utility of owning a little bit of more cotton.

Moreover, one can argue that in the futures market the supply and demand sides (S and D in figure 1) are interchangeable. One does not need to have cotton, or a desire to demand or supply it, in order to participate in the exchange. Here, the two universal laws of demand and supply collapse onto each other. They do not collapse as a result of the fact that there are no clear sides from which to locate demand and supply (they do exist separately and independently of each other), but because the *raison d'être* of being a part of the market is not a desire to demand or supply cotton. The object of supply and demand in the spot market is not the object of the market exchange in futures.

Nevertheless, the actual price of real-life cotton—in the example here, an amount close to USD 1.5 million, representing the worth of 1,000 metric tons of SLM—derives at least in part from the NYBOT cotton futures market, whose object of exchange is not related to the marginal utility of demanding or supplying a bit more cotton. The futures market is the derivative of the spot market where actual bales of cotton are exchanged, and the actual price of cotton is derived from the already derived practice of futures exchange. Whichever term one uses for the final destination of a price realization process (real, original, actual), this final outcome is by nature a derivative of its representation.

In this example, the buyer in April of 2003 had to move forward in time in order to locate the price of an actual bale of cotton. How, then, is the actual price of 60.00 cents per pound made in the futures market? In

Figure 3   A global trader in his office.

other words, what are the conditions of the making of the futures price? The answer to this question requires us to leave behind the hypothetical market participants and bring real traders back into the story (figure 3).

MAKING SENSE OF THE PRICE

John Hogan had worked as a cotton trader for more than forty years when I first met him in the summer of 2002. By 2003, he was working both as a market consultant and as the program director of the only professional institute in the world that trains global traders to work in spot, futures, and options cotton markets. I became one of his students when I enrolled in the professional trader training program he directs in Memphis, Tennessee. My class consisted of thirty-four trader students from twenty different countries. Except for me, all students in this two-month training, which counts as the equivalent of two and a half years of company in-house training, had either already worked in cotton markets or planned to work for an international cotton trading company. I was Mr. Hogan's only student who had no desire to supply or demand cotton, yet wanted to be trained as cotton trader.

In the first week of classes, Mr. Hogan realized my rather modest capacity to understand what was at stake in futures trading. After a week of training, I was still wondering about what was going on in futures markets. My questions were of the following type: "What do you mean by futures value? Is this a real market? Where is the cotton anyway?" His answers did not make sense until we discussed after class the reason behind my slow appreciation of how markets work. Over a cup of coffee, he asked what it was exactly that I did not understand about cotton futures. My problem was coming to terms with the fact that "real cotton" did not have a price in futures markets, although "real cotton" was priced according to futures. His answer clarified everything to me. Joking about the little black notebook I always carried with me, he said:

> I know you'll write this, too. You're always thinking about what the real price of cotton is. You always want to learn what the price is in real life. But the market does not trade on reality. It trades on perceptions.

What does it mean when one of the world's most experienced and successful international cotton traders thinks that markets operate on perceptions? Given that the market is about perceptions, do factors determining how we perceive the market have an actual effect on the market? How exactly do perceptions affect the shaping of the price on the ground? How are perceptions themselves produced, consumed, circulated, and contested?

The following day, I felt more comfortable in the trading simulation session. The relationship between perception, its representations, and reality was not an urgent issue, at least for survival during the trading exercise, which was based on a representation of the world cotton market. For Mr. Hogan, it was not important at all whether a derivative market (the futures) was less real than the one it was derived from (the spot). His main concern, and the one he wanted to impress upon us, was to attempt to predict what the market would do the following day.

This central concern is shared by almost all of the international or regional cotton traders with whom I worked and whom I interviewed. Their ways of attending to price-making did not differ greatly. The set of principles governing their everyday decision-making process was informed by a form of pragmatism, oscillating between positivist, antipositivist, and even constructivist assumptions about the external world surrounding them. They did not necessarily separate *what was* from *what others thought it was*. A strategic suspension of the correspondence between representation and reality in the way traders relate to and understand the market is important for their success. Yet a total denial of correspondence would be a catalyst for failure. Thus, a successful trader can juggle different ways of looking at the market, without relying too much on orthodoxy; for example, he should not always assume that there will be a decrease in price once there is a significant increase in the supply of cotton. Instead, an experienced trader will try to find out how market participants perceive market interactions and how their perceptions will affect these market actors' everyday practice.

The means to gather knowledge about perceptions in the market is to carry out *research in the wild* on a daily basis,[7] on all the key factors that a trader believes to make the market. Individual traders usually follow a daily routine of information gathering, based on their individual experience. Some start their day by browsing through financial indicators, while others switch on their computers to look at the figures that their intermediary trading company sends them. Large trading companies have employees, or even in-house economists, who gather and interpret everyday information for those who carry out trading decisions. The ways of doing research vary, but there are a number of sources everybody studies carefully, such as market reports.

MARKET REPORTS

Figure 4 is a popular and respected market report, dated April 11, 2003, published by one of the oldest global cotton trading companies. Founded in 1788 in Winterthur, Switzerland, only a few months before the French Revolution, the company is now run by the descendants of the Reinhart family. Unlike figures 1 and 2, this report is framed neither as a graphic representation nor as a cross tabulation of prices. It discusses the main factors that make the market and the changes to which the market, very much like an agent, reacts in either a bullish fashion (with increasing prices) or a bearish one (with decreasing prices).

The report opens with the observation that "the market reacted to the friendly USDA (United States Department of Agriculture) supply and demand numbers released before the opening." Traders rely on governmental, intergovernmental, and private agencies—such as the USDA, the International Cotton Advisory Committee (ICAC), and Cotlook, respectively—that gather information and post reports about global, regional and individual countries' cotton production and consumption figures. All international trading houses also have their own information-gathering networks, which rely mostly on their agents' and representatives' on-the-ground experiences in cotton-producing and -consuming countries.

A set of four fundamental market indicators is central to any market report, whether governmental or private. This set also constitutes the vantage point from which a trader can interpret how the market will behave

---

[7] *Research in the wild* is a term Michel Callon uses to refer to the way nonscientists produce knowledge (Callon and Rabeharisoa 2003).

REINHART
COTTON MARKET REPORT

phone: 972 301 3200
fax: 972 301 3284

New York showed some weakness early, but it only lasted until Thursday, when the market reacted to the friendly USDA supply/ demand numbers released before the opening. Option traders became aggressive buyers, forced to cover their exposure, as May03 moved toward 58.00. **May03 options** expired after uneventful trading today. For the week, May03 closed at 58.00 up 31 pts. and Dec03 settled at 61.38, gaining 138 pts. As of last Friday, **speculators** had slightly increased their net futures long position to 39.1%, from 38.8% previously. Next week's report will show them considerably less long, as a large percentage of their long futures position was held to cover their May03 short calls. The 2002/03 and 2003/04 **Cotlook A Indices** remained practically unchanged this week at 61.30 and 63.40, respectively. Starting next Friday, the **six-week AWP transition** period will begin. Provided the two indices remain the same, the cost of CCC loan redemption will increase by 210 pts. after this time frame.

Weekly **US export sales** amounted to 157,000 bales for last week, bringing total commitments to 11.14 million (480 lbs.). Main buyers were India (26,000), Turkey (24,500), China (24,500) and Mexico. Shipments totaled 390,000. With US shippers having completed two consecutive weeks of exports of over 350,000 bales, this should rule out any concern that, after a slow start, logistical problems may not let the US reach the USDA target of 10.8 million (480 lbs.) bales. **US 2003/04 crop plantings** continue in Texas (mostly completed in the Rio Grande Valley) and are beginning in the Southeast. However, the persistent cold weather in California is slowing the progress and forcing some replanting. 5% of the US crop was planted as of last Sunday, slightly behind last year's 6%, but the same as the five-year average.

Yesterday, the USDA released its **supply/demand** reports, increasing **US 2002/03** production by 70,000 bales to 17.2 million bales; domestic use (7.6) and exports (10.8) were left unchanged. Ending stocks increased by 100,000 (to 6.3). The 2002/03 **world production** decreased by 145,000 bales with major changes in India (−200,000), Pakistan (−100,000) and Syria (+75,000). **Consumption** increased by 725,000 bales, mainly in China (+500,000, now at 28.0 million), Pakistan (+200,000) and Egypt (+150,000), partially offset by reductions in India, Russia and Turkey (−100,000 each). No changes were made to previous years' figures anywhere. World **ending stocks** were reduced by 940,000 bales. Below, the USDA 2002/03 statistics (last month's in parenthesis) and the 2003/04 crop numbers compiled by Cotlook, ICAC, and our group. (The USDA will provide new crop numbers for the first time on May 12).

(million bales of 480 lbs.)	USDA 02/03	Cotlook 03/04	ICAC 03/04	Reinhart 03/04
Beginning stocks	46.46 (46.46)		40.9	38.5
Production	87.84 (87.99)	96.0	95.8	96.0
Mill use	97.80 (97.07)	98.3	96.6	97.0
Ending Stocks	36.62 (37.56)		40.1	37.5

China continues to purchase imported cotton, but not at the recent fast pace. We understand that mill stocks and their unreceived purchases cover, on average, only about two months of consumption, but that farmers and domestic traders are still holding large stocks. The official 2002/03 production figure of 22.6 million bales is widely accepted, including by the USDA. Consumption could be anywhere between 27.5 and 28.5 (USDA has 28.0). The government has announced measures to accelerate cotton selling and to provide stability to the market. Looking ahead to 2003/04, things appear very friendly for prices: Early projections point to another deficit-year; on top of that, the need to replenish stocks makes the scenario even more bullish. Also, many mills are considering buying new machinery to improve efficiencies and consumption. A number of export-oriented mills have apparently shifted their focus to the domestic market due to better demand and prices. This fact may not only give many Far Eastern countries a chance to regain market share, but also bodes well for a continuation of the upward trend in the world's cotton use.

OUTLOOK:
The USDA report showing a 1.0 million bale reduction in foreign ending stocks by July 31, 2003, may turn out to be another wake-up call for cotton buyers worldwide. Stocks are tight and the current guesstimates do not give much hope for relief during the 2003/04 season. We have been long-term friendly for prices since March 1, 2002 (May03 44.90). At that time we wrote that "lower 2002/03 crops will eventually bring higher prices." Since then, we have expressed our bullish long-term view on prices in more than 20 of our weekly OUTLOOK columns. We feel the same way today, especially for 2003/04.

REINHART , INC., Dallas   **www.reinhart.com**   April 11, 2003

Figure 4   Market report.
Source: www.reinhart.com. Accessed on April 18, 2003.

in the near future. First, market reports start out by locating stocks, for diminishing stocks are an indicator of rising demand or decreasing supply, which may increase the price. Production is another crucial factor, because an increase in world production may result in depressed prices. Mill Use, the third factor, is an indicator of supply: the more the mills spin, the more cotton they will need; therefore, a bullish effect on the market may occur. Finally, Ending Stocks locates the volume of carryover to the next cotton season, which, if low, may be an indicator of increasing prices.

As in figures 1 and 2, then, supply and demand figures are fundamental tools for locating the market. Yet, unlike in figure 1, these inferences, which help traders to locate the powers that move market prices, are treated as possibilities, and not as determinations in the form of universal laws. As an international merchant who trades West African cotton told me during an interview, "traders know that you never know." This is not an agnostic position; it simply means that it is not possible to locate an a priori logic of the market, for it has none.

The figures published in market reports are only estimates, and the product of observation as much as of negotiation among those who contribute to their making.[8] Traders know that representational tools used in markets, such as the statistics above, can never be finally and fully representative of actual levels of production and consumption before the cotton is produced and consumed. Traders always use this statistical apparatus with a dose of skepticism, for they assume that the manipulation of information through massaging the data is a powerful marketing strategy. It is not uncommon for regional traders to try to depress prices before and during the cotton harvest by overestimating production. Similarly, an international trading house hopes to affect the perceptions of market participants, from hedgers to speculators, by propagating a certain view of the market best suited to its own market position.

Therefore, although important, the figures supposedly representing levels of future production and consumption are only some of the many factors that interact in a market setting. This is also why both the traders and the reports themselves call the figures "guesstimates." In fact, full information is never possible, not because of the absence of tools that would allow traders to know more and in a more complete fashion, but because prices are realized, in part, through representational prosthetics. In a world of exchange where on a daily basis actuality is constantly in touch with indexicality,[9] both the existence of information and the lack thereof are similar prosthetic tools for realizing prices.

The fact that these market figures, such as those of supply and demand, have market-making as well as representative powers is a *sine qua non* piece of information that all traders must take into account in order to interpret successfully their possible effects on the making of the price. According to an Australian cotton exporter,

---

[8] For an ethnographical discussion of how these figures are produced see chapter 3.

[9] Indexicality is a concept Maurer borrows from linguistic anthropology (Maurer 2002).

A successful trader is the one who can make the market. You need power to do this, though. And not everyone can make the market. That is why they're all writing market reports, all of them. They say they provide their clients with information. Why then [do] they all write different things, and they all come up with different numbers? Partly because they have different market positions.

Another fundamental difference between the first two market representations and figure 4 is the appearance of the object of exchange and its position as agents that have independent capacities to affect the price. For example, the fact that a cotton tree as a living organism may react quite unexpectedly to changes in its environment is a crucial factor every trader takes into account.

In figure 4, the author of the reports use two words five times to refer to the object of exchange. The first is "cotton," a short-hand term used to refer to an already commodified object of exchange and its multiple forms, such as SLM. The "crop," on the other hand, is a rather alarming word for traders because the crop is open to all sorts of risk factors that can impede its growth, and, unlike in the futures market, here one cannot limit one's exposure to risk by using derivatives. Very much like grape crops whose annual variations affect the wine market, each year's crop has a different quality, and mills usually do not want to mix cotton from different years' crops in one layout. The outcome of the uncontrollable effects of nature on the crop is independent of and prefigures the effects of supply and demand. For example, according to figure 4, persistent cold weather in California at the beginning of April of 2003 slowed the progress of preparing the fields and forced growers to replant crops. This could have decreased production or delayed the crop's arrival on the market. Thus, climate, weather, and other natural effects, as well as how cotton farmers and traders deal with these natural forces, constitute factors that affect the price. For traders, nature is part of the calculation. The plant itself and its natural environment have a greater effect on the making of the price than on the representations of the market, such as figure 1. The way in which these effects are perceived is the fundamental drive moving the market, and that is why traders always consider the weather. Traders may expect the market to respond to these changes and try to react correspondingly, since they want to move the market before it is moved by others. All international trading companies either employ an in-house meteorologist or use one of their employees to track and record changes in the natural environment.

Once cotton is grown, ginned, and brought to the market after having been standardized by biologists, agricultural engineers, genetic engineers, and market experts, other factors begin to exert an influence on the making of the price. One of them is the traders' knowledge of what other traders know or do not know. For almost all cotton traders, whether regional or interregional, learning what China does as well as what others think China will do is an important asset. China, the largest producer and consumer of cotton in the world, is a large black box. The market report in figure 4 even includes an entire paragraph on China. In an interview, one cotton trader from Mexico said: "You never know what the Chinese will do." He continued:

> They say they don't have stocks, and then you have hundreds of thousands of bales. You know what happened a few years ago. They underestimated Chinese carryover, we made our decisions accordingly. We were all wrong. Suddenly the Chinese had more cotton than the figures said. First I didn't believe what I saw on a market report a friend had sent me. The price collapsed because everyone thought that the supply would be much higher.

Here it becomes clear how perceptions can have real effects on the everyday workings of the market. In this case, miscalculations resulted in underestimating Chinese carryover. Traders around the world assumed that the world supply was contracting quickly and managed their positions accordingly. Then, China declared its actual level of stocks, and because the information had come from the source itself, one representation of the market was undermined. Cotton prices declined, helping those who kept in mind that one never knows, and teaching once more the importance of the obligatory skepticism that traders always embrace and use effectively.

In such a mercantile universe, rumors and speculations from "a certain Chinese market analyst" can be as powerful as supply and demand figures for governing trade decisions. The sharp increase in the futures price of cotton in New York on September 26, 2003, was explained in terms of neither weather nor contracting supplies. According to one report, "rumors about sales to China led to a hectic and volatile trading activity at the New York futures market and prices made new highs."[10] Because it is not easy to create, disseminate, and sustain rumors, they are not the most frequent factor moving the market. Yet, in their everyday conversation, traders discuss rumors frequently. They mock them and tease each other while referring to rumors proven to be false; however, they also take great pleasure in talking about the ones that helped them make money, because nobody "knew" that they were accurate.

Which rumors can one trust? Can rumors be a basis for trading decisions? I asked these questions to all the international trading house representatives I interviewed. The interviewers did not mention that the committees carrying out trading decisions ever took rumors seriously.

---

[10] Reinhart Co. Market Report, No. 43/39, 26.09.2003.

Still, almost all of them referred to a particular rumor that moved the market. "We don't take them seriously," explained a trader sitting on a bar stool while watching a Weather Channel program, "you cannot refer to a rumor and ask your boss to borrow and invest in trade, referring to what you have heard from so-and-so."

> *But I heard that rumors move the market and everyone takes them seriously.*
> I take them seriously, too. They are crucial. I don't know why, it is not scientific to refer to rumors, we don't talk about them. But we know there are companies who disseminate rumors. And specs are affected. When specs begin to do things, then you know that rumors are working. So even if you don't find it scientific, you have to take it seriously.
> *Then you talk about them in your meetings.*
> Yes, we do, because sometimes not taking a rumor seriously can cost money, because others may take it very seriously.
> *Did your company ever circulate any rumors?*
> My company never does this.
> *But there are rumors that you guys do, too.*
> Yes, I heard that. It is just rumors.

Although rumors are circulated in trader circles and can occasionally move the market, they are usually contained in a series of statistical and informative reports. For example, the *Spec-Hedge Report*, as it is referred to by traders, contains crucial information on the trading activity in the NYBOT cotton futures exchange. The report summarizes the market in terms of a distribution between speculators and hedgers, and then divides each group in terms of their market position: long or short. Then each party is grouped under house and customer accounts. Any trader who buys or sells more than 50 contracts or 5,000 bales of cotton, an amount close to that grown by between 500 and 1,000 farming families in the Turkish and Egyptian villages in which I conducted fieldwork, must be registered with the Commodity Futures Trading Commission (CFTC)[11] as a house account, for they have a larger influence on the market than do individual investors.

Long-position holders are those who buy cotton contracts in order to sell them soon, whereas "shorts" are those who sell cotton contracts to make money when they buy them back in the future. Because speculative trading is conducted without trading a single bale of actual cotton, all of these spec positions should be closed before their underlying future date. For example, if specs are 60 percent long, one assumes that "longs" will

---

[11] The Commodity Futures Trading Commission is an independent agency created by the U.S. Congress in 1974. It is the regulator of commodity futures and option markets in the United States.

sell their cotton contracts, for they cannot wait and accept delivery of the commodity. Such a situation will have a bearish effect on the market, depending on the number of speculative positions.

Official market reports are crucial tools for making the market for cotton traders. Their date and time of publication are always fixed. Traders take special care to mark these days in their calendars. For example, Tuesdays are marked for the *Spec and Hedge Report* published by the NYBOT, Thursdays for the *U.S. Export, Sales and Shipment Report* by the USDA. The *Four Months and Older Cotton Certified Report* is published on the first day of every month, the *U.S. Crop Report* on the twelfth day, and on the thirtieth day the *U.S. Cotton Consumption Report* arrives in the traders' mailboxes or fax machines. There are also annual reports, such as that of the International Cotton Advisory Committee (ICAC), summarizing the year's main events and discussing their possible implications for the market.

What is commonly referred to as the world market price of cotton appears in a crucial market report published by an influential, privately owned, Liverpool-based company: Cotlook Ltd. Originally published as a four-page document at the beginning of the twentieth century, it is now a daily publication read by all international cotton traders. Like the dailies of the nineteenth century that helped forge the imagination of the nation, these publications facilitate not only imagining, but also engaging in the temporal topography of commodity exchange that we call the global market. This point is crucial for understanding global markets. Imagining these temporal locations of exchange happens through engaging with them, by using prostheses like world prices.

It is almost impossible to come across a cotton market report that does not refer to Cotlook figures or an international cotton trader who does not keep an eye on them. These indices also play a central role in how the market report in figure 4 summarizes the making of the world market for cotton traders. What traders understand as the global price of cotton appears in this representation of the market as Cotlook Dual Index System.

Cotlook Ltd. maintains an information-gathering network in order to receive quotes from all of the major cotton-growing regions in the world. The prices of forty-five different cotton types from the most expensive long-staple cotton to lower-quality shorter counts, grown by fifty million farmers from thirty-three countries, are tabulated under the title *CIF North Europe Quotations for Principle Growths*. A few minutes after it is published—in other words, also produced as a commodity—each weekday at 2:30 p.m. GMT, this price table circulates around the globe, reaching all major traders and merchants. Learning cotton prices comes at a price, too: traders pay an annual fee of USD 6,105.79 to receive these reports.[12] Many small regional traders fax these reports to each other in order to share the cost with their colleagues.

Cotlook market experts carry out what they call a "pricing routine" on a daily basis, by gathering quotations through corresponding with hundreds of cotton traders who sell or buy these crops. Cotlook does not disclose the identity of the traders from whom it receives quotations; however, by and large these traders are known by their colleagues. The pricing routine starts in Memphis, Tennessee, usually after 2:00 p.m. U.S. Central Time, with telephone calls, e-mails, and faxes from merchants who may have speculative or actual positions in the market and with whom the agency has been working for years. Nonexporters and small companies are not consulted in this routine. It is important to note that the cotton prices gathered are not firm offers, representing the monetary worth of an actual bale of cotton, but quotations that represent prices around which buyers and sellers are willing to sell or buy. They are not the prices made in recent sales either, for once the market is made traders are not particularly interested in previous actual prices. The quest for the price in global markets is an engagement with the future, not with the past.

Furthermore, these quotes include the transportation cost of cotton to Northern European ports, although most cotton does not arrive in these ports. Although textile mills have moved from Northern Europe to the Third World, posted world cotton prices continue to incorporate the cost of transporting cotton to Europe. These quotes also take into account insurance, profit, and agents' commissions.[13]

For one of the senior representatives of Cotlook, "the difficult part is to find out representative offering prices." Market experts know very well that merchants may intend to move the price quotes according to their position. Moreover, merchants also talk to each other on a daily basis and may try to forge a common market position depending on their mutual interests.[14] How, then, can one know that the quotes that market experts receive from merchants accurately represent the price? "Full

---

[12] The price includes daily reports, CIF Quotes, and weekly reports. It was £3,659.76 or 5,193.89 Euro on October 7, 2003.

[13] Cotlook recently introduced a new selection of quotations for Far Eastern Asia delivery, but they do not inform the making of the A Index, discussed in the remaining part of the chapter.

[14] Price depression is the most frequent goal of the merchants, for they sell more cotton when cotton prices decline. This is because mills tend to use more cotton and less polyester, a side-product of petroleum, when cotton prices are relatively cheaper than oil prices. Moreover, merchants need to use less capital when prices decrease. This is also why, whether in the United States or Egypt, they have a class interest in depressing prices to an optimal level, so that farmers can continue to produce.

accuracy is impossible," according to one of the experts who gather these quotes:

> Because you never know the price. What you learn is various offering prices. There is nothing you can actually cross-check to see whether these prices are accurate. Think about the A Index. Can you really compare it with something else? You can't. You simply can't. . . . Imagine that we get ten offers from the Memphis area. What are you going to do when the offers you get have a range of 800 points? This means 8 cents per pound. This is a huge difference, far exceeding the basis. So what we do is to understand what is behind the prices.
>
> *What do you mean by "behind the prices"?*
>
> This is very important. We ask around. We try to learn the market positions of those who send us quotations. We may end up funding a merchant buying like crazy. He will fax us an offer much below what he is willing to pay. We know this. It is experience. We then try to understand whether he is low or high relative to others. Then we decide what to do. We can pretty well tell when someone would like to put it [the price] up or down. Then we make up our mind, and set a point that we think represents the market price. But it is not a simple average, we may leave a few offers we think inaccurate aside. I think we are pretty good at this, because these quotations are regarded as world market prices by everyone, including the United States, European Union, and Egypt. The SEAM also uses our indices as a basis.[15] People trust us to make this decision. Because they know that we don't have a market position whatsoever. We don't trade futures, options, and cash.

This pricing routine is carried out in the same way in all other cotton-producing regions in the world, by going beyond the price itself and locating the way in which the politics of representing and negotiating the price is performed. "During the compilation of our reports, we collect offering prices from many sources," reads the company's report, "[. . .] our assessment of them is inevitably a somewhat subjective process" (Anonymous 2002). It is this subjective intervention in the process of price realization that secures the strength of the report's representative "objectivity" and power. Experts know that they are not trying to reveal an invisible price; they are intervening in relations of exchange to make a prosthetic price.

After gathering these quotations and then "editing" them by going beyond the offer itself, Cotlook Ltd. publishes two indices, A and B, which together are regarded as the world market prices of cotton. These two indices are called the Dual Index System. A and B refer to two separate

---

[15] SEAM is a website that brings together those who want to trade cotton in an internet-based cash market.

indices made up of the quotations received for middling- and coarse-count cotton, respectively. Duality refers to the co-presence of two quotations, the Current and the Forward, in one table of indices—the former for the shipment of cotton at a nearby date no later than August-September of any given year, and the latter for shipment in the future no earlier than October-November of the same year.

The A Index is produced by taking the arithmetic average of the cheapest five quality-specific quotations for middling cotton with a staple length of 1 3/32 inches, produced in the United States, Mexico, Brazil, Paraguay, Turkey, Syria, Greece, Spain, Uzbekistan, Pakistan, India, China, Tanzania, the African Franc Zone,[16] and Australia. The B Index represents the world prices of lower-grade cotton with comparable quality, usually with a staple length between 1 1/16 and 1 1/32 inches, grown in the United States, Brazil, Argentine, Turkey, Uzbekistan, Pakistan, India, and China. After receiving quotations from merchants trading cottons from these countries, the editors locate a price that, according to them, best represents trading levels. They then take the arithmetic average of the cheapest five offers and post it as Current B and Forward B.

When cotton market reports, newspapers, or magazines refer to world cotton prices, they are referring to these indices. According to figure 4, the Current and Forward A Indices are 61.30 c/lb and 63.40 c/lb, respectively. Unlike figure 1, the price of the market report in figure 4 does not aim at representing the monetary worth of an actual bale of cotton or a bushel of corn, as Marshall would have put it. The price is not made in the crossing point of two lines, at a location where they maintain a balance. The index is regarded as the world price of cotton precisely because it does not aim to locate a point where supply and demand meet each other. Everyone, from traders to market experts, knows very well that the coming together of what figure 1 calls "supply and demand" is a temporal and scattered practice which cannot be captured by a metaphor based on space, as Robinson showed years ago and Maurer reemphasized recently (Maurer 2002).

The index, not the price, is realized in a pricing routine whereby quotations are regarded and edited *individually* and brought together by arithmetical framing, and not by geometrical positioning, as in figure 1. The indexical price of figure 4 is not a geometric price, which is a representation of what figure 1 would call a real price. It is the intersubjective dynamism of what the experts at Cotlook Ltd. call the pricing routine that

---

[16] The African Franc Zone countries include Benin, Burkina Faso, Ivory Coast, Mali, Niger, Cameroon, Senegal, Chad, Togo, Congo, Gabon, Guinea-Bissau, Equatorial Guinea, and the Republic of Central Africa; however, only quotes from the first nine countries are included in the A Index.

makes it possible to locate a point around which prices can be negotiated over time.

The index-derived nature of the price is crucial in the sense that the index does not refer to something other than that which it manufactures, but it is not circularly referential either (cf. Robinson 1980). The A Index is indexical for the market price it constructs through the pricing routine. The market as such appears as a map of relations of exchange that occur within a field of power relations. It is crucial at this point not to assume either that "the market happens" and then the index emerges, or that the index makes the market itself because, as we have seen, the pricing routine is carried out as a process parallel to the marketing of cotton. Pricing routine and exchange routine are simultaneous and interdependent processes. The index that informs the daily trading practices of traders is already informed by the daily practices of the very merchants who use it on the ground. The Cotlook A price represents the traders' perceptions and interests, as located in terms of the worth of a pound of cotton (in our example, 61.30 cents). This price of 61.30 cents is a prosthetic device, and not necessarily the monetary worth of an actual bale of cotton. It is an apparatus that helps traders to locate the dynamics of exchange, the prices around which buying and selling are carried out. This, in turn, provides traders with tools for the realization of the prosthetic price, because this price is based on what traders think the price is/should be as well as what market experts see "beyond their prices." The index is made up of perceptions—this is precisely what the market is based on according to Mr. Hogan.

How exactly do such perceptions in their new indexed form inform actual prices? Traders whose everyday practices are represented in the supply and demand graph of figure 1 prefer the reports in figure 2, the table of the futures market, and in figure 4 when they attend to the conditions of the market, not only because they think that with their help they can make sense of the interactions of the market, but also because the arithmetic price of Cotlook, which is *indexical* to everyday perceptions, has a direct effect on the actual price of cotton. This is true, not only because of the index's power to shape or be shaped by the perceptions of traders, but also because the U.S. government, whose cotton exports in 2001 and 2002 represented 39 percent of the world cotton market, accepts the A Index as the world price of cotton and furthermore uses it to locate the levels of various forms of subsidies, thus contributing to the realization of the price in a quite effective way.

The United States, the largest cotton exporter and second-largest producer in the world, enacted two farm bills in the last decade, the Farm Security and Rural Investment Acts in 2002 and 2008. These bills made the United States the largest subsidized cotton-growing and market system in the world. Roughly speaking, half of the total income of the 25,000 cotton-growing companies and farmers comes from the U.S. government. There are four essential components of the 2002 bill related to cotton growing and exchange. In all of these components, identification of the world market price of cotton is essential. According to the first, the Non-Recourse Loan Program, all cotton growers are eligible to receive a loan on their crop following its harvest, which is fixed as 52.00 c/lb until 2008.[17] After using this option, the vast majority of farmers pay back the loan. The second component of the bill introduces a new dimension to the first: if the adjusted world price of cotton is lower than the fixed loan rate, then the farmers are required to pay back only the adjusted world price to redeem the cotton, not the original 52.00 c/lb loan they received from the U.S. government. The third component usually is deployed in situations where there is a tight supply. Farmers in these situations can sell their produce immediately after the harvest; they can still borrow from the government, but only if the world price is less than the loan rate.

The last component includes a three-step competitiveness provision for which location of the world price of cotton is essential. Step 1 (Discretionary Adjustment Program) is designed to nominally reduce the world price of cotton so that more subsidies can be extended to the U.S. cotton sector. For example, if the Secretary of Agriculture thinks that U.S. exports are lower than expected, and if the world price of cotton is lower than 115 percent of the loan rate, the bill authorizes the secretary to nominally decrease the world price of cotton used for the U.S. pricing mechanism. In other words, this is the adjustment of the adjustment.

When the world price of cotton is lower than 134 percent of the fixed loan rate for four consecutive weeks, Step 2 (User Marketing Certificate Program) is deployed, so that the difference between domestic and world markets can be paid to U.S. textile mills and U.S. cotton exporters. The payment is the difference between the lowest quotation for U.S. Middling with a staple length of 1 3/32 inches and the A Index as published by Cotlook Ltd. Step 3 (Limited Global Import Quota), the last provision, is applied when the domestic market price exceeds the world price of cotton, so that the Secretary of Agriculture can allow a certain quantity of foreign growth to be imported to the United States. However, it is rare to observe the opening of this quota, for the United States barely imports any cotton at all.

In all of these different ways of extending subsidies to U.S. growers and traders, the price of cotton in the world market plays a central formative role. The ways in which this price is located can have consequences far exceeding the importance of the indexical price. Because of the ways in which traders relate to the market, and because the indexical price is

[17] Premiums and discounts are applied for different cotton qualities.

taken for granted as the actual price, another market agency, the U.S. government, is pushing the processes of price realization to a whole new dimension: by relying on the A Index, the USDA calculates an Adjusted World Price (AWP), using the following formula:

$$(2 \times \text{Current A}) + (1 \times \text{Forward A}) /3.$$

The end result then is adjusted for shipping, quality and location differentials, taking as basis the U.S. cotton quality[18] and ports. The resulting Adjusted World Price (AWP) is announced every Thursday afternoon at 4:00 pm U.S. Central Time.

The AWP is another frequent focus in cotton market reports. On April 11, 2003, the date on which figure 4 was published, the AWP was 48.22 c/lb, whereas the Current A Index was 61.30 c/lb. The nature of the Current A Index, from which the AWP is derived, undergoes a metamorphosis during this interesting moment of price realization in world markets. Although the two prosthetic prices are similar in nature because they do not represent the price of an actual bale of cotton, it is their different capacities and formative moments in shaping actual prices that make them quite distinct. The index is a tool for engagement in the market, whereas the AWP is the deployment of the tool itself. The already derivative nature of the A Index is not only assumed to be the price, but also made to be the world price of cotton after filtering it through various steps of adjustment.

The AWP loses its indexical character through two main processes: first, the USDA assumes it to be referential and thus capable of representing the world price of cotton. Because the only way to determine a world market price is to calculate a price by indexing the relations of exchange around a commodity, the assumption of its referentiality is almost a necessity for anyone who aims to locate the price to freeze a moment of correspondence between the indexical price and an imaginary bale of cotton. Second, once assumed to be referential and adjusted, the A Index is used as a tool of further realization of the price, by making it a reference point according to which the universe of U.S. subsidies is constructed. This temporary and imagined moment of freezing ongoing and dynamic relations of exchange each Thursday afternoon at 4:00 p.m. U.S. Central Time makes this nonstop activity of exchange possible. In order for the price to be realized in all of its forms of appearance, it is necessary to make such calculative breaks.

This moment of price realization in world markets also shapes the future realization of prices in cotton-growing regions around the world, by

---

[18] Strict Low Middling (SLM) 1-1/16 inch, leaf grade 4, micronaire 3.5–3.6 and 4.3–4.9, strength 24–25 grams per Tex.

affecting all prices, indexical or not and thus contributing to the making of the price as an index. Therefore, depending on the moment that one chooses as the vantage point from which to look at the market, the indexical price and the referential price of cotton can be seen as derivatives of each other, while still preserving their prosthetic quality of indexicality and referentiality, respectively.

For example, if one considers the moment when the A Index is posted and then used to derive the AWP, one may conclude that the AWP is a derivative of the index. Yet, if one considers the moment after the AWP is published, taking into account the production of the A Index, the index then can be seen as a derivative of the AWP. However, the writers of the index insist that their report refers to or represents nothing more than its own making, a point which is underscored in the reports of Cotlook Ltd. As in the NYBOT futures market table in figure 2, all reports end with a disclaimer, and also perhaps a reminder that no report draws "a true picture of the market," for the report can only be used as an index, not as a referent.[19]

The A Index and the AWP as two world prices mutually shape each other. However, the fundamental difference between their production processes should not be overlooked. They are both prosthetic prices; yet the representative power of the AWP relies on the indexical power of the Cotlook A, and not vice versa. The fact that the AWP is produced by a government agency does not constitute a radical deviation from the processes of price realization as a whole. With or without government intervention, it is this pricing prosthetics that makes price realization possible in world markets. The AWP is just another adjustment in the process of the realization of the price, because the actual price of cotton in our example (USD 1,436,558 [62.84 c/lb]) is not visible in any representation of cotton world prices. It has disappeared and has been replaced by prosthetic representations, such as P, the AWP, the NYBOT futures price, and the A Index, none of which refer to the price of any actual bale of cotton, while at the same time they all participate in different ways in the realization of an actual price of cotton, that is, 65.15 c/lb.

Optional Prices of Cotton

Before concluding the discussion of price realization in international markets, there is one more price of cotton that needs to be taken into account. This discussion will bring us back to the supply and demand graph in figure 1, via a very complicated process that draws on extremely

---

[19] See, for instance, *Cotton Outlook*, June 7, 2002, 20.

simple yet effective assumptions about relations of exchange in particular and the nature of social relations in general. The discussion of the options price of cotton is the vantage point for the market report in figure 4. No market report can miss referring to the options price; no international trader can work without making it a part of his price offers.

The firm offer that the hypothetical trader makes to the hypothetical buyer, "basis 515 points on, for the next two hours," means that he is willing to sell his cotton 5.15 c/lb above the December 2003 price in November of 2003. The date of the deal is April 4, 2003; yet it would be in November that the 5.15 points were to be added to the December 2003 price if the buyer accepted the deal. However, the futures price skyrockets from 60.00 c/lb to74.09 c/lb in October of 2003. If it were possible to pay a premium to the merchant so that the mill did not pay, let's say, more than 70.00 c/lb in November, even if the price rose to 90.00 c/lb, it would be a great risk-limiting option for the buyer, a terrific risk-trading possibility for speculators, and a quite effective service to merchants whose customers need to be protected from risk, so that they can continue buying from them. Such a risk-controlling option was made possible in 1984 through the introduction of cotton options trading by the NYBOT. The options market is a derivative of the futures market. The primary condition of possibility for the options market's functioning is the presence of an active futures exchange. The object of exchange in the cotton options market is neither the commodity itself, nor its future value. Rather, the object being traded is the right but not the obligation to buy or sell a futures contract on cotton at a predetermined price within a specific period of time. There are two kinds of option. A call option entitles its owner to the right, but not the obligation, to buy a cotton futures contract, whereas a put option entitles its owner to the right, but not the obligation, to sell a cotton futures contract.

Options trading can be seen as an insurance activity because traders engage in the options market primarily to fix a price floor for a specific commodity in the future. Just as one insures a car by paying a premium, merchants guarantee that the price they peg to the future value of cotton will not exceed a predetermined level. If one wants more protection, one has to pay a higher premium. Similarly, in cotton options, too, if a mill wants to secure a cheaper price, it has to pay a higher premium. These premiums are the prices paid to buy an option contract. One key difference between the car insurance market and the cotton options market is the fact that in the latter anyone who would like to sell insurance can be a part of the options market. Since one does not need to demand or supply cotton to trade in the futures market, one does not need to buy or sell actual bales of cotton in order to trade in the options market. Merchants use options markets to provide their customers with a fixed price, and speculators use them to make gains by trading risk.

Each options transaction is between a buyer (a holder) and a seller (a grantor). Because the object exchanged between the two parties is not cotton but its future price, each options contract is framed around a price. It is the premium paid to fix the price at a certain level that is changing. Therefore, for each contract month and year, there is an individual option; furthermore, there is a call and a put option for each individual price. For example, a December 2003 70.00 c/lb call option gives its owner the right, but not the obligation, to own one cotton futures contract for a fixed price of 70.00 c/lb. How much does one have to pay in order to fix the price? The price of the fixed price of cotton can be located in figure 5, which represents the options market as posted by the NYBOT.

Figure 5 identifies the price of the December 2003 70.00 c/lb call option as 39 points, which means 0.39 c/lb. In other words, one has to pay 0.39 cents to be able to fix the price of cotton in December of 2003 at 70.00 c/lb. Similar to the supply and demand graph in figure 1 and the futures market table in figure 2, location of the price here entails finding the point where two lines cross each other: the line of the strike prices of a particular futures contact, and that of the price of the option of owning it.[20] Like the futures market table in figure 2, figure 5 is also published by the NYBOT for representation purposes only, furnished without responsibility for accuracy. It does not aspire to be *real*.[21] Again, similar to figure 2 and unlike figure 1, this representation of the market locates moments of exchange in a temporal arrangement, not as a spatial location as a graphic form of P. The prosthetic price is again realized in a temporal universe.

Yet there is a fundamental difference between figure 5, which essentially is a derivative of figure 2, and figure 2 itself. What makes the options market possible is a set of formative assumptions about the workings of markets, and the tool of its realization is a formula that draws on these presuppositions. It is true that all markets are made possible in part because of the assumptions of individual buyers and sellers that inform the way they relate to each other. But these assumptions inform their practice in an exogenous manner and are only a part of a universe of diverse interacting dynamics. In contrast, in options trading assumptions about the functioning of markets act on the market itself by pricing the object of exchange, that is, the option of buying or selling a commodity.

---

[20] Figure 5 depicts only a portion of the December 2003 options prices. The original list is many times longer. Because it presents all prices for each of the ten cotton futures contract months between May of 2003 and March of 2005, it is not useful to reproduce it here in full length.

[21] See the note at the end of figure 5.

New York Board of Trade
COTTON NO. 2 (CT)
Friday, April 04, 2003
1 NORTH END AVE. 13th FLOOR, NEW YORK, NY 10282 TEL. - (212)748-4094 FAX - (212)748-4000
OPTIONS

MONTH	STRIKE	P/C	DELTA	OPEN	HIGH	LOW	CLOSE	PRICE	CHANGE	VOLUME	OI	CHANGE	EXER
Dec 2003	62	C	0.4151	0 0	0	0	0 0	201	+11	1	1960	+1	0
Dec 2003	63	C	0.3638	0 0	0	0	0 0	167	+10	0	1841	0	0
Dec 2003	64	C	0.3156	0 0	0	0	0 0	138	+8	102	1475	+63	0
Dec 2003	65	C	0.2711	0 0	110	110	0 0	113	+6	13	1183	+3	0
Dec 2003	66	C	0.2305	0 0	0	0	0 0	92	+5	50	797	+50	0
Dec 2003	67	C	0.1941	0 0	0	0	0 0	75	+5	0	708	0	0
Dec 2003	68	C	0.1618	0 0	0	0	0 0	61	+4	0	1188	0	0
Dec 2003	69	C	0.1337	0 0	0	0	0 0	48	+3	0	400	0	0
Dec 2003	70	C	0.1095	0 0	0	0	0 0	39	+2	7	1072	+2	0
Dec 2003	71	C	0.0888	0 0	0	0	0 0	31	0	0	122	0	0
Dec 2003	72	C	0.0715	0 0	0	0	0 0	25	+1	0	80	0	0
MONTH	STRIKE	P/C	DELTA	OPEN	HIGH	LOW	CLOSE	PRICE	CHANGE	VOLUME	OI	CHANGE	EXER
Dec 2003	62	P	0.5848	0 0	0	0	0 0	397	-19	0	13	0	0
Dec 2003	63	P	0.6361	0 0	0	0	0 0	462	-20	0	0	0	0
Dec 2003	64	P	0.6843	0 0	0	0	0 0	531	-22	0	0	0	0
Dec 2003	65	P	0.7288	0 0	0	0	0 0	604	-24	0	0	0	0
Dec 2003	66	P	0.7694	0 0	0	0	0 0	681	-24	0	0	0	0
Dec 2003	67	P	0.8058	0 0	0	0	0 0	763	-24	0	0	0	0
Dec 2003	68	P	0.8381	0 0	0	0	0 0	847	-25	0	0	0	0
Dec 2003	69	P	0.8662	0 0	0	0	0 0	932	-27	0	0	0	0
Dec 2003	70	P	0.8904	0 0	0	0	0 0	1021	-27	0	0	0	0
Dec 2003	71	P	0.9111	0 0	0	0	0 0	1111	-30	0	0	0	0
Dec 2003	72	P	0.9284	0 0	0	0	0 0	1204	-28	0	0	0	0

Figure 5   Options market.
Note: The information contained in this report is compiled for the convenience of subscribers and is furnished without responsibility for accuracy and is accepted by the subscriber on the condition that errors or omissions shall not be made the basis for any claim, demand or cause of action.
** Includes adjustment(s) by reporting firm(s), notices and/or expit transfers.
"B" indicates a bid price, "A" indicates an offer price, "N" indicates a nominal price.

The price is calculated with the help of a formula originally published in 1973 by two Nobel Prize winners, Myron Scholes and Fischer Black. According to the formula, the price of a call option is a function of the current price of the object of exchange, the cumulative standard normal distribution of random processes in life, the option strike price which is fixed according to the needs of those who want to set a floor price, the interest rate, the standard deviation of stock returns, the time until the expiration of the option, and an exponential term fixed at 2.7183. Maurer has shown that the formula "is a partial differential equation dealing with random processes," originally put together to understand "the random behavior of small particles bumping against each other in a solution or a gas" (Maurer 2002). One of the scientists who worked closely with Black and Scholes was Emanuel Derman, a particle physicist with a Ph.D. from Columbia, who was recruited for Goldman Sachs to develop the Black and Scholes formula to make it applicable to bond markets. Fischer Black was also working for Goldman Sachs and became one of Derman's mentors. Their collaboration produced another formula that prices bond options, the Black-Derman toy model. For Derman, particle physics and markets are not very different (Derman 2004).

Many of the assumptions on which the formula draws—such as the presence of fixed interest rates, the absence of transaction commissions, and the impossibility of dividend payment during an options life—are relaxed in the model for the cotton options market. Yet there are two assumptions that cannot be relaxed or modified because they are the building blocks of the formula: first, it is assumed that price distribution is a stochastic process. If observed over time, drawing on an infinite number of observations, prices would represent a normal distribution. Second, it is assumed that markets, from which the options markets are derived, are perfect in the sense that the prices they produce represent the free interaction of the forces of supply and demand, without any interference from factors other than these two forces during the exchange. The equilibrium of forces that balance themselves on price is the idea behind the formula. To Derman, there was also a personal touch by Black: "[he] was genuinely in love with the idea of equilibrium" (Derman 2004; Stern 2004). It is these two assumptions that make it possible to create the table of the options market in figure 5. The most complicated picture of the market then draws on the simplest representation of it. In other words, Alfred Marshall's representation of the market, the supply and demand graph of figure 1, is the logic behind the actual market setting as represented by figure 5. It is not the presence of these logics in life that make the market work; it is the assumption and imposition of their presence that performs the market.

Other than serving the daily formatting functions, these assumptions about how markets "should" work are also used extensively in crisis situations when "the market begins to act unexpectedly," according to one cotton trader.

> The market can do anything. They don't let the cotton futures market increase or decrease more than 300 points a day. But in reality they can.
> *What do you mean by "in reality"?*
> In reality, traders can continue to buy; speculators can continue to sell, etc. The price can go anywhere. It can even go down to zero. You don't want this to happen. You can't predict what will happen in the market.
> *But this is what free market means, no?*
> Yes, this is the free market. But if you let it free, it'll kill us. We have to protect ourselves from it. That's why NYBOT stops trading if the price fluctuates by more than 300 point. After a limit-up,[22] you have to know where to start next morning.

The morning following the limit-up, traders locate the point of "where to start" by calculating the futures price, drawing on a simple formula derived from the Black and Scholes formula. The synthetic price, as it is called in trading circles, equals the closing price of cotton futures plus the price difference between corresponding put and call options. This new price is assumed to be the price of futures, if the market has been left free to trade, thus naturalizing an already prosthetic price.

In crisis situations, such as a sudden increase or decrease of the cotton futures prices, the market is halted by the very agents of its maintenance; models of reality are required to be more radically deployed in order to control the effects of unexpected market moves. It is also via these occasional interventions that the price is realized in world markets. It is important to understand that these "market interventions" are not exogenous to the market. They are endogenous to the making of "free" markets.

Conclusion

Price realization in the world cotton market is performed and maintained by constant intervention in the making of the markets and their prices, through different forms of perception, standardization of the object of exchange, various calculative tools, rumors, and indices. At times, it is also formatted by the direct intervention of market boards and formulas,

---

[22] He is referring to the 300 points or 3 c/lb increase of the cotton futures price.

drawing on assumptions about the neoclassical political economy of things. Markets are constantly intervened in and maintained. This is their condition of possibility, and not an exceptional state.

In this context of market relations, realizing the price is a power relation in itself, for the actual price is not realized in the spatial universe of supply and demand. Yet, to a certain extent, the acceptance of an unmediated relationship of causality among what is called supply/demand and the price is one of the major and central interventions in the process of price realization, by embedding Marshall's supply and demand graph (figure 1) into the cotton options market (figure 5) through the Black and Scholes formula.

Supply and demand graphs are among the crucial heuristic devices used by market analysts, economists, and to a certain extent also by traders in order to imagine and represent the process of price-making. As one of the most popular microeconomics textbooks states on its first page,

> Economics proceeds by developing models of social phenomena. By a model we mean a simplified representation of reality. The emphasis here is on the word "simple." Think about how useless a map on a one-to-one scale would be. The same is true of an economic model that attempts to describe every aspect of reality. A model's power stems from the elimination of irrelevant detail which allows the economist to focus on the essential features of the economic reality he or she is attempting to understand. (Varian 2002)

It is the elimination of "irrelevant" detail that makes these devices possible. Figure 1 is neither a correct nor an inaccurate representation of reality, because there is no reality other than what it represents; it is internal to the formation of reality. It is an authoritative and institutionally authorized statement, as well as a powerful intervention in the realization of the price. This possibility and its success make it central to price realization, and not its correspondence to an actual price-making process.

Price realization is implemented by deploying several tools, from the pricing routine which realizes the A Index and the AWP, to the Black and Scholes formula that realizes the optional price of cotton. In all these moments of realization, the taken-for-granted correspondence between a representation and "reality" is a formative technology of power that performs well. Yet, depending on the moment of exchange, even this correspondence is suspended, for without taking strategic breaks from these assumptions of correspondence it is not possible to execute successful trading decisions. This is true not only because the indexical nature of world prices makes it tautological to claim a correspondence, but also because such a strategic suspension is a technology of relating to a market that trades on perceptions, as Mr. Hogan would put it.

If the very idea of understanding the market and the deployment of such a technology in actual market settings are among the building blocks of markets and their prices, how can one attend to market relations without putting together another definition of the market that becomes a part of its own operation? One possibility is to analyze processes of price realization in a dynamic and heterogeneous context of power/knowledge relations without categorically distinguishing the authorities of power and knowledge. This can be done by locating markets in the multiple sites of their making, in a field of power that prefigures the ways in which their prosthetic prices are realized.

In the market field, one formative element (such as neoclassical assumptions on the nature of market exchange) can be used in multiple contexts and even in conflicting ways, depending on what strategic choices traders make. This is evidenced by the discussion of how neoclassical assumptions enable as well as undermine different modalities of commodity exchange in the world cotton market.

The *prosthetic price* is a key concept for understanding how different price forms are realized in market fields. In order to realize prices in a market field, such as that of the global cotton market, prosthetic prices are produced and deployed by a group of market actors from economists to traders, from market researchers to governments. Prosthetic prices equip those who exchange cotton "with tools, competencies and resources" (Callon 2002). The actual price of cotton is made through the deployment of various prosthetic prices, such as the World Price of Cotton, the Adjusted World Price, and the A Index. They do not set the actual worth of a bale of cotton; yet they do inform price realization in various ways.

The ways in which the market's power field is made visible contribute to the making of the market, because it is only in relation to this indexical world of representations that actual trade takes shape on the ground. Without framing the market field following the indexing logic deployed in figures 1, 2, and 4, traders cannot operate. It is through these frames that traders imagine a unitary temporal topography of exchange in the world. Various frameworks used in economization—such as supply and demand graphs, market reports, and futures and options price tables—serve as interfaces of market activity in global trade. Helping market actors carry out calculations and planning to govern their trading practices, these frameworks also lend themselves to traders as locations of market activity and price realization.

The fact that the world price of cotton, such as the one given by the A Index, does not set the monetary worth of a bale of cotton does not mean that the world price of cotton is either real or false. It is a prosthetic price, a tool of engagement with the market field, which simultaneously helps traders imagine a market field by consulting various frameworks of economization. These frameworks (such as figures 1, 2, and 4) constantly inform further moments of price realization; they intervene daily in order to create and sustain the conditions for producing the effect of a definite correspondence between supply/demand and the price.

The AWP (48.22 c/lb), the Cotton A Index (61.30 c/lb), the New York Futures Price of December 2003 (60.00 c/lb), and the December 2003 70.00 c/lb Call Option (0.39 c/lb) are all prosthetic prices that help to set the actual price of cotton—that is, 1,436,558 USD (62.84 c/lb) in the hypothetical trader's example given in this chapter. In the example, the actual price was realized for two hours, but disappeared because the buyer did not accept it. It would have been possible to call the trader before this time period expired and ask for his firm offer, because the tools of price prosthetics—from the pricing routine to the making of futures prices—are maintained on a daily basis. They are represented by reports, produced as constants, misunderstood, gossiped about, transformed by the natural habitat and the crop, interpreted with the help of research in the wild, sometimes imagined as products of a neoclassical free market, deployed to stop the free market with the aim of protecting market participants such as farmers and merchants, and finally guesstimated as a force in making the market.

The tools of price realization are developed through various technologies of pricing prosthetics in a market field, where many components interact in multiple and heterogeneous ways. These include neoclassical assumptions and discourse, institutions (such as the New York Board of Trade), architectural and institutional or formulary designs (such as trading pits and options pricing techniques), regulations (such as those of the Commodity Futures Trading Commission), and scientific interventions (such as the Black and Scholes options pricing formula). It is within the price realization moments of world markets that actual prices appear real; they are vividly conceived as real and converted into actual money. What allows the making of an actual price is to realize it within this process. The market price is made possible and visible through the tools of these calculations, not in the coming together of the two lines of supply and demand as depicted in the graph.

In that sense, markets are neither embedded in social relations nor disembedded from them. They are fields of power operating on dynamic and heterogeneous platforms of power/knowledge relations; these relations reflect the logics of economization as informed by asymmetrical relations of power among human and nonhuman actors. The way to approach them, then, is to locate how different market participants understand and engage in the sustenance, production, and contestation of these mercantile fields of power. In order to do so, one has to open the black box of the prosthetic and actual price realization processes even wider. The following chapter aims to accomplish this by discussing the everyday universe of world trade by following 2,000 bales of cotton as they move in the world.

CHAPTER 2

Market Maintenance in the Worlds of Commodity Circulation

WHAT HAPPENS TO COMMODITIES after their price has been realized? Studies of the market rarely address this question, assuming that the market transaction comes to an end once the actual price is accepted. Yet in actual exchange relations the market transaction begins only after the price is accepted. Furthermore, not infrequently the deal is called off, depending on what happens during the execution of trading decisions. Acceptance of a price is a promise only, whereas the execution of the trading decision is the realization of this promise. Without shipping of the commodity and receipt of the amount representing the commodity's worth, the market transaction does not take place.

Scholars have demonstrated the importance of focusing on the social life of things in order to understand economic relations among humans. Following the ground-breaking work of Strathern and Munn, which has underlined that the role of things in the exchange process should not be taken for granted, Appadurai has argued that things and humans are entangled with each other in processes of circulation (Appadurai 1986; Munn 1986; Strathern 1988). Thomas has taken one step further and empirically shown how market transactions draw on categorically different modalities of circulation, making it impossible to assume that markets dissolve once the price is realized (Thomas 1991). Guyer has discussed the asymmetries produced by different modalities of circulation even in single markets, by looking at the metamorphoses of things as they are pushed around in the market (Guyer 2004). We now know that the circulation of things in the market has to be more rigorously studied if one wants to understand markets better (Weiner 1992; Keane 2001; Miller 2001; Myers 2001). Changing the vantage point from price realization to commodity circulation in global markets, this chapter follows 2,000 bales of cotton as they move from the United States to Turkey to better understand how global markets work on the ground.

Documenting the routes of circulation in the world cotton market, this chapter analyzes the everyday institutional and trader practices that maintain global commodity markets on the ground. The present discussion will show that the very circulation of commodities requires everyday maintenance work and demonstrate that market maintenance makes possible the stabilization of price realization processes—in other words, there can be no global market without market maintenance.

Stretching the notion of market action to cover the very execution of buying and selling decisions opens an entirely new avenue for understanding markets. The agents of world markets build a platform from the interaction of capital, knowledge, and network in order to relate to and profit from the market. On these platforms of trading, simultaneously human and nonhuman things are constructed, such as "human bridges," through the networking that ensures that traders simultaneously know and make the market. On this platform, gift and commodity exchange do not exclude each other. Gift exchange is a technology of power for those who exchange commodities, who need to network to be able to better know and make the market. However, the global traders need thousands of other agents to maintain the world market and continue working on the bridges traversed by commodities, gifts, and documents. Mapping the world of all market actors and their interaction in global cotton trade, the chapter concludes by presenting a theoretical framework for understanding global market maintenance and its contribution to the study of markets in general.

The World of Cotton

In 2003, around fifty million farmers from eight-one countries produced 88,034,000 bales of cotton, each containing 480 lbs of lint cotton—an amount more than enough to produce eighteen T-shirts for every person on earth. This cotton was grown on 300,507 square kilometers of land, an area slightly larger than Britain and Switzerland combined. Compared to other cash-earning crops, cotton holds the largest area of production in the world, followed by sugar cane, sunflowers, coffee, and tobacco.

In 2003, the largest ten cotton producer countries accounted for more than eighty-five percent of world production; the largest six producing countries—China, the United States, India, Pakistan, Uzbekistan, and Turkey—produced more than seventy-five percent of cotton consumed in the world. In the same cotton season, the spinning mills of 118 countries consumed 97,933,000 bales of cotton. The largest ten consumers bought more than three-fourth of all bales produced. In the same year, 30,609,000 bales crossed international borders to be consumed in a foreign country. This was nearly one-third of all cotton produced in the world, making the world cotton market the largest of any global agricultural market. No other agricultural product travels to such an extent.

With the exception of the United States, all major cotton importers are Third World countries. The first ten major buyers account for more than sixty percent of world trade, while the ten major cotton exporters dominate the world market. Their cotton trade volume accounts for more than two-thirds of the world cotton market. Only the United States and Uzbekistan covered more than half of the world cotton demand in the 2002–3 marketing season.

Thousands of small local traders, hundreds of regional traders, and tens of international merchants make up this world of circulation. Most world cotton trade is carried out by private companies. Of a total of four hundred companies that trade at least 67,000,000 bales of cotton—more than two-thirds of entire world production—only a handful are cooperatives or government companies. The largest nineteen cotton sales companies—which include twelve private international trading houses, three government companies, and four cooperatives—handle at least 17,453,267 bales, corresponding to slightly less than twenty percent of all cotton produced in the world. These large enterprises are followed by fifty companies—forty-four private trading houses, four government companies, and two cooperatives—whose combined trading volume is up to 45,929,650 bales annually, slightly less than half of world cotton production. The third group of companies consists of six government companies, one cooperative, and thirty-six private establishments; its total annual trade is somewhere between four and ten million bales. The rest of the cotton produced in the world is traded by hundreds of smaller companies.

World cotton trade figures and estimates do not, however, reflect the actual level of consolidation in the cross-border circulation of cotton. There are no official figures published on the volume of cotton annually traded by international trading houses. Still, almost all of the interviews I conducted with the representatives of these trading houses underlined the high level of consolidation in the world market. The ten largest companies are estimated to trade up to 21.35 million bales of cotton. It is safe to claim that these companies handle more than two-thirds of the annual world cotton trade. The story of the 2,000 bales of cotton told here starts in a trading room of one of these global companies.

WE HAVE ON THIS DAY SOLD TO YOU AS FOLLOWS

In early April of 2003, Pamuklu İplik A.Ş., a spinning mill in Bursa, Turkey, needed to buy cotton. The cotton had to be delivered to its factory no later than May or June of 2003, because the factory's stocks of cotton were decreasing fast. Like all cotton merchants, the owner of the mill, Mr. Özcan, had been closely following the market. To do so, he always looked at the Cotlook Dual Index and the pricing quotations that the Cotlook experts gather from merchants and their agents around the world. At the time of our interview, he had already read all the figures I analyzed in the previous chapter. He knew that the A Index was 61.30 c/lb. He had learned from his father, the founder of the company, how to use these pricing prostheses effectively. "You know that merchants always quote higher prices so that they can have a better bargaining position when it comes to cutting a deal," he said while showing me the Cotlook Report faxed to him by one of his cousins.

> There is no way that I can pay 61.30 c/lb.
> *What are you hoping to pay then?*
> We'll see. . . . I'll try to go down to somewhere between 50 and 52 cents.
> *The New York Futures Price for May 2003 is 57.69. Can't you base your price on this?*
> No, these are American ways. We don't do that. There are mills that do the American way, futures and stuff. What I really care is how much I will pay in the end. Look, here it says 57.69. Can I pay 57.69? It is still too much. Besides, the futures price is not the price of cotton. It is something else. We look at it and then make an individual price. The A Index and the Futures price help us a lot though, I mean, we don't cut a deal relying on them, but they are useful.
> *What is their use for you?*
> When you don't have the A Index or the futures or what have you, you are lost. You don't know what is going on. You can't know whether you are paying high or low, you cannot plan, you cannot see the future. They are like compasses, showing us where the market is going. I know in the end I will not pay the A price or any price other than the one I accept. But the other prices guide us. They help us make up our minds.

"Other prices," as Mr. Özcan calls them, are prosthetic prices that help him fix his own actual price in the market. His success relies on using prosthetic prices effectively. Two weeks after Mr. Özcan had collected quotations from agents—whom he knew by name, with whom he had had several lunches and dinners, and from whom he had previously received numerous gifts—he asked for a few firm offers. He received three offers from three different agents representing three different cotton trading houses. They were 52.50 c/lb, 52.15 c/lb, and 52.05 c/lb, representing potential actual prices for the specific cotton quality and amount he sought to buy. Those prices were valid for one day only.

On April 29, 2003, he ruled out the first offer which was 0.35 cents more than the cheapest bid. The remaining two offers had a difference of

0.10 c/lb, which in gross terms meant 1,000 USD for 2,000 bales of cotton for him. (The amount corresponded to the monthly salary of four workers.) In the afternoon, he made up his mind and signed the sale contract. The contract was with ICTH Inc., an international cotton trading house based in Texas, represented in Turkey by an intermediary trading agency based in Izmir, İTA A.Ş. Mr. Özcan chose to pay 0.10 cents higher, instead of taking the cheapest offer.

> *You didn't choose the cheapest. Can I ask you why?*
> Well, it was not cheapest, I mean, it was the cheapest. True. But in terms of money only. It had hidden costs. Yes, the difference is 1,000 USD. . . . The cheapest bid had hidden costs. The agent who made the cheaper bid is not someone you would like to work with. . . . The trading house he represents is not my favorite either. Once they sent me terrible cotton. It happened once, but when you buy hundreds of bales, once is enough. So it was risky, very risky, I swear to God. Instead of having a bad night's sleep, I pay a bit more and am sure that what I order, instead of what they send, will be here soon. You know, I already sold the yarn I will produce with this cotton coming from the United States. What would I do if there is a problem?

Containing the rich and slippery universe of unexpected problems is the main motivation of the two parties who signed this contract. Before the two thousand bales start their journey from the United States to Turkey over a trading bridge, the bridge itself has to be constructed and then continuously maintained.

Setting an actual price of cotton, 52.15 c/lb, is the beginning of this relationship of exchange, not its end point. As argued by Thomas and revisited by Callon, in order to carry out the exchange itself, the object of exchange has to be defined clearly; then, its ties to the original owner, ICTH Inc., should be cut carefully and reconstructed again as a relationship of ownership between the buyer and the object of exchange. The object has to undergo an operation of decontextualization, dissociation, and detachment for it to be bought and sold then established in a new relationship of ownership (Callon 1998).

The sale contract that Mr. Özcan signed chronicles and contains this operation through a series of moves. First, it describes cotton as Memphis SLM, with a micronaire of 3.5 to 4.9 NCL, a staple length of 1 1/16 inches, and a strength of 26 GPT. This standardization is the first step allowing for cotton to be exchanged, for cotton as a generic term does not mean anything concrete to either its buyers or its sellers.

The quantity is fixed as 2,000 bales of approximately 500 lbs per bale. Yet the weight basis is not the multiplication of 2,000 by 500, for cotton gains or loses weight during shipment because of different levels of humidity. This is also why ICTH Inc. writes 500 lbs in the contract instead of citing the U.S. standard bale weight of 480 pounds.

The remaining clauses of the contract specify the procedure of payment. Ten percent of the price has to be sent to the company one week before the shipment. The rest has to be sent one week before the ship carrying the cotton reaches Turkey. The first 1,000 bales will be sent to the buyer in May of 2003, and the rest no later than June of 2003. In case the buyer does not claim the shipment on time, the seller can charge an additional 1.5 percent per month for the expense to store it at the port. Insurance is covered by the seller and incorporated into the price.

Word by word, the contract documents the parameters of the cotton exchange between the two parties. The totality of these clauses and how they relate to each other summarizes the ways in which a market is made and maintained in a global network of exchange. Moreover, each individual clause itself is a summary of the relations of power, exchange, and production that precede the immediate moment of exchange. To better understand the anatomy of relations visible in the contract, we have to analyze the supportive environment that contextualizes the making and enacting of contracts.

THE SHIPMENT IS BROUGHT TOGETHER

Well before ICTH Inc. sold the two thousand bales to Mr. Özcan, the company had started buying cotton from U.S. cooperatives, farmers and other merchants, who store their cotton in warehouses from Virginia to California. Following the arrival of bales in warehouses, an employer of the warehouse cuts two samples from each bale and sends them to one of the USDA's thirteen grading laboratories. The USDA's classers grade these samples according to their leaf grade, preparation, and extraneous matter, with reference to standards that the USDA maintains. After this first round of locating cotton as a standardized commodity, the classers use High Volume Instrument (HVI) systems to measure and assign a numerical value to samples. Each value represents one cotton bale according to the different qualities of fiber length, length uniformity, strength, micronaire, color, and trash content.

Classification systems for cotton have developed according to the relative power of producers, mills, and merchants. As a rule, farmers resist further standardization of their cotton, because they know that the demands of the textile industry inform the way in which their cotton is classified. Textile mills want farmers to produce better-quality cotton, yet they do not want to pay more for this better quality. A good example of this situation can be seen in the chart prepared by the USDA to locate

"Premiums and Discounts of 2001 American Upland Cotton." The chart takes SLM 41, leaf grade 4, staple length 34 as the base quality of U.S. cotton, and prescribes discounts for lesser-quality cotton and premiums for better-quality crop. Out of the 1,188 combinations of different grades, staple lengths, and leaf content of the 2001 crop, only four percent of grade combinations were eligible for the label "premium." The monetary punishment for lesser-quality crop is so severe that the monetary reward for a better crop is negligible.

After being graded according to what the USDA calls "universal cotton standards," each cotton bale is assigned a permanent bale identification number. With the help of this number, both the owner and potential buyer can retrieve the bale's data file. International merchants usually replace these permanent bale tags with their own company tag in order to hide the statistical identity of their cotton and to redescribe the cotton according to their own market and bargaining position. Thus, these standardizations are both a facilitator of and an impediment to trade. According to different contexts, they are either used or hidden.

After they have been standardized and assigned an individual number printed on cotton identification coupons, cotton bales acquire a legal identity when they are issued an electronic warehouse receipt by a privately owned company, EWR Inc., which is supervised by the USDA. The warehouses open a file for each new cotton bale that they receive and send individual information to EWR Inc., which then makes security checks and issues a legal electronic warehouse receipt (EWR) for each bale. The way to make a global cotton market is to individualize each of its building blocks.[1]

Since 1995, these electronic warehouse receipts have circulated in relations of exchange within U.S. cotton markets. The bales they represent are not transported to the new owner's location until they are sent to their final consumers. In each moment of exchange, a new electronic circulation is launched by the computers of the buyer, seller, intermediary financial institutions, and EWR Inc.

The circulation of cotton in the domestic U.S. market starts after the seller, having reached an agreement with the buyer, sends the list of EWRs to the clearing company, EWR Inc. The company then runs security checks, issues a receipt of the exchange, and sends it to a bank that acts as the intermediary agency between the parties of exchange. After the bank has received payment from the buyer, it instructs the clearing company to assign the new owner as the title holder of the bales. EWR Inc. then deletes the previous owner's name from the EWR and substitutes the buyer's name. The exchange is accomplished as soon as

---

[1] I owe this observation to Julia Elyachar.

the buyer and seller receive a confirmation note from both the bank and EWR Inc. Unless the cotton is ordered to be shipped to a new warehouse, no one touches any cotton in this relationship of exchange. The thing circulated here is the cotton bale's permanent identification number and its ownership.

Two Thousand Bales to Go

A few months before the bales were shipped to Turkey, ICTH Inc. received a note confirming the purchase of 2,000 EWRs. The vice-president of ICTH, Mr. White, who signed the sales contract, then asked his company's Export Traffic Department to initiate the routine of the exchange. According to Mr. White, no sale is final until the buyer accepts the delivery of the cotton and the seller receives payment; signing the contract is just a moment in the making and maintenance of this relationship of exchange:

> One thinks that after you sign the contract everything is over. This is hardly the case in cotton markets.
> *But you signed the contract, set the price, and the deal is cut. What exactly is not over now?*
> You see, an old cotton trader once said that there are one hundred lessons one should learn to be a good trader, and that each year traders learn only one lesson.[2] Most probably, if everything goes as we planned, there won't be a problem. Nothing follows these plans unless we carefully carry out the daily work of enacting the contract. The spinning mill in Turkey can reject the bales by claiming that it is not the cotton they want. They may be right or wrong. This is not the issue.
> *But HVI machines can solve the problem. By carrying out another test one can prove that the description of the contract matches the cotton shipped to them, right?*
> Well, theoretically yes. But it does not work that way. You take three samples from the same bale and run them in the same HVI machine, you'll get three different results. There is still room for maneuver there. When one looks for a reason to screw a contract, it is not difficult to find one. For example, the mill may figure out that I sold the same cotton for a cheaper price to a company which is located a few miles away from them. Or they may realize that they could have taken a cheaper price from someone else. This is human nature. If you lose interest in honoring a contract, and if you can still stay in the business without honoring it, you can do it.

[2] Five different cotton traders, one Egyptian, one Mexican, and three from the United States, told me the same story with the same teaching and attributed it to their grandfathers.

What else could happen?

The cotton has to be shipped on time. For this, we have to follow a routine. If we ship it late, we may lose the customer. If we ship it early, we may end up paying carrying charges in the port. But imagine that everything went OK and we shipped right on time. Then there is a huge amount of paperwork to carry out to claim the money sent from the bank. In this business we worship documents. Without them, you can't have the market work this way. Bankers, mills, traders, shippers, forwarders, agents, controllers, what have you, produce tons of paperwork. You see, I have to send many documents to the bank to secure my payment. It is in the interest of the bank to release the money as late as possible; after all we sell cotton, and bankers sell money. . . . Endless formalities! On the one hand, these formalities are required to have a healthy trade relationship. . . . But on the other hand, it is not infrequent for banks to refer to a few missing documents, or to a few missing details in the documents, to defer the payment for a few days.

After the contract is signed by the sales department, it is the traffic department of ICTH Inc. that carries out the everyday routine that Mr. White explained above. Traffickers are assigned to carry out three basic operations to maintain the exchange and execute it on the ground.

First, the traffickers connect two different markets, cotton markets and shipment markets, by negotiating freight rates for all sales contracts signed on Cost and Freight (CNF) or Cost, Insurance, and Freight (CIF) bases. It is crucial for international merchants to determine the cost of transportation before they carry out trading negotiations, for the competitiveness of their prices depend partly on decreasing the cost of transportation. Moreover, they have to work with reliable partners because the timing of the delivery has increasingly become one of the most important price components of cotton, since a great majority of spinning mills work on a just-in-time inventory basis.

The traffic department also makes sure to find the most economical way to transport the cotton from the domestic warehouses to the port. Monitoring these two processes of transporting cotton requires a daily routine of controls that ensure the global flow of cotton. Related to these two functions, traffic departments also keep an eye on problem areas of world trade in regard to the movement of cotton. In times of trade congestion, the movement of cotton can be slowed down, or the cost of transportation can rise because of the limited supply of vessel space. The ability to detect these congested areas contributes to the competitiveness of the quotes that the company sends to potential overseas buyers.

Secondly, the traffic department observes the ways in which the bales to be sent abroad are gathered from various warehouses in a timely and orderly manner. Coordination of the movement of commodities requires

Figure 6   The trading room of an international cotton trading company.

daily attention to the intersection points of the routes on which the cotton travels, because the cotton's movement stops at every junction. Once it stops, it takes time and much work to make it move again. Maintaining close personal relationships with warehouse officers helps during times of crises, because a small personal favor often turns out to be crucial to make things move a bit faster. In addition to observing the workings of the warehouses and maintaining personal relations with their managers, international cotton merchants in the United States also keep a list of warehouses that do not meet their standards. This black list is published and updated by the American Cotton Shippers Association.

The last function of the traffic department is to carry out the work I have described above, but this time it is the circulation of paperwork rather than the circulation of commodities. It is only by replicating the movement of commodities in a world of their representations that it is possible to intercept and monitor the global circulation of things (figure 6).

In addition to the export traffic departments of international cotton trading houses, specialized international freight forwarders carry out the maintenance work of international trade. Many international traders do not have their own export traffic departments and rely on the services of forwarding agents who, according to my informants, reconstruct the whole trade relationship by documenting it step by step, in order to be able to monitor the movement of commodities and to facilitate their circulation.

In this new route of circulation, the object of exchange is replaced by the bill of lading, and the price of the object of exchange is replaced by the letter of credit. The forwarding agents, whether they consist of the traffic departments of international traders or independent freight forwarders, make possible the double movement of these documents on the routes of cotton exchange, by creating a series of documentations which represent the physical circulation of commodities.

The bill of lading, which is generated by the forwarder who has the power of attorney on behalf of the seller, represents the ownership of the commodities to be exchanged. The person who owns the bill of lading owns the cotton itself; exchanging it represents the exchange of actual cotton. Similarly, the letter of credit is a document that, very much like a personal check, represents the monetary worth of the commodity. The buyer or its representative agent asks a bank to open an irrevocable letter of credit on behalf of the buyer, so that as soon as the necessary documentation representing the closure of the trade reaches the bank, the seller can cash the amount specified in the letter of credit. All letters of credit specify the fulfillment of certain conditions before the seller can have access to the funds that the letter of credit represents.[3] After receiving the terms and conditions of the letter of credit from the buyer's bank, the seller passes the information to its forwarder, who will then be responsible for all steps in closing the trade. The forwarders then contact their domestic bank to secure the payment that the buyer's bank will send. Following this, the domestic bank communicates with the buyer's bank abroad to secure its client's payment by charging a service fee.

Now a new bridge of exchange is constructed. Instead of dealing directly with the buyer and seller, the forwarding agent uses a financial intermediary to decrease the risk of payment failure, by subcontracting the collection of the payment to a bank that has the resources, networks, and agents to initiate an international financial settlement case against the bank abroad in case the buyer's bank does not send the guaranteed payment.

The president of one the five largest cotton-forwarding companies in the world described the necessity of introducing more agents as follows:

> It looks as if there is one buyer and there is one seller when cotton is sold. This is hardly the case. There are invisible people in this business. We all need them because what we call trade is a jungle of risk. Once the contract is agreed upon, how safe is this transaction? The buyer can pay for

---

[3] International trade based on open account receivables dominates world trade and is extensively used instead of the letter of credit system. Its logic of operation is not very different from that of the letter of credit, which is more frequently used when trade partners know each other well.

what he does not get. The seller can ship and not get paid. They have to be protected. They have to make sure that the shipment arrives in its final destination, while at the same time the payment reaches the seller. My job is to make things go smoothly. But I have to protect myself too, right? So just as the seller buys my services, I buy the services of banks. The buyer's local bank can be bogus. Even an international bank can go bust. So I use another bank to secure the payment on behalf of the seller. The bank then requires me to provide the necessary documents so that it can protect its own interests.

What kinds of other documentation do you have to put together?

It depends on the nature of the trade and the country of destination. I tell you, the documents are endless. We use hundred of forms, each standing for a little part of the trade. We deal with bills of lading, dock receipts, certificates of origin. There are shipper's export declarations, export licenses, sailing schedules, packing lists, stowage plans. If the country of destination requires fumigation and other things, there is documentation for these additional measures. We have to put together phytosanitary applications, inspections, and certificates. The list can go on like this.

A document is after all a piece of paper. How can these documents protect you from this jungle of risk?

It is not the document that protects us. It is its power that protects us. Let me give you an example. To secure the payment, one has to put together documents required by the letter of credit and then send them to the bank. You need the bill of lading, you need a commercial invoice, and the packing and weight list of the cargo. Securing these documents means that you actually carried out all the steps to make sure that the trade is conducted according to the requirements of the contract.

Can you tell me what these steps are?

The first thing one should do is to study both the contract and the letter of credit very carefully. If we think that there are problems with the letter of credit, we may need alterations or clarification to get rid of potential loopholes. After making sure that the letter of credit is workable, we call the warehouse to make sure that bales are ready to go. We book with the transportation company and make sure that we have space in their vessel and that the vessel will arrive in the destination port before the expiration date of the letter of credit. We then line up trucking and advise the port warehouse about the arrival of the cargo. The USDA needs to be updated about all international sales, so we send them a report. If fumigation is necessary, we arrange it and send instructions; after receiving the documents that make sure the fumigation is carried out properly, we call the inspectors. We then sign an insurance contract, get loading reports, container numbers, and seal numbers, get hold of the certificate of origin of the cotton approved by the chamber of commerce of the region the cotton is coming

from, give a copy of the letter of instructions to the shipper, put together
the master copy of bill of lading and an SED [shipper's export declaration]
document for the ocean transportation company, and send the SED to the
U.S. government. The vessel leaves the port, but the work continues. Now
we have sent the cotton, it is time to bring the money for the customer. We
put together all the documents required to get the payment for our customer, like a letter of transmittal with payment instructions, commercial
invoice, original letter of credit and bill of lading, phytosanitary certificate,
inspection reports, packing list, stowage plans, insurance certificate, and
anything else the letter of credit requires. We then deliver these documents
to the bank. They need time to process them, and they do not necessarily
do it very fast. So we have to call them and get updates. After they clear all
the documents, they release the payment. Then we invoice our client.
What happened to the bill of lading? Now the bank seems to own the cotton.
My bank sends it to the buyer's bank as soon as it gets the necessary documents from both me and the buyer's bank. Depending on their relationship
they will negotiate the payment. Usually the bill of lading is sent to the
bank representing the buyer in exchange for a promissory note. The buyer
then contacts his bank, and in exchange for the bill of lading he pays the
amount he decided to pay for the exchange. After receiving the bill of lading, he brings it to the port and claims his cotton. That is it.

In fact, that is not it. Although the entire trade relationship is reconstructed in the route of document circulation, so that the agents of trade
can intercept the processes of commodity exchange whenever necessary,
there is still more work to be done to maintain the market. The last task
to be done is to make sure that the documentary route of the reconstructed circulation of commodities matches the actual route of commodity circulation. Even if the documentary circulation is carried out
flawlessly, one party of the two routes of exchange can claim that the actual exchange does not match the documentary exchange. For example,
the buyer can claim that the cotton he received did not match the qualities
of the commodity specified in the letter of credit.

No one can guarantee a perfect match between the documentary circulation of things and their actual circulation, for the way things are represented in documents and the relations of their documentary production
is a technology of power in itself. There are two agents independent of,
yet related to, all other actors of world markets, who work to contain
this slippery ground of the relationship between the circulation of things
and the circulation of their representations: controllers and arbitrators.
Controllers are hired by international cotton merchants to ensure that
the documentation of exchange and the actual circulation match in all
steps of the cotton's voyage. Furthermore, they inspect the ways in which

the cotton is handled during its circulation. Controllers maintain the correspondence between documentary and actual circulation, by following a routine that draws on three main operations.

First, they inspect the shipped cotton to make sure it matches the qualities of the cotton specified in the sales contract. This is done either by supervising the processes of cutting samples from the bales, or by the controllers' carrying out the sampling themselves. In the latter case, they cut two samples from five to ten percent of the bales, from two sides of each bale, and have them graded. The experts of the controllers carry out both HVI testing and hand-classing.

According to the president of one of the largest controlling companies, it is not possible to rely on machine testing only, "because the HVI readings may vary from climate to climate. Moreover, there may be deviations of measurement resulting from the machine itself. Although all the HVI machines are calibrated frequently to ensure a standard measurement, and although samples are conditioned before they are tested, hand-sampling is still dominant." Standardizing the standards themselves requires constant attendance; yet it is almost impossible to perfectly standardize measurements. This is why hand- and eye-classing are still popular and desired.

Sampling is carried out twice: first, a preshipment sampling is done in the country of origin in order to locate the cotton's qualities before it starts its journey to the port where it is going to be claimed by its new owner. Before the cotton is claimed in exchange for the bill of lading, it is sampled again by controllers, to ensure that the quality did not change during transportation.

Secondly, controllers either supervise or carry out the weighing of the cargo, again in two locations. Preshipment weighing ensures that the quantity shipped matches the quantity written on the contract. Similarly, postlanding weighing is done to determine the quantity of cotton arriving at its final destination. Other than sampling and weighing, controllers supervise truck and container loading and sealing before shipment as well as container opening and seal breaking in the destination port. The last operation of the inspectors is to write a standardized research report on how the cotton was handled and transported to the port of destination. This report can then be used as a point of reference for assessing the documentary circulation of commodities and whether the actual circulation matched the way it is represented in the documentary circulation.

The final major agent in the maintenance of world markets is the arbitration boards, whose services are central in making the circulation of commodities possible. All sales contracts have clauses on "rules applicable" and "arbitration." These two conditions of contracts locate in advance the ways in which any future disagreement will be solved, in case other agents of the circulation in documentary and actual routes fail to maintain the market. The largest and most powerful arbitral authority in world cotton trade is the Liverpool Cotton Association Limited (LCA), who had also been chosen as the arbitration medium by ICTH Inc. and Pamuklu İplik A.Ş., the signatories of the sales contract mentioned above. Until the middle of the twentieth century, Liverpool was the epicenter of the world cotton trade. Today, not even a single pound of cotton arrives in the city; yet close to seventy percent of world cotton trade is still carried out under the LCA's arbitral authority.

Once an international cotton sales contract chooses the LCA to be its arbitral authority, the contract is framed within nongovernmental, yet governing, bylaws whose constitution is the LCA Rule Book. Since the rule book itself has been developed in a nation-state, all contracts are simultaneously made under British law. It is also because the seat of arbitration is in Britain that all contracts are framed by British law. Yet the LCA bylaws enjoy a high degree of autonomy, as they are written and maintained by an international membership committee, mostly composed of merchants. Trading companies usually choose arbitration instead of litigation because arbitration is cheaper, faster, more private, and less traumatic for future relationships between trading partners. However, this also comes with a disadvantage: arbitral decisions are not as binding as court decisions. It is the practicality of this private realm of law that makes it more desirable when compared to the public realm of state laws.

When a dispute arises, trading partners try to settle it among themselves by introducing discounts or surcharges. For example, if a spinning mill receives a cotton shipment whose grade is lower than was specified in the contract, the mill can either reject the cotton if there is a rejection clause in the contract, or accept it and pay less in return. The seller, however, can refuse to be paid less and ask for arbitration. Such crises emerge when the documentary realm of circulation and the actual exchange of commodities do not match each other; sometimes their correspondence actually collapses. The further maintenance work of market-making is then carried out by arbitral authorities such as the LCA. When a trade dispute cannot be solved by a settlement, the LCA is asked to intervene and appoint arbitrators. It is the appointed arbitrators who reach a decision on the case, not the LCA itself. Arbitrators are usually selected from those who have been working in the cotton business long enough to be regarded as informed and experienced referees.

The commencement of arbitration begins when one party of a sales contract informs the other party that it is launching an arbitration process to resolve the dispute. The LCA then appoints an arbitrator to the case. The parties can reject the appointed arbitrator if they can come up with a legitimate reason—such as showing that the proposed arbitrator has been a trade partner of the party who asks for settlement. After the arbitrator is accepted, he or she proceeds to carry out research and to locate the problem, mostly by checking the problem areas where documentary circulation does not match actual circulation. After locating those problem areas, the arbitral authority issues awards that must be paid according to a timeline fixed by the authority. The names of those companies who do not abide by the arbitration results are published in a black list called the "LCA Default List."

Still, the list is not all that "black" for many parties of the world cotton trade. Between 1996 and 2002, more than fifty percent of all awards issued by the LCA arbitrators were not honored.[4] The names of these defaulted firms are published in the list. For a spinning mill owner from Turkey, whose company's name has appeared on the LCA's default list, the list means "nothing." Because, as he says:

> . . . even if you are on the list you can still do business. You can change your company's name. If there is a problem of trust, you can even send cash, and this fixes the problem. After all, what is at stake for the merchant is to have his money. The LCA list is a list of people who upset merchant interests. All of their arbitrators are merchants. They know each other from previous business. They have dinners and stuff. The LCA is the merchants' police. We don't trust them.

Many textile mill owners believe that the LCA is a merchant organization that represents mercantile interests only. It is not easy for a mill owner to win an arbitral award. Almost all of the mill owners I interviewed agree with this view; it is widely accepted that awards are biased toward merchants. According to the LCA's director-general, too, this is a widespread belief:

> The majority of our members are merchants. Moreover, half of the board members are international merchants. The LCA is believed to represent merchant interests more than spinner interests. It is true that the majority of the decisions we make are in favor of merchants. But large mill owners can be a part of the LCA and lobby it to change these bylaws in accordance with their own interests. They don't do this.[5]

Although they have reservations, the majority of spinners and cotton buyers all over the world still sign contracts that specify the LCA as the arbitral authority. This is because there is no other private authority whom they can trust more than the LCA. For a mill owner in Mexico, "the LCA is the best of the worst. It does its job OK. You know that you

---

[4] Personal correspondence with R. M. Williams, Director-General, LCA, June 12, 2001.
[5] Personal correspondence, June 12, 2001.

are more likely to lose if you have a problem with a merchant and you go to his house to solve it. But we use LCA bylaws because they give a shape to trade. It is not bad in this business." This is also what the LCA's director-general told me about the main function of his association: "We are imposing a sort of discipline to the international cotton market, a sense of equilibrium based on good trade." It is this formative role of the LCA and its success in arbitration that makes it the largest and most powerful arbitral authority in world cotton trade.

We Hereby Confirm the Arrival of . . .

In accordance with the sales contract I analyzed above, the first half of the two thousand bales arrived in the Turkish port in May of 2003; the rest reached the same port in late June. The seller accepted the cotton in exchange for the bill of lading and sent the buyer the money he had promised to pay. Yet, behind this seemingly simple relationship of exchange, there was a whole group of actors and practices that made the cotton exchange possible.

For each actual commodity circulation taking place in the world today, there is a parallel process of documentary circulation that maintains commodity markets and creates tools that intercept their making. In the world cotton markets, as soon as a contract is signed, a documentary route of circulation is made. The creation of this new route entails representing all of the objects (cotton, money, monetary value, standards) and subjects (seller, buyer, their agents, controllers, arbitrators, financial intermediaries, forwarders) in a new context and facilitating their interaction in an orderly fashion. This new route of documentary circulation provides all parties of exchange with tools for intercepting, correcting, and sometimes resisting the ways in which the exchange is carried out. Without this documentary circulation, no global commodity exchange would be possible.

When one takes a closer look at this parallel realm, however, a new logic of encounter between agents slowly begins to appear. Buyers such as Mr. Özcan do not necessarily choose to take the cheapest bid. They may decide to choose the second-best offer or even the third-best, thus accepting the loss of thousands of dollars in a single trade. Yet losing some money provides them with better tools for intercepting the process of exchange. Similarly, sellers subcontract the shipping of cotton and even the handling of the payment itself to a freight forwarder, thus losing money and sharing some of their income with intermediaries who make their trade possible. These intermediaries in turn contact other intermediaries to protect themselves from risk. For example, they may instruct a bank to act as an intermediary to process payments; the bank then puts together another documentary realm to control the circulation of money and receives payment for its services.

Market maintenance renders possible the everyday making of world markets between sellers and buyers. No understanding of a market is possible without paying attention to the individual characteristics of market maintenance tools, from representation to documentary mapping, from standardization to arbitration. However, beyond the routines of exchange directly aimed at maintaining the circulation of commodities in the actual and documentary routes of exchange, there is one last set of activities to consider. Here, I refer to how international merchants create and deploy these maintenance tools in a realm adjacent to the world of commodity exchange. I will discuss this by focusing on the everyday working of an international trading house, ICTH Inc, who signed the sales contract mentioned above.

The Market Platform: Capital, Knowledge, and Network

All trading companies draw on concrete platforms, according to the vice-president of ICTH Inc., one of the ten largest cotton trading houses of the world. Whoever wants to be successful in the market, be it a trading house or an individual, has to develop a successful platform:

> The platform is composed of three things: capital, knowledge, and network.
>   This is what makes a trading company work.
> *Do all international cotton trading companies work this way?*
> They may have different operating systems, but they all stand on the platform
>   I am talking about. They need capital to buy cotton, so that they can sell
>   it later. They need to know how a market is made, how to calculate risk.
>   They need networks to have knowledge and capital. One has to have all of
>   them. You lack one, you are out of the game.

To be in the game, a metaphor often used by the cotton traders with whom I worked, the first requirement is to be able to finance trading decisions. The capital necessary for financing both the purchase of cotton and the running of the company either comes from the company's own reserves or is borrowed from banks.

> Capital looks as if it is the most important part of one's platform. It is not.
>   Yes, it is true that without capital you are nothing. But if you have only the
>   capital, you are nothing, too.
> *Can you explain?*
> Well, there are many people with money who don't know what to do with it,
>   right? If they don't know what to do, they don't have knowledge. If they

don't know people, they don't have a network. When they don't know how to learn, their money is useless. So they sell it to others.

What does "to know" mean for you?

Knowing is to have a working business plan and being aware of one's operating costs,[6] overhead,[7] cash flows, and position awareness.[8]

But this is to know one's company. Is it enough?

Of course not. This is the beginning. Because knowing is to have a capacity to manage risk. A successful management of risk is based on calculating how much that risk is worth. Then we decide whether we want to buy the risk or sell it.

How do you build this capacity to know?

We have agents everywhere in the world. They write us reports. We follow other market reports, too. We follow the weather, politics, China, everything related to prices. It is not only us. Everybody does this. We all look at the same [. . .] information, but always reach different conclusions.

Network seems to be a part of knowledge then. Can you talk about network?

Capital, network, knowledge. They are all a part of each other. Network is a bunch of people coming together. It is a bridge. Creating a network is absolutely crucial for this business.

What makes it so important?

Actually, without a network, without having these human bridges to reach other people, you can have neither capital nor knowledge.

These last comments of the vice-president summarize almost all of the twelve interviews I conducted with high-level managers of international cotton trading houses whose combined market position covers more than two-thirds of the world cotton trade. The raising of capital, production of knowledge, and forging of networks represent the universe of everyday market-making carried out in the buildings where international merchants work. The last task, however, is categorically different from the first two. Networking is an instrumental activity carried out by traders, sometimes with great enjoyment, sometimes with great boredom.

According to traders, networking starts with knowing how to relate to others and to win their "friendship." The first step is to learn about the people with whom one wants to trade. This is also why the very first

---

[6] The operating costs of a cotton trading house are composed of variable costs such as interest, warehouse expenses, insurance, freight, currency adjustment factors, commissions paid to various agents, bank charges, controlling and forwarding charges, port fees, and bale fees.

[7] The overhead consists of the total fixed costs of a trading house. They are wages and bonuses for the personnel, office rent, utilities, and communication, travel, and entertainment expenses.

[8] The position refers to a company's long and short positions in the spot, futures, and options markets.

lecture to which I listened in my market training in Memphis, Tennessee, was on the cultures of the world. All student-traders were given a cultural handbook, which in a nutshell summarizes the main cultures of the world and locates them on linear scales stretching between a bipolar world of collectivism and individualism, fate and control of one's life, one-thing-at-a-time people and many-things-at-once people, monochronic and polychronic conceptions of time.

During the course, the lecturing anthropologist asked us to locate our own nation-state on these scales. There was a deep silence in this "multicultural" class, as the anthropologist called us. This was partly because it was the first day of class and partly because we did not know what to do. On all of these scales, it turned out, the United States was located on the one side, always representing one extreme, immediately followed by the United Kingdom, Germany, and France. These are considered monochronic and individualist societies who do one thing at a time and believe in self-control instead of fate. The Third World, however, usually had "collectivist" and "polychronic" societies who do many things at once and believe in fate.

A cotton trader from Mexico called the anthropologist's lecture "bullshit" and whispered: "You know what? This woman is telling us is wrong [sic]. Mexicans are like this, Egyptians are like that. Chinese think honor is the most important. Americans are individualist and Indians are collectivist." We were listening to the lecturer unveiling the last culture scale. She wanted a Chinese student to locate China on a scale of locus of control. The Chinese student was asked whether her culture believed in an internal locus of control that assigns more active agency to individuals, or an external one that assumes life to be more fate driven. The student's English was a bit rusty, and she frequently referred to her speaking electronic Chinese-English dictionary. A few seconds after she was asked to locate China, she probably pressed a wrong button on the translator. Suddenly, a surprisingly high metallic female voice spread from the little machine to the classroom: "Irrelevant."

None of the traders in the class, including those from First World countries, took these scales seriously. When they were asked to comment on them, they tended to resist the scales, alluding to "changing things" in their countries, by citing how Americans talk about religion and fate all the time, or by simply dismissing the categories in which they were asked to frame their cultures. Yet none of them dismissed the importance of networking and the necessity to be sensitive to the differences between cultures.

Traders usually use three main technologies of networking. The first is attendance at annual dinners and conferences organized by the industry. Every year, many business gatherings are held in different parts of the world. The Liverpool Cotton Association's annual dinner in London is one of these opportunities to meet new people and revitalize old relationships. The International Cotton Advisory Committee's annual meetings also provide forums for traders and those who work with them to come together, establish new relations, and make business deals. These gatherings also provide traders with an image of a unified global market to which they can relate. Individual dyadic relations of exchange can be brought together as a unified market, either in frameworks such as world cotton prices and supply and demand graphs, or in these industry meetings. Following the event, almost all organizers of these gatherings produce publications such as magazines, which cover the meeting and make clear who attended and contributed, by including as many photographs as possible.

The second technology of networking is to send letters, e-mails, or cards on important holidays. Traders send hundreds of Christmas, Hanukkah, or Eid al-Fitr cards to their associates, clients, and potential clients. Birthdays and other anniversaries are also important occasions for networking. Various traders told me that they keep a list of birthdays of almost all their clients, so that they can congratulate them on the correct date.

The last technology of networking is more direct and frequent: gift giving in its multiple forms. The most frequently given gifts are the following: visible and nonpersonalized small items gifted by companies to other companies; institutionally less visible, personalized gifts given by companies to individuals; and visible personal, yet not institutionalized, gifts given to individuals.

Small gifts are usually presented on behalf of the whole company to the whole group on the receiving end. They may consist of calendars, small office items, or local crafts from the gift giver's country, such as a picture or a small carpet, historical paraphernalia, or an illustrated coffee-table book. These gifts carry the least weight in securing a close relationship, for they are the least personalized. Usually, they are put away somewhere in the receiver's office. Not infrequently, their origin is forgotten. Yet it is the moment of gift giving that makes it an effective technology of networking, for it creates a short moment of closeness between the two parties. It is usually not the gift itself that creates a moment of intimacy, for frequently the gift is not valuable to either party's personal life. The building block of "human bridges" in this technology of networking is the performance of gift giving and receiving, not the gift itself.

To illustrate this type of gift exchange from my own observations: an Uzbek trader brought a wall carpet, slightly larger than a letter-sized sheet of paper, to a cotton trading company in Memphis. Both the gift giver and the receiver were smiling, shaking hands, and posing for a photograph while performing the networking. A few days after the performance, I had lunch with the Uzbek trader and asked him about the gift he gave to his American colleague. "I hate these little carpets," said the trader, "they are so old, traditional. They remind me of the lives of my grandparents. But what can I really bring them as a gift? It is almost a rule to give these cultural things." I met the gift receiver a few weeks later and in passing mentioned the gift he received. He looked at me briefly and said, "Yeah, tell me about it!"

The second type of gift giving is institutionalized and visible. It includes small but relatively expensive items, such as liquor, fountain pens, palm pilots, cell phones, and the like. These gifts are given to people who are close to decision-making circles and usually consumed by the friends and family of the receiver. They are more effective for establishing and maintaining contacts. In comparison to the previous category, they are less visible and more individualized. The performance of giving and receiving these gifts is less important, for they are usually sent by mail. However, the gift's relatively higher monetary worth makes it more memorable in terms of an established intimacy between trading partners.

The last form of gift giving is the most effective and frequently used networking technology in commodity markets. It has two basic forms: first, it can consist of taking a client or a group of clients out for an expensive dinner or lunch. This form of gift is so common that it has become second nature to commodity circulation. It is not the object of exchange but the time consumed during the gift's exchange that constitutes the main focus of both the gift giver and the receiver. The immediately visible gift giver seems to be the one who pays the check. Yet, in the actual performance of the exchange, the one who pays the check receives the time of the gift receiver, thus creating a vivid if somewhat enforced reciprocity. It is rude to turn down a dinner invitation, but once accepted it is also rude not to thank the person who, actually, is the receiver of the more precious gift—that is, face-time.

Secondly, this more personalized form of gift can take the shape of an even more expensive treat, such as a holiday paid by the gift giver. It is rare for the gift giver to accompany the receiver; thus, the performance of giving and receiving is rather insignificant. Still, the worth of the gift is so decisive that it is usually regarded as the most effective technology of networking, even if it is the most infrequently used one. This type of gift is also the limit of the socially acceptable technology of networking, for anything beyond that can be regarded as bribery, whose exchange structures a specified course of action for the receiver.

Conclusion

In the previous chapter I analyzed how world market prices are realized in a relationship of power within a global market field. The conditions for making a world price of cotton are based on the prosthetics of pricing, which deploy several tools—from the Pricing Routine, through the A Index and the AWP, to the Black and Scholes formula—that contribute to the making of the actual and optional prices of cotton. Based on a strategic assumption of the correspondence between a representation (the prosthetic price) and reality (the actual price), these price realization technologies are formative technologies of power that also perform.

However, when we change the vantage point from that of price to that of the commodity circulation in order to approach world markets, a new set of everyday market-making and maintenance work becomes visible. It is not only the world price of cotton that needs daily attention, but also the very circulation of commodities that requires at least four different, yet related, sets of everyday market maintenance activities.

The first set is made possible by the making of an actual price, based on prosthetic prices. Analyzing the signing of an actual sales contract, I have showed that it is by taking into account the "other prices," as the buyer put it, that trading partners can bargain. The signatories of the sales contract are aware of the prosthetic universe of prices surrounding them. By using the contract as a context of negotiation, the buyer in this case took 52.15 c/lb as the actual price of cotton. The seller then sent the cotton in two shipments to the Turkish port in April and May of 2003, and the buyer claimed his cotton in May and June of 2003.

Embedded in this first set of everyday maintenance work where an actual market is made are two simultaneous market activities that allow the execution of trading decisions. The actual exchange of cotton is reproduced in a documentary route of circulation, which simultaneously provides buyer and seller with the tools to exchange cotton. This requires the introduction of a whole new set of actors to the world of exchange. From the moment when the two thousand bales were gathered in the United States, to the moment when they were claimed by their new owner in Turkey, warehouses cut samples from the bales and sent them to the USDA. The USDA's human and nonhuman graders classified the bales and then assigned them permanent identification numbers; based on these data, the bales acquired an electronic warehouse receipt issued by EWR Inc. Then, they were readied to be shipped by traffic departments and freight forwarders, who created the documentary route of circulation, putting together endless documents representing everything in the trading relationship, from the exchange act to the commodity and its price.

It is the creation of this documentary circulation of representations that allows the circulation of commodities; yet even this vast parallel world is not enough to ensure the actual circulation of commodities. As we have seen, each step of representation opens up possibilities for contestation, for the very documentary realm relies on a correspondence between things and their representations. Depending on one's market position or the way in which circulation is carried out, the correspondence can be challenged at any point.

This "jungle of risk," as the president of a forwarding company put it, has to be contained. This requirement introduces the services of controllers and arbitrators, whose job is to ensure that the documentary route of circulation matches the actual route of circulation. However, their capacity is limited, for there are always loopholes, no matter what one does to ensure correspondence. A perfect match between actual and documentary routes of circulation is not possible because there are no objective criteria to check the level of correspondence. Controllers do their best to monitor the actual circulation of things and compare them with their documentary representations. Their reports serve as reference points in arbitration cases. Still, as soon as one actor does not recognize the power of the sales contract or honor the award issued by the arbitral authority, the maintenance and thus the making of the actual market collapse.

This is why it is crucial for merchants and traders to introduce a supporting universe of networks within the two routes of the documentary and actual circulation of things. This networking constitutes the second set of activities that make a market possible. Both their capital and its effective deployment are based on the traders' knowledge and networks, as the vice-president of an international cotton trading house put it. Knowing is an instrumental activity in building a capacity to manage risk, to contain the "jungle." For this, the company needs a network, "a bunch of people coming together," a "human bridge," constructed by having agents all around the world, agents who can reach customers and "know" them. Because, as the vice-president of the trading house said, "without a network, without having these human bridges to reach other people, you can have neither capital nor knowledge."

Nothing is as vital to a successful trading relationship as networking. Nothing is as effective for networking as learning about and meeting people and exchanging gifts with them. Regularly organized business meetings provide traders with opportunities to establish new relations and renew old ones. Sending e-mails, letters, and cards strengthens already constructed human bridges which connect those who exchange commodities with each other. However, not only commodities travel over these bridges. Gifts also circulate during the networking activities of international traders, maintaining the human bridges.

The making and maintenance of world markets in the documentary and actual routes of commodity circulation are thus made possible by a different kind of engagement with the market. It is through constructing human bridges by networking that one can simultaneously know the market and make it. Gift and commodity exchange do not exclude each other. Gift exchange is a technology of power for those who exchange commodities and also need to network to be able to better know and make the market.

From the vantage point of traders then, the world cotton market is based on a simultaneous circulation of commodities and their representations. The agents of these routes of circulation, however, are more numerous than the immediate universe of the two market agents in the neoclassical life-world of the relationship of exchange. These agents build a platform from the interaction of capital, knowledge, and network in order to relate to and profit from the world market. A handful of global traders needs thousands of local agents to maintain the world market and continue working on the bridges traversed by commodities, gifts, and documents.

To better understand the cotton world markets, then, one has to write the story of the market's making also from the vantage point of the other side of the bridge: from that of the local traders and farmers. The last four chapters of this book will tell their story.

CHAPTER 3

Markets' Multiple Boundaries in Izmir, Turkey

THE PREVIOUS TWO CHAPTERS have presented an empirical discussion of price realization and global market maintenance in world commodity trade, concluding with a discussion of how world traders draw on trading platforms and connect them to regional markets by means of so-called "bridges." This chapter moves from the global traders' end of the bridge to the other end: that of regional market actors. After all, the practices of global price- and market-making are always articulated in particular geographies of encounter.

The nature of the interaction of these different locations in the global market should not be assumed to resemble a trade relationship between a "global" merchant and a "local" sales broker. Such relations between global agents and local intermediaries draw on encounters between different agents who have asymmetrical mercantile platforms; yet they are still local agents. The interaction of the global and local markets is a relationship of derivation, not of encounter.

Indexically global things—such as the A Index, the AWP, or the World Cotton Market as it appears in statistics—are derivatives of their local articulations. The derivation of global things is based on technologies of indexing, such as the pricing routine of Cotlook Ltd. Just as cotton's global price is realized by bringing together sixteen local prices and creating a prosthetic index, the global market is a universe of indexical possibility. It is produced not only by bringing together dyadic encounters of exchange, but also through the making of the prices of distant, yet related local markets. Only after the creation of dyadic actual prices in their local geographies of realization has been made visible does it become possible to produce global prosthetic prices. In other words, an analysis of the world market would not be complete if it did not include a discussion of its local articulations whence the market's indexical nature is derived.

How, then, are regional markets made, their prices realized, and trades executed? Finally, how do these "nonglobal" regional traders, merchants, and brokers understand the market and relate to the world commodity markets? This chapter addresses these questions by focusing on relations of exchange and their various technologies of production as deployed by regional and local traders based in Izmir, Turkey. By discussing the everyday workings of cotton exchange from the vantage point of regional traders, I will explore how world markets are articulated in locales such as Izmir, attending to the voices of those who make such articulations possible.

Contributing to the emergent literature on the study of markets, this chapter analyzes the processes and types of price-making in the Izmir Mercantile Exchange (IME). Describing how a variety of prices are produced in multiple locations of a single commodity market, I argue that the market prices of cotton at the IME can best be seen as devices that traders produce and deploy in order to pursue their trading objectives. These devices turn cotton into a calculable and exchangeable entity whose value can be negotiated through various forms of bargaining.

The cotton is priced in three forms at the IME: *rehearsal price, transaction price*, and *market price*. Such a rich world of price realization in Izmir is made possible by drawing on the dynamic boundaries of the market. Empirical research suggests that markets have multiple boundaries in Izmir, as all market price forms are produced in four temporally and spatially specific places: in the *pit*, in *postpit*, at the *Closing Price Committee Meeting*, and at the *Permanent Working Group on Cotton Meeting*. Drawing on ethnographic research on the production of market boundaries, I argue that prices can best be seen as prosthetic devices produced in multiple market places in a single geography of trade. As we will see, instead of "setting the price," traders produce various price forms to prevent or foster exchange. Prices are never set by a mere coming together of supply and demand. They are made, produced, and challenged by a multiplicity of actors in a market process that happens in a variety of trading places.

Pit Trading in the Izmir Mercantile Exchange

The exchange of two thousand bales sold by ICTH Inc., the international merchant house based in Texas, to Pamuklu İplik A.S., the spinning mill in Bursa, Turkey, was made possible by ICTH Inc.'s representative agent based in Izmir, Turkey. It was through ITA, the company that represents ICTH Inc., that the price quote was faxed to the buyer. After the trade was concluded, the representative earned a commission for his services of bringing together buyer and seller. ICTH Inc.'s vice-president explained the importance of his agents' services when I met him in the lobby of the Peabody Hotel in Memphis:

> Agents are our trust belts. Without them you cannot do business overseas. They know their local markets. They know what we don't know. If you have an agent you trust, you cannot change him or overrule him and do business

with others just because they have a better offer. By the way, good offers are usually too good to be true.

These "trust belts" are crucial connections between cotton markets. It is through their intervention that cotton bales cross borders. These agents do not only connect international sellers with local buyers, they also relate international prices to local prices, because for the most part they serve as sales brokers. They bring together local demand and supply in their own domestic markets, thus providing a comparative scale of price quotes for potential buyers. Their specialized knowledge and the networks they sustain build their platform for engaging with the market. What exactly is it that they know? How and where do they bring together buyers and sellers in such a transnational and domestic market context? The pit at the Izmir Mercantile Exchange is the place to look for answers to these questions.

The cotton trading pit of the IME has historically been one of the important nodes of world cotton trade. As the first and largest commodity exchange of the Ottoman Empire and its successor state, the Turkish Republic, the IME's cotton pit (in Turkish, *korbey*), hosts the trade of thirty-five percent of lint cotton in the country. The earliest recorded cotton prices in the United States are quoted for cotton imported from Smyrna (Izmir's old name) and Barbados, in Philadelphia shillings (Baffes 2004b). Large-scale cotton-growing emerged in the settlements of Virginia (1621), North Carolina (1664) and Louisiana (1697), with the help of the cotton seeds that merchants from Smyrna and the surrounding areas carried to there (Smith and Cothren 1999; Baffes 2004b).

More than four centuries later, every weekday around 11:30 a.m., traders, brokers, spinners, ginners, and their representatives enter the exchange building in Izmir. As they tour the trading pit and try to read the market, the number of traders reaches between 100 and 120. Strolling around the pit, traders observe their colleagues' body language and actions in order to locate subtle traces of weakness or strength, self-confidence or insecurity, alarm or tranquility.

The pit is located in the grand cotton trading hall of the IME. The hall is home to small trader offices surrounding the space. The pit, resembling two small amphitheaters opposite each other, has the capacity to seat approximately 120 persons. All traders wear an identification card before entering the pit, which has reserved seats for all who have the right to enter. The remaining persons must stay outside the pit, but not the market. The pit has two entrances into its center. The IME employee sitting at the center is responsible for registering sales and documenting bargaining and exchange. Four circular rows of seats, each higher and longer than the previous one as they ascend, help the traders, observers and officials

Figure 7   Cotton traders in the pit at Izmir Mercantile Exchange.
Source: İTB (1996).

sitting shoulder to shoulder to see and hear each other without difficulty (figure 7).

Trading opens at 12:20 p.m., when an IME employee invites the traders to enter the pit and take their seats. This call takes place as traders walk around the pit or wait in the lobby right outside the hall. It requires a few calls for all traders to take their place, because traders drag their feet a bit before entering and taking their predetermined seats. Being too eager affects the price so directly that no trader can risk looking like someone with an urgent need to sell or buy.

Ten minutes after it opens, pit trading terminates exactly at 12:30 p.m. Following an open outcry system, bid and offer cry-outs frame the trading in terms of four dimensions. First, they specify the amount of cotton in terms of truck loads. Each truck is expected to carry approximately ten metric tons of ginned cotton; however, the amount can exceed ten tons, depending on the relative size of the truck. Second, the offer locates the quality of cotton by specifying its standard and original location of production such as "Standart 1," "Garanti," and "Bergama." Third, the offer includes a specific price in Turkish lira for each kilogram of cotton. Finally, the offer specifies the payment terms, such as "in advance," "in one week," or "in two weeks." The acceptance of the cry-out is indicated by saying "write." In the pit, the word is a bond enforced not only by the rules and regulations of the IME, but also by peer pressure. It is rarely possible for a trader to change his or her mind after accepting the bid.[1]

At 12:30 p.m., with the ringing of a bell, trading in the pit terminates. In an interesting contrast to their slow entrance, the traders leave rapidly. Individual dyadic prices are made in these ten minutes. However, the end of pit trading is not the end of trading at the IME. Trading continues after 12:30 p.m., until 1:15 p.m. For another 45 minutes, traders walk up and down in the area between the pit and their booths, making comments, jokes, bids, and offers as they pass each other, while constantly holding in their hands their cell phones connecting them to their clients. Trading can continue after 1:15 p.m., but it rarely does. Prices made after 1:15 p.m. are not considered representative of the day's prices.

After 1:15 p.m., the meeting of the Closing Price Committee consisting of leading buyers and sellers, exchange brokers, and merchants takes place. Following deliberation and the study of all registered transactions in and outside the pit, the committee writes a price report. This document establishes the closing price of the market and the day's turnover, closely watched by other traders around the world.

The Rehearsal Price of the Pit

The official publications of the IME draw on a neoclassical logic for explaining how the price is set in the market: "The price is made in the immediate universe of the pit which provides traders with the necessary platform for demand and supply to come together and to result in a market price" (İTB n.d.). These documents refer to the exchange as an "institutionalized market place" based on five pillars: the commodity, the seller, the buyer, the legal structure, and the organization of the exchange (İTB n.d.). "The objective of mercantile exchanges is to create all the necessary conditions to achieve free competition, in other words, to make the laws of supply and demand work. It is in this way that mercantile exchanges come quite close to being ideal free markets" (İTB n.d.). As a result of this "almost ideal market setting," it becomes possible for commodities to be traded at their "real values" (İTB n.d., 18).

Traders agree with the way their organization sees its functions. "Here is the market," whispered an experienced exchange broker into my ear while we were sitting in the pit. It was the first day of my field work.

---

[1] However, one can stretch a bid somewhat if the accepted offer turns out to be worse than the market price set later in the day. In situations such as these, payment terms can be relaxed in an informal manner.

Trading had started a few minutes earlier, after the exchange officer, with a cordless microphone in his hand, had invited the traders to the pit at least three times. I looked around and saw a universe of encounter almost invisible to the naked eye. I had read all the rules and regulations of the exchange and even conducted a few preliminary interviews about the everyday workings of the exchange beforehand. I was not among the least informed visitors in the cotton hall, but it took a while for me to realize that traders were actually trading. After an exchange broker cried out "write," I leaned towards my host and asked: "What happened?" "I'll explain it to you later," he replied. The ten minutes of trading passed rapidly for me, but at a snail's pace for my host. With the ringing of the bell, the traders quickly emptied the pit. The sales officer of TARİŞ (Union of Agricultural Co-Operatives for the Sale of Figs, Raisins, Cotton, Olives and Olive Oil), representing the largest seller in the market, was the fastest to leave. He was followed by five other agents, some of whom chased the TARİŞ representative.

I left the pit with my host and watched him show a potential client the cotton samples he kept in his booth. Another trader came to the booth, entered it, and listened to their conversation. I could see others looking at my host, his potential customer, and the other agent who was listening. I stepped outside to the then almost empty pit and decided to take a look at the electronic board where the world prices of cotton were projected, just to keep myself busy since I felt out of place. A waiter interrupted my studying the world prices. He handed me a cup of tea, sent by another exchange agent. I looked around to spot him and caught his gaze as he accepted my gesture of thanks by gently moving his head up and down. I stood there, right in between the pit and the booths surrounding it, sipping from my cup and trying to register what was going on in the market. It would take close to one hundred formal and informal interviews and three months of observation for me to begin to appreciate what "here is the market" meant for the cotton traders of the IME.

"This is the market," said another exchange agent two months after my first day in the pit. He was the oldest and perhaps the most respected trader at the IME. He had been active in export markets all his life, until 1987, when Turkey became a net cotton importer for the first time in history. "Gin owners, speculators, exporters, importers. . . . Everyone is here. Buyers and sellers call them, ask what the market is. They say, buy me two trucks of this and that," he said, pointing to the traders around us with the same hand with which he held a constantly ringing cell phone set to Mozart's *Rondò Alla Turca*. Deciding that he had kept the caller waiting long enough, he apologized and took the call while shielding his lips with his right hand, a common gesture to prevent others from understanding what he said. After a few seconds, he hung up and continued:

Here, everything depends on trust. Once you say "write," it is written on the board. Once it is written, the deal is cut, the market is made. Your word is your bond. You cannot later say that you misunderstood this or that. People would laugh at you. You lose your reputation. You are not taken seriously. The hall is made of one hundred and ten years of trust, institutionalized around this pit.

But not all trade is carried out in the pit.

Yes, the pit is only the beginning. It sets the stage. But even before the pit trading starts, things begin to happen in the hall, the market begins to appear. We observe each other before the pit. We want to learn the level of rejected cotton.[2] We probe the market by reading other brokers' faces, the way they talk on the phone, the way they approach each other. This doesn't take a long time if you are experienced enough. I have been working here for decades. So it is very easy for me.

The pit?

Yes, then we enter the pit. We make more deals outside the pit. But it is the pit that makes this possible. You sit and look around, traders start making offers and bids. I sell this, I buy this. Depending on the price, you make your decision, and if you are buying, you say, for example, write me a truck.

The everyday performance of trading both in and around the pit is crucial for pricing cotton. On the one hand, it would be misleading to claim that it is only the performance that structures price levels; on the other hand, it would also be problematic to argue that it is the unmediated workings of supply and demand that make the price. This is because the levels of supply and demand should be located by various market agents in order for them to have any effect on the market. "Market forces" have to be perceived and processed by traders. The making of supply and demand is not independent of the traders' perceptions of supply and demand, and it is only through institutionalized filters and deliberations that their effects are felt by market agents. It is also through speech acts and bodily performances that traders locate the invisible hands of the market. Performances are central for the everyday working of trading pits.

Another exchange broker explained to me the working of the pit and its role in bringing together supply and demand of cotton with the help of analogies and rhetorical questions that depict, in his own words, the way market forces of supply and demand are mediated in trading floors on the ground:

---

[2] Rejected cotton is the commodity whose quality is contested. Buyers can reject the cotton sent to them if they are not sure about the quality, until an arbitrator of the IME solves the problem.

The pit makes sure that demand and supply meet each other in a disciplined way. And it is through the pit that the exchange carries out this intermediary role. The supply and demand are made there. So the pit is an instrument for the exchange. How does a carpenter work? With a saw. How does an exchange make supply and demand? With the pit. So the pit is the tool for making a market. Where is Shakespeare's *Hamlet* played in Izmir? It is played in the theater. The pit is the theater of the market.

It seems to me that there is more than crying out "I sell this," "I buy this," or "write."

The pit is a performance place. Traders and brokers are in a situation similar to that of poker players. Traders know that, when they sit in the pit, their facial expressions, the way they talk and the way they don't talk, the time they enter the discussion and when they don't, everything they do and don't do are crucial. Imagine that your client calls you and orders you to buy twenty tons of cotton at that day's price. You know that you have to buy, or else the factory will stop. What happens when others also know that? You can't be selling at a price lower than the market price. But you don't know the market price. What if the market price turns out to be lower than the one you took? You can do it once, do it twice, and then you lose your customer. We have to catch the market price and if possible make it. We'll do everything to make the price. We look as if we don't want cotton, we pretend that we're not interested; we probe others, and watch what they do. We have to do this as if we were not doing this. Yet, however cool you are, your body [. . .] reveals what is going on inside. This is how we read each other and decide what to do.

Trading performances have their own limits. On the one hand, they are effective ways of bargaining; on the other hand, their effect depends on one's market position and power in the pit. Traders are aware of their colleagues' market power in terms of the volume they buy and sell, but they do not know when they take these positions. If a trader overperforms in the pit, without necessary means to supporting his performance, he usually fails to meet the market price. One exchange broker made this mistake of overperformance and made a deal without probing the market effectively. It was the first time he spoke in the pit since I had started to observe traders in the cotton hall. Another broker, whose market position was one of the largest in the IME, explained to me what happened on that day when I met him in his office:

It is not possible for everyone to make the price at the İME. It requires a strong heart. It requires courage. It requires experience. Our job here is to create stability. We are responsible to those who trust us. This is the spirit that informs us in the pit. But some people make too many zigzags. There are two different groups in the exchange. The first group just talks in the pit for satisfaction. . . .

I mean, like a real actor. We all have the same gun, but a different number of bullets. We all know how much ammunition we all have. For example, today one man wanted to buy. Of course, we didn't sell. I don't let others make the price. I make it. What happened to this man? He bought the same cotton spot cash, but others bought it on credit. We all know each other. If you follow what is going on in the hall before the pit starts, you can make the price. Not many people can make it. I would say only five to ten people are really good at what they do. Their power relies on their experience and the firms they represent.

The limits of performance in trading and the effect of performative acts on making prices are related to the performer's market power. Those who observe these performances in the pit always perceive them in reference to the performer's market position and the firms he represents. This is why when these "five to ten people" come to the pit, the entire atmosphere changes. Moreover, when one of them does not join the session that day, the pit is even more affected.

According to another exchange broker whose absence can move the pit, observing individual traders is enough to probe the market. For him, the way individual traders behave and feel that day creates a synergic whole, a specific air—*hava* in Turkish. To him, traders affect each other and also interact in a rather unconscious way to produce a combined effect that cannot be observed by looking at individual traders only. The market has to be "smelled."

Once you enter the pit, you are all ears and eyes. What one really has to do is to smell the air in the pit to locate the supply and demand of the day. Traders may be talking to you, but at the same time they watch what is behind you. Before going to the exchange, I always do research and study the market. You can't make the price if you don't study it. I make projections, and relying on them I observe traders and smell the air in the pit. If the business is hot, I can read it in advance. I read the market's pulse. In our exchange, traders make many beautiful maneuvers. For example, if I don't go to the pit, if they don't see me there, they know what it means.

Whether they smell the air made up of a synergic whole that the traders co-create, probe the market by carefully registering how others act before and during the pit session, or perform in such a way as to cloak their intentions, so that it may be possible to gain a better bargaining position, traders rely on various forms of bargaining to affect each other's perceptions. Trading performances in the pit have immediate effects, visible only after the session terminates. According to a broker who has had a seat in the pit for at least two decades, "the pit is nothing compared to what happens afterwards. The pit is the trial run on the market. You try to make it there and then get your deal later. For every deal cut in the pit, there are three deals outside it." His rather conservative estimate was challenged by another trader a few days later:

> The pit is a total show. It is not the market where the prices are made. They are made later. I'd say only ten percent of trade takes place during the ten minutes of the pit session. Brokers and traders try to fix a price there so that they can make money later. For example, they would say 1.60 in the pit, but sell later for 1.50.

If the pit is "nothing" compared to "what happens later," and if pit trading constitutes only a fraction of later trading, then what makes it the place of the market for traders? One immediate answer is that, through the temporal and spatial framing of the way in which supply and demand meet, it becomes possible to engage with the market. It is the pit that brings them together and helps buyers and sellers to meet each other. Otherwise, the market would be "everywhere" and could not be effectively engaged. Although partially valid, this answer cannot take into account the fact that the vast majority of trading takes place outside the pit, both temporally and spatially. Instead of seeing the pit as the market's place, a more adequate answer would locate the pit as a design of intervention in the making of the market. It is misleading to assume that there is only one boundary between the market and the nonmarket. Markets have multiple boundaries, even in their immediate universes, like the IME. In other words, markets have various places with various price forms, even in a single geography of trading. However, one has to be careful when using geographical analogies to make these different market "places" visible, for these boundaries are not only spatial but also temporal. The cotton market at the IME has multiple locations, strategically separated by temporal and spatial limits.

Traders, when they are in the pit, perform and watch performances to weigh their validity. By and large, the pit is a preparation for the postpit trading that takes place before 1:15 p.m. Working to produce a price in the pit is an investment in performance. These pit prices will very soon become a point of reference in making deals during postpit trading. By quoting the prices made in the pit, traders discuss strategies with their clients and then readjust them according to the price levels of the day. The pit prepares the ground for marketing, by marketing cotton itself, though in smaller amounts. It is important to note that many traders use theatrical analogies to describe their everyday experiences in the pit. It is either "a place that looks like a theater where Shakespeare is played," or just "a show" that "real actors" put on. Yet actual transaction prices are made in this "show."

This new form of price produced in the pit for postpit trading presents an interesting puzzle: these prices are made to exchange cotton. They are actual transaction prices. However, they are also prosthetic prices. They are used as devices to affect postpit trading, which constitutes around ninety percent of actual trading at the IME. As a result, this interesting price form is an actual price, but, at the same time, it is a prosthetic price. Drawing on the traders' analogies, I call this price form the *rehearsal price*, for it is caught in the middle of actual performance and nonperformance—traders rehearse actual trading by using rehearsal prices. The volume that they trade as they rehearse trading is only a fraction of the volume they trade after the pit. The price produced during pit trading is a rehearsal price also because it is produced to probe and make the market. The rationale of its existence is not to make a transaction, but to affect the postpit trading price. However, these rehearsal prices are also transaction prices, because cotton is exchanged after these prices have been taken. For the price to be rehearsed, it has to be taken by a trader. As soon as one hears the cry "write," a rehearsal price is produced. In any given pit trading session, depending on the season and the volume of the market, tens of different rehearsal prices can appear. All of these prices are used as devices that enable traders to strategize their trading moves during the postpit session. In contrast, what happens when no trade takes place during the pit session and no rehearsal price is made? Traders still produce a form of price rehearsal by making bids and offers that are not taken.[3] The absence of rehearsal prices does not indicate that no rehearsal has taken place. A rather explicitly displayed disinterest may actually be indicative of an urgent interest. In the next section, I will discuss an empirical example of how rehearsal prices play a significant role in postpit trading.

The Transaction Price of Postpit Trading

After the pit session closes at 12:30 p.m., traders either return to their booths or walk in the circular space between the pit and their office cubicles. Immediately after the pit session, they call their clients to reconsider their trading decisions, depending on their ideas about the rehearsal prices. If they represent buyers, they would do their best to buy cotton on terms better than those made during pit trading. Of course, those who represent sellers are motivated by the opposite objective. Sellers try to take a price slightly higher than the rehearsed prices in the pit. Thus, when they rehearse prices, buyers always try to pull them down, whereas sellers try to make them appear high.

---

[3] It would be a tautology to say "nothing happened in the pit today," because even if nobody makes a bid or offer during the session (a very infrequent event), it still means something valuable for traders.

The centrality of rehearsal prices in the making of markets becomes even more visible during postpit trading. Bargaining always takes place in reference to rehearsal prices, either by taking them seriously, or by looking down upon their importance, depending on one's market position. The following instance of bargaining between two exchange brokers, which I witnessed together with at least four other traders, presents a case exemplifying both technologies of power:

A: So you say 1.60?
B: You heard it. You know the cotton.
A: It is high. You know C sold it for 1.55 a few minutes ago.
B: Why don't you go buy from him then. But who buys his own cotton, eh?
A: OK, OK, 1.60 it is, payment in a week. Shall I call the factory?
B: Go ahead.

In this round of bargaining, the rehearsal price played a major role in two respects. First, the buyer mentioned it in order to point out that the seller's price is higher than what was taken a few minutes ago in the pit. Indeed, a few minutes earlier one truck of Bergama cotton had sold for 1.55. This was a rehearsal price, made for later use. However, the seller recognized the power of the rehearsal price only to a certain extent. B accepted the fact that the bargaining had to be around 1.55; yet, he alluded to the fact that the rehearsal price was made to depress the actual prices after the pit session. The question "who buys his own cotton?" was meant to decrease the power of the rehearsal price, by rhetorically underlining the fact that the price was an investment for later use, to structure the possible range of prices in postpit trading. He suggested that the rehearsal price was "rehearsed" between two traders who work for different companies, but buy and sell for the same yarn producer.

Immediately after the seller had challenged the rehearsal price itself, the buyer, who already was willing to pay up to 1.625 for the same cotton, made the deal. His client's factory needed the cotton. Being very experienced and strong—one of the "five to ten people who knows how to make the price"— he managed to buy for less than he had anticipated. The trade was a success. For the seller, however, the trade was neither a success, nor a big failure. He had to sell immediately, for the ginning factory that owned the cotton needed cash soon, and the factory owner had ordered him to sell for as high as possible, but no cheaper than 1.60.

I interviewed both A and B after this exchange took place. A, who had successfully bought for less than he had expected, let me know the range his client had given him. Immediately before the trade had taken place, during the pit trading, A had looked terribly disinterested. B, a broker representing relatively less powerful clients, had to sell. He did not skillfully cloak his feelings of urgency. He was still a bit upset at having sold the cotton at his lower limit. It was A's power and his performance's strength that put together a well-rehearsed price.

The first boundary of the market—the one located between the pit and the postpit, which is demarcated by time (12:30 p.m.) and space (the outer circle of the pit)—holds together and makes possible trading performances that produce the rehearsal price. Once the first boundary is crossed, transaction prices are made during various sessions of bargaining. As these sessions take place, the forces of demand and supply are performed, registered, contested, and perceived differently by traders who have diverse market positions, information, orders, and thus performances. These technologies of mediation, interpretation, translation, and performance structure the effects of supply and demand on the ground. Without the mediation of these technologies, supply and demand would be nothing but ineffective abstractions.

Postpit trading has an enormous volume. The rehearsal prices, as prosthetic devices, are used extensively during postpit trading. This second market place hosts the great majority of trading in the İME. Hundreds of truck loads of cotton are sold and bought, producing hundreds of transaction prices, some higher and some lower than the rehearsal price.

Crossing the boundary between pit and postpit trading also allows buyers and sellers, represented by brokers, to meet each other individually and make individual dyadic prices. They utilize the prices made or rehearsed during the pit session and center their trading and bargaining strategies on these prices. One main difference between pit and postpit trading is that trading in the pit is an individually performed and publicly observed act. After the pit, trading can still be observed by others, but only to a limited extent. The traders' individual encounters are scattered. Their place in the market is not as fixed as it is in the pit; they move in it, literally, by walking up and down in the space between the pit and the walls of the mercantile exchange building.

Another central difference between these two locations of the market concerns the visibility and registration of trading. All trade in the pit is registered as soon as a deal is cut, by saying: "Write!" This literally means that the trade is registered and that the names of the buyer and seller, the quantity of the sale, the price, and the payment conditions are written down. All sales are visible in the pit. Both because of the level of visibility and the requirements of pit trading, traders cannot always choose their trading partners, for anyone who says "write" can take the bid or offer.[4] In postpit trading, however, traders have more freedom to choose their

---

[4] It is possible to make a bid or offer to a specific market agent by directly spelling out his name, but this is a rather rare occurrence in the pit. I would like to thank Hayri Özmeriç, a trader from the IME, for correcting me on this point.

trading partners. This is crucial because, according to the cotton traders, no two offers are the same, even if they include exactly the same amount, price, and payment conditions. The trading records of sellers and buyers always play an important role in making a deal. Traders tend to choose bids or offers made by a relatively more trusted trader. For this reason, traders may choose not to reveal their deals in postpit trading. Traders may also choose not to reveal their sales, for it may allow others to gain an insight into their trading policies and it may put them in a better position to guess their moves in the market in the near future.

Making the Market Price of Turkish Cotton

These various rounds of postpit bargaining, which draw on rehearsal prices and are carried out in dyadic form, continue for another 45 minutes and end as traders begin to leave the cotton hall around 1:00 p.m. Many registered and unregistered trades take place in the market during the postpit session. Although it is illegal to carry out an unregistered transaction, they are frequently performed, for the hands of the market can indeed be invisible if wanted. But it is not possible to render the market price invisible. Just before the trading day ends, one crucial market activity remains: members of the Closing Price Committee come together at 1:15 p.m. to locate the market price of cotton. The market price is a price form that is shaped by the deliberation among the committee members. Without it, the dyadic relations of exchange that take place scattered in time and space could not be brought together. It is this interception of the market process that allows for the market price to appear. Because it entails a daily routine of deliberation and yet another form of bargaining, it connects by definition market positions to power, usually by mirroring power relations on the market. The committee has historically consisted of large-scale traders and a few smaller sales brokers who are included to present an image of equality. Deliberation goes on without disagreement, especially when market activity is low. Yet, when the trading volume rises, it becomes more difficult to locate the price.

The first difficulty consists of linking the rehearsal price of the pit with the transaction price of the postpit. Market agents know that rehearsal prices are simultaneously prosthetic devices and transaction prices. By definition, these rehearsal prices are made to appear lower or higher than acceptable levels, in order to be able to trade in desired future prices. However, the actual, scattered prices of the postpit trading are not rehearsal prices; they are not made as investment to be appropriated for future use. Still, they draw on rehearsal prices, and only in reference to them is it possible to make these transaction prices. When the number of rehearsal and actual prices increases, the range within which they oscillate becomes wider. In these situations, it is more difficult and strategically important to locate a market price that represents these different trading levels. The second difficulty of locating the market price arises because postpit trading provides traders, to a certain extent, with an invisible ground of interaction. They do not have to register their trades. Legally, all trades have to be registered, but in practice there are many ways of not registering a deal immediately, or after the deal, or sometimes even at all.

The committee follows a few rules of thumb to establish a range of representative transaction prices and trading levels. Only registered prices are taken into account. Traders may make a deal in the cotton hall after pit trading and still keep it private. These unregistered deals are not taken into account in locating the price of cotton. Because one cannot know for sure the level of invisible trading, since it is not documented, it may be misleading to post prices depending on not yet posted transaction prices. This challenge does not make the Closing Price Committee helpless in filtering out possible tactics of manipulation. For example, when a seller and buyer representing the same company or brokerage house make a registered deal, their trade and price are not taken into consideration.

The market price is usually set by looking at transaction price levels that do not vary greatly: rehearsal prices always set a range of bargaining before transaction prices are taken. Yet, sometimes, especially when the trading volume increases, it becomes more difficult and contentious to set the market price. In these situations, deliberation takes more time, and another round of bargaining takes place, affected on a daily basis by the market power and positions of the traders. To give an example, on one day in 2003, after one market price announcement, TARİŞ—the cooperative representing cotton farmers—protested to the committee, did not recognize its decision, and asked the IME Board to include a cooperative member in the committee. It did not take long for the IME to include TARİŞ in the committee, and since then the committee has been regarded as more representative of the market players.

The committee's coming together helps us locate yet another market place in the halls of the IME. Now all trading has been carried out, and the prices have been rehearsed and then realized in various rounds of transaction. This third location of the market—spatially still located in the cotton hall of the IME, yet temporarily located "outside" of marketing—is the place where the *market price* is produced. At this point, we should take note of the fact that, in order for the market to produce a price, market participants leave the immediate location of marketing and recreate another one by using social technologies drawing on arbitration and deliberation. The market price of Turkish cotton traded in Izmir is set in this third location of the market. This is also the market price that other cotton traders and market analysts around the world take into account as they carry out their daily routine of trading and research.

ANOTHER MARKET PLACE: THE PERMANENT WORKING GROUP ON COTTON

These three temporal and spatial places of the market—the pit, the post-pit, and the Closing Price Committee meeting—are not the only locations where prices in their multiple forms are made in Turkey. Over lunch in an upscale restaurant in Izmir, an experienced cotton trader told me: "Tomorrow, we'll determine the supply of this coming cotton season." Slowly reaching for his beer, he continued, "Everyone will be at the IME tomorrow, the ministry, the cooperative, traders, and cotton research people. You can see the real market there." Learning the fourth *real* location of the market since I had started my urban field work ten weeks earlier, I asked:

What do you mean by determining the supply?
I studied economics. It is true that supply and demand come together to make the price. This is what takes place at the IME. But before it happens, we have to discuss its amount and fix it somehow.
Before what happens?
You know. The supply. What you see in the market depends on what you want from it. I cannot accept a declining production figure before the new season starts. If it declines, if I, as a trader, say that it is going to decline, the price will go up, so I'll sell less cotton. So I have to find more capital for turnover and make less money. So we do our best to present a higher supply figure.

The next day, after postpit trading had ended and the Closing Price Committee decided on and posted the market price of Aegean cotton, not all traders left the IME for their offices or warehouses. Some went to the IME's historical conference room to join the meeting of the Permanent Working Group on Cotton, a gathering described by the above trader as another "real market place." This new market place was comprised of bureaucrats from the Ministry of Agriculture, traders, economists, agricultural engineers, a few large landowners, and the officials of TARİŞ, the cotton sales cooperative representing farmers producing more than a quarter of the crop in the country.

Returning from lunch with a sales broker, I entered the conference hall and sat with a few traders and a ginning factory owner. A bit worried that I arrived only after the first ten minutes of the meeting had passed, I leaned toward the ginning factory owner whom I had interviewed during my rural fieldwork and asked whether I had missed anything. "Nothing," he replied, dismissing the importance of these first ten minutes, "regular stuff, welcoming, underlining the importance of cotton for the country and using scientific techniques to develop the cotton sector, etc. The real stuff is yet to start."

Indeed, it was yet to come. The director of the Nazilli Cotton Research Institute ended his opening remarks by commenting on the importance of the committee for the Turkish cotton sector. Moving his eyes from the text he was reading to look at his audience in a recognizably more serious way, he closed his speech by saying: "We have to be very careful in estimating the supply levels, for they will affect cotton prices greatly. So we have to discuss the matter very seriously and reach a decision that best represents the interests of the cotton sector."

This was not an easy objective. There were three major groups in the meeting, with three different sets of motivation prefiguring their approach to cotton supply estimates. Traders, merchants, and brokers comprised the first group who had an interest in depressed prices, because lower prices would allow them to trade larger volumes. As a result, they would do their best to prevent the caucus from producing an underestimated production level, for a forecast of decreasing supply would push up prices. The second group, the large-scale landlords and the cooperative representatives, had the reverse motivation. Obviously, they would benefit from increasing prices. Thus, they had an incentive to prevent the overestimation of the production level, for a higher supply would depress prices. The ministerial representatives, however, did not care for the price levels as much as these two groups. Their main purpose was to note the cotton supply levels as accurately as possible, in order to inform the Minister of Agriculture so that he would be able to ask for an accurate amount of money for agricultural subsidies from the annual budget of the Prime Ministry. A wrong estimate would result in a problem in his budget.

It did not take long for these three positions to gain visibility in the meeting. After the cooperative representative had presented his production estimates for the 2002 crop—there would be a considerable decrease in production—traders, merchants, and the ginning factory owner sitting next to me simultaneously began to fidget and shift their body weight from side to side in a rather uncomfortable manner, displaying their disagreement. A few went even further and voiced their disagreement by making loud noises of discontent and flying their hands over their heads, as if trying to get rid of a fly.

Merchants and brokers, however, did not present a figure of their own. Although the research department of the IME had worked on estimates, they were understaffed and lacked the funds necessary for carrying out a complete survey. There was an ongoing project that monitored production levels by using satellite remote sensing imagery, but it was not yet effectively in use. After a long and heated deliberation, the caucus reached a consensus that made everyone unhappy, but content. The estimated cotton supply was pinpointed as lower then the previous season. Still, it was determined to be higher than the cooperative's estimates and lower than most of the individual traders' guesses.

Cotton supply is not only a function of its production, but also a matter of everyday market politics. This is why the traders who invited me to this meeting thought that it was another location of the market, for the very processes of price-making are also intercepted in meetings like that of the Permanent Working Group on Cotton. Its decisions inform trading decision and, thus, the very making of the price in all its three forms.

Yet, the mood of consensus disappeared quickly when the next item on the agenda was introduced, the production cost of cotton, making the differences in perception even more observable. After a rather lengthy presentation on the techniques of estimation and data-gathering, the Cotton Research Institute representative finally revealed the institute's estimate of cotton production cost as 1.10. This estimate created such an uproar that for a good ten seconds chaos ruled the meeting hall. A ginning factory owner, whose main occupation was to fund indebted farmers to secure an annual supply of cotton for his enterprises and then sell his cotton at the IME through his agent sitting close to him that day, told me in a quite irritated manner: "This is a lie. A straight lie! What kind of a cost is this? Even if one gives two lira to the peasant, he would say 'oh, I go bust.' It is their nature. It is a lie. The cost is not more than 0.40. I myself am a farmer. I know it."

The anger in the hall somewhat calmed down as the speaker stepped down from the podium and attention turned toward the cooperative's representative. His estimates dragged down the institute's figure, yet still not low enough for the merchants. The land-owner's estimate of 0.60, however, pulled the production cost estimate even lower, injecting into the meeting a more peaceful mood.

The cost of production is important for the making of prices, even if in a rather indirect manner when compared to the role of supply estimates. A high cost estimate would fuel the grievances of the farmers and the cooperative. Furthermore, it would make historically low cotton prices look even worse. Finally, a higher cost estimate would also contribute to the negative public image of brokers, merchants, and traders. From the government's perspective, however, a higher cost estimate would corner the government, giving the opposing parties ammunition to criticize it for not extending enough support to the farmers.

The institute's calculations of the cost of production treat farmers as workers with a forty-hour work week, enjoying national and weekend holidays and earning a minimum wage. In short, the institute's estimate calculates all costs by attaching a monetary value to them, following the standards that the Ministry of Labor and Social Security sets for all workers. Yet the mercantile opposition was fierce enough to both silence the institute director and force the caucus not to consider the institute's estimate, taking it out of the arithmetic average calculated by adding the landowner's, the cooperative's and the exchange's estimates, then dividing their sum by three. An arithmetical formula helps the three parties reach a consensus.

The estimate for the cost of production, like that of the supply, is "determined," as the ginning factory owner told me over lunch, in yet another place of the market, where the forces of supply are negotiated and the cost of production is calculated within a context informed by various interests crossing class, status, and scientific boundaries. Furthermore, the Ministry of Agriculture's representatives remained silent, preferring the registration of lower estimates. They were aware of their limited power in economic decisions because of the standby agreements that the government had made with the International Monetary Fund. They also knew that they would be criticized harshly if a high, yet more accurate, cost estimate was published.

Meetings such as that of the Permanent Working Group on Cotton are peculiar locations of the market and rarely considered to be market places in the literature. However, it is in these meetings that the very building blocks of markets—supply and demand—begin to take shape. The coming together of supply and demand is probed, prefigured, and even produced as estimates by a caucus representing all market actors. The making of rehearsal prices, transaction prices, and market prices is directly affected by this last location of the market. This is why the very meeting itself should be seen as a market activity, as central as trading itself, thus rendering the Permanent Working Group on Cotton Meeting a new market place where various prices are made.[5]

CONCLUSION

The exchange of cotton takes place in the various locations of the market. The institutionalized universe of the market is demarcated by multiple boundaries. Pit trading, the point of entry to the study of cotton

---

[5] For more information on how trading decisions are executed and trading platforms constructed and maintained, see Çalışkan (2005), 223–31.

trading in Izmir, is framed in temporal and geographical limits, bringing traders together every day for ten minutes between 12:20 and 12:30 p.m. It is in this temporal and spatial location that "the theater of the market" takes place. Market players produce *rehearsal prices*, a heterodox form of price caught in the middle of indicative and transaction prices. This price form is taken to exchange cotton; yet, it is made to exchange only a very limited quantity of the commodity, rendering it a rehearsal for the actual volume of trade that has yet to be reached during postpit trading. The pit price is a market device deployed and produced by merchants in order to strengthen their position as they make actual transaction prices. The rehearsal price is a device because its making is a simultaneous investment for postpit trading, but at the same time it is an actual transaction price, for actual cotton is exchanged following its acceptance. This process of rehearsing the price during pit trading draws on various trading performances and represents the effects of the perceived levels of the demand and supply of cotton.

Once this first boundary of the market is crossed by leaving the pit at 12:30 p.m. sharp and by entering the second location of the market, the postpit, traders begin to use these rehearsal prices to negotiate actual transaction prices. Postpit trading, during which traders are not brought together as closely as in the pit, produces actual transaction prices. However, both the traders and their prices are scattered in this second place of the market. Hundreds of registered and unregistered prices are made in this most vibrant location of the market. More arresting still, this is not the place where the *market price* emerges.

At the end of postpit trading, the market price appears in a categorically different setting: the Closing Price Committee meeting. Following a heated process of bargaining and haggling, the committee makes a decision on the market price of cotton as it is produced in Izmir. The committee members remove the highest and lowest market prices from the list of prices they receive from the IME administration and take the weighted arithmetic average of individual transaction prices that have been registered. The market price is made by using an arithmetical formula in a process of heated bargaining and discussion. The market price is not set by a mere coming together of demand and supply, as neoclassical price theory suggests, but produced in a political process of deliberation. To study a market and its prices is to study these processes.

Demand and supply also play their role in yet another surprising setting. Before traders perceive their effects, they are negotiated in committees specifically formed for this task.[6] The actual demand and supply

---

[6] For an analysis of how the perception of supply and demand contributes to the making of prices and exchange volumes, see Odirici and Corrado (2004).

figures of any market are known after the market is made. Before the market is made, one cannot know these figures for sure. It is misleading to deduce the price from the levels of supply and demand, for prices in their multiple forms are made *before* these levels are known. In meetings such as those convened by the Permanent Working Group on Cotton, the perceptions of "what the market will be" are discussed and negotiated, and figures such as supply volume or costs of production are literally produced, thus further informing the ways in which prices are made as market devices. Regardless of what the actual cost of production and supply will be, the effect of their estimation is the product of a deliberative market process. The actual figures of supply and cost only manifest themselves after the cotton is consumed and thus disappears.

Hence, it is more appropriate to see prices as prosthetic forms produced, deployed, resisted, and, at times, abused by traders. Seeing the market price as a summary of a market activity is misleading, for every summary reflects the vantage point of its writer. Markets draw on many stories informed by a diverse set of constraints and interests. So do prices. In Izmir, market prices are produced in three main forms, in four different market places. Studying the market from the vantage point of the price, then, requires us to look at the very production process of prices as market devices. Future research on the anthropology of prices as market devices has great potential to provide us with tools to address this pressing need.

Ethnographic attention to price production and market-making also helps to approach markets as sociotechnical contexts whose working can be studied and critically questioned in a novel way. Seen as prosthetic devices, it becomes impossible to perceive prices as a more or less neutral convergence of the forces of supply and demand. Making visible the very processes that produce various price forms can help those who are affected by these prices to become more active participants in the making of prices. As we have seen in the discussion of the making of the three price forms at the IME, people constantly intervene in and maintain markets. This is a precondition for the possibility of existence of markets, and not an exceptional state. If this is the case, *laissez-faire* acquires a new meaning, for letting some people, but not others, produce the price and make markets directly affects the livelihood of those who make and consume the very commodity whose price is produced amid relations of power. The next chapter provides this conclusion with an even stronger empirical case study that has the potential to introduce yet another theoretical novelty in market research: the act of institutional trading without an exchange in Alexandria, Egypt.

CHAPTER 4

A Market without Exchange:
Cotton Trade in Egypt

GLOBAL MARKETS DRAW ON MULTIPLE forms of trading practices. From electronically organized exchanges in the United States to informal futures trading in India, one can observe a dynamic universe of interaction in world trade. The presence of organized exchanges such as the NYBOT and the Izmir Mercantile Exchange brings together scattered instances of trading. The exchange building also helps researchers to observe and understand more easily the making of global markets. Yet many trading relations do not take place in exchanges. Thus, a market study that did not take into account commodity markets without organized exchange would be incomplete. Focusing on cotton exchange in Egypt, this chapter introduces Alexandria into the picture in order to round out the study of regional markets and their interaction with global and local relations of commodity exchange. It will provide a case study of how a trading regime without organized exchange can be fully integrated into a global market.

Even though it is a major cotton-growing country and helped create institutional designs of capitalist trade relations with the world's first cotton futures market, Egypt has no institutionalized cotton exchange.[1] Unlike Izmir and New York City, Alexandria lacks a mercantile building that brings together merchants under one roof, around one pit. Still, it is home to a very dynamic market where public and private trading houses compete for cotton and profits. How can we understand the ways in which traders relate to the market regionally and globally in such a setting? What types of mercantile prostheses enable Egyptian market-makers to attend to the conditions of trade? Finally, how are markets made and maintained in Alexandria?

This chapter discusses how Egyptian traders carry out everyday market maintenance and price realization in the absence of an organized exchange. Following a discussion of the workings of the cotton market

---

[1] In 1994, a new spot exchange was opened in the Mina al-Basal district of Alexandria. However, the exchange was a superficial measure to present the World Bank with a case of market development in the country. Lacking any substantive activity, the exchange has not even seen the trade of a single bale of cotton on its premises since its opening.

from the vantage point of Egyptian regional traders, it explores how world markets are articulated in a locality categorically different from Memphis, New York City, or Izmir. After analyzing market exchange in Alexandria, I will discuss how Egyptian traders relate to the countryside on the one hand and external markets on the other. By doing so, I will locate the ways in which trade connects social positions to power and show how the Egyptian trading regime relates to the making of a world market. We will see that the main technologies of Egyptian market-making as derivative engagements are not substantially different from the trading relations I analyzed in the cases of Izmir and Memphis, despite the lack of an institutionalized mechanism of exchange. The presence of an institutionalized exchange thus does not necessarily change the main dynamics and technologies of a market arrangement. It forces traders to find individualized ways of inventing and deploying market devices that reflect the dynamic universe of global markets.

In addition to presenting a case study of market-making without an exchange building, the analysis of Egyptian cotton trading practices contributes to the study of a world market in two other, major ways. First, Egyptian farmers grow long and extralong staple cotton, an input commodity used for spinning the world's highest-quality yarn. The fact that there are only a handful of countries where this type of cotton can grow provides us with an effective vantage point for studying price-making and the market within better-defined internal boundaries.

Second, bringing Egypt into the analysis provides us with an opportunity to discuss a test case for almost all the major global social experiments of modernity. It was during Egypt's colonization that major technologies for governing populations and their political economy were produced and developed. Following decolonization, the country became the center of global attention again, as an exemplary forerunner of planned development projects in the import-substitution industrialization era. Nasser was the beacon of Third World development; his image still haunts the Egyptian countryside. Anwar Sadat's *Infitah* or open-door economic policies after the 1973 war with Israel and, later, Hosni Mubarak's policy choices prepared the ground for Egypt becoming a test case for the last major global transformation of the world—that is, of neoliberal reforms. Study of the Egyptian traders' mercantile platforms, therefore, provides the analysis with a perspective that takes into account the social geography of all major market and development experiments of world history.

The World's First Cotton Futures Market and Its Historical Setting

Since the early nineteenth century Egypt has been a leading center of cotton trade in the world. Commercial cotton-growing in Egypt began in the early 1820s. In less than two decades, cotton became the main source of income for the landed class. The world's first formal futures contracts were exchanged in Alexandria in 1861, almost a decade before the opening of New York's cotton futures exchange (Baffes 2004a, 2; Baffes and Kaltsas 2004).

The end of the nineteenth century was the beginning of a new era in the making of world markets. In 1865, John Pender, a textile merchant from Manchester, financed the installation of the first cable connecting both sides of the Atlantic Ocean, hoping to enable traders to have real-time quotes for the first time in history (Hugill 1999). This initiative failed, and it was not until 1875 that the Siemens Company began to operate the first reliable cable connection between Britain and the United States. However, even before that, in 1865, the Indo-European Telegraph Company had launched services between India and Britain, and in 1869 the Anglo-Mediterranean Telegraphy Company had connected Egypt and England via Malta. Three years later, another cable connected Egypt and England to East Asia and East Africa. Moreover, the introduction of the steamship reduced the time necessary to cross the Atlantic Ocean from two months to two weeks.

By 1880, five major cotton exchanges—Alexandria, Le Havre, New Orleans, New York, and Liverpool—were connected to each other, exchanging spot and futures contracts by cross quotations (Garside 1935). At that time, more than half of the bales produced in the world crossed borders, to be unpacked in a location different from the one in which they had been grown. Today, after decades of neoliberal reforms and trade regimes imposed by the World Trade Organization, only thirty percent of cotton is exported.

Under British colonial rule in Egypt, Alexandria's importance in the world cotton market grew even further. In 1892, the opening price of the Liverpool Cotton Exchange was based on the closing prices of the Alexandria and Le Havre cotton exchanges. Moreover, Liverpool's closing price prefigured the opening prices of New York and New Orleans (Baffes 2004b, 17).

During the first half of the twentieth century, Egyptian cotton trade was dominated by a non-native merchant class: before the 1952 revolution, less than five percent of cotton merchants were Egyptian. The main organization representing merchant interests, the Alexandria Cotton Exporters' Association (Alcotexa), was founded in 1932 by primarily French-, Italian-, and Greek-speaking merchants and by colonial settlers, some of whom also represented the world's major cotton merchants. Between 1932 and 1960, only three Egyptians served as Alcotexa presidents.

The end of World War II marked the emergence of anticolonial struggles everywhere. A coalition forged by the Free Officers Movement took control of the army and later proclaimed Egypt's independence. The new regime headed by Nasser was aware of the importance of cotton for the country's economy and decided to use the state to restructure trade. The exchange was closed between 1952 and 1955 and briefly reopened in 1955. In 1956, the world's attention focused on the exchange again, but this time not because of its power in world trade. Three days after being elected president, Nasser gave his famous speech on the nationalization of the Suez Canal Company from the balcony of the Alexandria Cotton Exchange building. Later, a fire destroyed it, eventually leading to its collapse. Today, a parking lot has replaced the building that housed the first cotton futures and second commodity futures markets of the world.

Nasser made sure that no cotton was exported or internally traded without the authorization of the Egyptian Cotton Commission. As he nationalized the cotton business, the world's first cotton futures exchange lost its importance; in 1961, a century after its inauguration, it was closed. Cooperatives and planned marketing replaced the order that the exchange had imposed. Starting in 1961, all farmers had to be members of an Agrarian Reform Cooperative or an Agrarian Credit Cooperative. At the end of 1961, about one-seventh of all lands owned by large-scale landowners were transferred to small land holders and tenants (Bush 2002, 8). These developments helped reduce poverty in the countryside and promoted economic growth, and also made sure that the government controlled the growing of cotton and its marketing channels.

Nasser's death in 1970 marked a turning point in Egyptian politics. Sadat reversed the policies of the former regime and prepared the ground for market reforms in the country. In 1981, Sadat was assassinated, and his vice-president Mubarak replaced him, but not his neoliberal economic policies. From the mid-1980s onward, the decline of workers' remittances and the increase of rent provisions to the domestic allies of the regime created an unsustainable economic climate. Foreign debt payments became the major source of government spending. During the 1980s, debt servicing amounted to twenty-five percent of the total foreign exchange revenues of the country, reaching a record forty percent at the end of the decade (Bromley and Bush 1994). Further need for external borrowing made the Egyptian government approach the International Monetary Fund (IMF) and the World Bank to secure financing. In 1986, full-scale neoliberal structural adjustment reforms arrived in the country.

Alcotexa and Cotton's Associate Price

Until 1994, no cotton trade could take place in Egypt without government authorization and the involvement of a public trading company. Cotton trade was carried out by six large public companies using three major agricultural cooperatives as their buying agents. In 1994, at the personal invitation of the Egyptian Prime Minister, Mahmoud Wahba, a U.S. economist and businessman, opened the first private cotton-trading company of Egypt, the National Cotton Company (NCC). The objective of Law 210, which allowed the privatization of the cotton sector, was to set domestic cotton prices according to global market prices. He was welcomed to the Egyptian market with huge fanfare, with the participation of all important persons involved in the cotton business. In 2002, a cotton trader who had been vice-president of one of the six public cotton companies at the time told me NCC's story over lunch.

> . . . when he came for the first time, a big reception was given in Helwan Palestine Hotel. Even Prime Minister Sidqi was there. The Minister of Economy, all important people were there. The main idea was to introduce this man to every significant person in Egypt. We were told that he was a professor of economics and knew how markets work. He gave a pompous speech, looking down upon all of us. Then he came again for the second time. He brought with him the chairman of the New York Cotton Exchange and the chairman of the Chicago Exchange. They came all together. Five ministers, three undersecretaries. . . . Every important person in the cotton sector had come to see them. They gave us a lecture about cotton exchange. Osman Helmy[2] stood up in that meeting and told them that in Alexandria we had the first cotton futures of the world. They seemed not to know this. Wahba had a huge residence in the Semiramis Hotel. He was introduced to us as the son of an Egyptian cotton trader. But I know all the names in the cotton business. Wahba didn't ring a bell. I asked him about his family. He turned the conversation so that we would not have to talk about it anymore. His father was a *fellah*. Well, usually peasants are very wonderful people. Anyway, everyone was impressed by him. His interest in the market was so big, so big for someone who never worked in cotton before. He got a permanent room at the Nile Hilton and a permanent fat salary. He wanted me in this company, too. I knew what was coming, and so I declined. He bought a villa in Cairo, and then a flat in Alex[andria]. The first year he made a huge profit thanks to the state. He then bought an oil company; he was an oil man anyway. He thought that oil and cotton are the same. After all, he was the market expert! He rented eleven ginning mills. Next year, he went bankrupt; and the national bank had to bail out all the debt. But he took his money out, he was smart. He said: "I know how markets work." The cotton market is not the oil market.

Thus, privatization in Egypt started with a trauma, but this did not keep Egyptian investors from opening private trading houses. In less than a

---

[2] Osman Hemly is one of the most experienced Egyptian cotton trading agents in the world. He is generally regarded as the master of cotton trade in Egypt.

decade, between 1994 and 2003, twenty-two private cotton trading houses opened in Alexandria, outnumbering their public competitors. Their interaction and export are governed by Alcotexa, an institution inherited from the country's colonial past. No Egyptian cotton can be exported without Alcotexa's authorization. The association is managed and financed by its members, and its most important function is to provide traders and merchants with a tool for making their markets visible and prices manageable. Unlike their colleagues in Izmir or New York City, the merchants of Alexandria do not come together under the roof of a cotton exchange building to trade the commodity. However, very much like other merchants, they come together to make and maintain the market.

Alcotexa executes three main activities. First, by producing reports about both the Egyptian and the world cotton market, they make the market appear real and ready for the traders' interaction. Yet, as we have seen from the ways in which reports are written and supply and demand figures made in other instances, in Alexandria, too, market forces are identified by the market participants. As in every other place in the world, merchants always predict a great harvest, increasing supply, and a shrinking demand before the harvest. Their ideas about the market change as the cotton changes hands.

Alcotexa's *Cotton Gazette*, a publication older than the Republic of Egypt, plays an important role in this. Compiling statistical information estimated and produced by experts, it brings together the markets. It also publishes photographs and articles of people related to the cotton sector, articles in which they usually propagate their ideas on what the market will do next.

Secondly, Alcotexa serves as an arbitral authority. As we have seen in the previous two chapters, trade is made possible by the forging of a documentary realm of circulation parallel to the world of commodity circulation, and markets are made by matching these two realms. The final function of the association is its most important one: it sets the export price of Egyptian cotton. Once a week, on Sundays, the managing committee of the association comes together and determines an index of minimum export prices for each variety and grade of cotton grown in Egypt. This price then becomes the minimum price of cotton for the following week. Because all export contracts need the association's approval, traders are required to post either this or a higher price.

The making of the price in Alexandria poses an interesting puzzle for understanding the realization of cotton prices in world markets. Alcotexa is not a government institution. Between 1994 and 2000, the private merchants did not have the power to control the association, even though they were an important part of its management. In 2001, private companies reached an absolute majority in the association's management and prevented government companies from holding membership in the managing committee. In 2002, the president of a public company summarized Alcotexa's transformation as follows:

> They threw us out of Alcotexa. Now we have a private sector monopoly in Egypt. Can you believe that? This is privatization. They [the private companies] are sixteen. We are only six. Although we are bigger, we all have the same number of votes. Until now, public companies have been dominating the administration. But we lost. This is the disadvantage of elections. But although we are out, they know that we are important. They always ask us questions, because they are just learning how to run a trading company.

Every week, Alcotexa members come together and discuss the minimum price to be set. Members keep a number of factors in mind before locating the price of the Egyptian market: first, they check world cotton prices by considering them in their prosthetic universes. The NYBOT futures price is consulted to see the direction of the market. One of the reasons why these prosthetic prices are effective devices for price realization is the fact that all prices around the world are made in reference to them. Second, Alcotexa members check the A Index of Cotlook Ltd. This index already incorporates the merchants' way of seeing the market, because, as we saw in the first chapter, it is the average of different quotes from the main centers of cotton trade in the world.

The association's price sets the minimum worth of a base grade and type of cotton; in reference to this price, the minimum prices of other types and grades are determined. However, setting the price does not mean that this is an actual price to be used for transactions. Although it is legally not possible to go lower, it is common for traders to cut informal deals with their clients at prices lower than the Alcotexa one. Whatever the actual price is, it surely is not the association's price. This situation is parallel to all the market prices we have analyzed so far. All of the world prices of cotton are prosthetic in nature, whether they are realized in New York City or Izmir. They are not taken to exchange commodities.

However, the price made in Alexandria is categorically different from both the world prosthetic prices of cotton and the IME's rehearsal price. It is not produced as an index; yet, like an indexical price, it still does not set the actual worth of a bale of cotton. It is not a rehearsal price either, for it is not produced in a pit where traders exchange cotton by rehearsing its price. Still, similarly to prosthetic and rehearsal prices, the Alexandria price draws on the everyday politics of market-making in associated practices of trade. The association of a market comes together, in the same way in which the closing price committee comes together at the IME after every trading day, and sets the price. One may call this new price form the "associate price."

It would be misleading to argue that any trade regime can produce associate prices, because the cotton concerned here is extralong-staple cotton (ELS), which occupies a niche in the global cotton market. As the most expensive cotton in the world, ELS is used to produce high-quality yarn for fine and expensive garments. Since Egypt and the United States have a hegemonic position in the world market, their private sectors, or "markets," can afford to forge these associate prices. The same cannot be said for medium-staple cotton.

Egypt has been the world's largest exporter of ELS cotton for almost a century, having a share of up to sixty-five percent of the world export market. Since 1980, Egypt's Giza 45, 70, and 88 varieties, the best ELSs in the world, has declined in production. This decline has coincided with the time period when United States–based international financial institutions began advocating free market reforms in Egypt, under the precept of attaining Egypt's comparative advantage through the effective working of the market.

However, the more free market reform steps were taken, the fewer farmers produced the highest-quality cotton. In fact, within a few years Egyptian ELS production declined to nineteenth-century levels. Starting from 1984, the void in world production created by neoliberal reforms began to be filled by about 1,000 heavily subsidized U.S. agricultural companies. As a result, in the eight years between 1980 and 1988 Egyptian ELS production was halved, whereas U.S. production quadrupled.

Armed with the aggressive marketing strategies of the United States Supima Association and with the help of subsidies, United States–produced ELS caught up with its main competitor in the world market in 1987. In one decade after becoming the main competitor to Egyptian cotton, the United States increased its market share more than fivefold, depressing the Egyptian share to less than twenty percent of the world market. Paradoxically, the very same free market reforms that aimed at integrating the Egyptian market into the world market led to the shrinking of Egypt's share in world trade.

Realization of the associate price at Alcotexa has an additional advantage, other than the deployment of a market-making tool to interact with the ways other competitors behave in the market: Egyptian private merchants use these associate prices to reap profits by playing on multiple boundaries of public and private, formal and informal, market and nonmarket. Between 1960 and 1980, cotton traders working for public exchange companies maintained an effective mercantile platform that at some point managed to dictate almost half of the world's ELS market.[3]

---

[3] For the history of Egyptian success in world cotton markets prior to 1950, see Goldberg (1988).

With the launch of "promarket" reforms, private merchants' power grew, and these merchants, the very representatives of a free market, began to contribute to the association's realization of prices. This is another example of why government intervention in the market should be interpreted as merely another intervention, for markets constantly experience intervention by different actors contributing to their making and maintenance. In the 1990s, private merchants began to dictate the conditions of market maintenance and price realization. This puzzling situation is rarely addressed in the literature on economic reform. The making of associate prices prevents public companies from setting a price of their own. Furthermore, these regulations do not allow public companies to decrease their prices in the short term in order to be able to grasp a larger market share in the future. Public companies are required to register their sales at equal to or higher than the associate price. For private companies, anything goes.

Public companies are more transparent as a result of the many internal checks and balances. They cannot produce documents that may appear to meet the requirements of Alcotexa. Private companies, however, have invisible hands that can produce "proper" documentation when necessary. These forgeries are easily disguised, and only a few people—mostly the company's partners—know about them. This is one of the ways in which invisible hands make the market in Egypt and abroad.

This interesting interplay of market boundaries and associate prices presents a dilemma for public companies. The sales manager of a public company described the situation in the following way:

> Now we have the free market of our former colleagues. These private merchants and their sales people were all trained in the public sector. When they resigned to have better salaries in the newly founded merchant houses, they took with them all the contacts, customers, and trade secrets. My former clients call me and say: "Look Fatima, we want to buy from you. But private companies have better deals." Before privatization, things were more transparent. If I had a price, my customers knew that this was the best I could do. There was trust. Now I can't even trust my customers. They tell me: "This private company has a better deal." They cannot have a better deal for that grade of Giza 70. Because it is lower than the Alcotexa price. But we all know they do have better deals. So even when there is no lower price in Egypt, customers say there is. They exaggerate it. Now we can't know.

Public companies are required to use the exchange rate posted by the Central Bank when sending price quotes or firm offers to companies abroad, whereas private companies use informal and free market exchange rates that depress their cost relative to public companies. This is an effective subsidy for private merchants, preventing government companies with a large client portfolio from being competitive, an objective of the privatization of the cotton sector. Thus, private merchants acquire both the international clients and traders of public companies.

The pace of this transformation should progress slowly, for if it went too quickly, the private sector could not absorb the rich and hard-to-sustain client portfolio of the public sector. If the transformation of the cotton trade in Egypt follows the present trajectory for another decade, it is safe to assume that public trading companies will disappear. A public trading house director also predicts such a future:

> Private companies also play on the fluctuation of the dollar. The public sector receives payment through public banks. We cannot use our foreign exchange in the private market; instead, we have to use the National Bank's rates. I'll give you an example: today the [exchange] rate is 4.61 LE. But you cannot simply buy as many dollars as you need, if you want to import stuff, or for God knows what reason. So if you want a lot of dollars, say a million dollars, you need to buy it from private dealers, who sell it for 5.20 LE. This is the private sector. It is illegal. It is informal. But this is what they are doing in Egypt. Private cotton traders also make money out of this scheme. When private merchants get their dollars in exchange for cotton, they sell the dollar in Egypt to those who need it the most. So they make money this way, too. We [public companies] cannot make money under such conditions. We'll go bust soon.

Another interesting difference that contributes to the unfair competition between private and public companies derives from a similar logic of transparency and formality. Public companies cannot formally hire child labor younger than twelve years of age for their seed cotton processing facilities. Their labor cost is higher, not only because of this restriction, but also as a result of giving social benefits to public officials and workers. A public company whose business portfolio is one-third of that of a private company usually employs three times as many workers and officials. It may seem that private companies are more effective in terms of a cost-benefit analysis, but only to a blind eye.

Private companies almost without exception either employ children younger than twelve, or subcontract the employment of children to another private agency. Moreover, they deny their workers social benefits and proper insurance. Although working in a government company in Egypt is not the most desirable job, without exception all mid-level employees and workers prefer to work for public companies. Public companies are more transparent, more formal, and contribute more benefits to society when compared to the private companies that thrive in nontransparent corners of illegal and informal sites of privatization.

Another public company's sales manager registered his protest as follows:

How can I compete this way with private merchants? I want to compete. I know the cotton business, I have many contacts, and I know everyone in the world. But they don't let me make my price. This is the free market in Egypt. This is the free market in the world. Maybe all they want is to get rid of us. Ten years ago we had 1,200 employees in this firm. Now we are 530. Other public companies had to lay off workers, too. In the private sector they employ only a handful of people with decent salaries and benefits. The rest are almost [like] slaves. Only a few have fat salaries, the rest are extremely poor. In my company we could not even hire one person in any job in the last ten years. The kids they [the private companies] put to work cannot open their eyes in the morning, they want to sleep, so small are they. [Private companies] want me to work for them. How can I really leave my company in good conscience?

WE SPEND ALL OUR TIME IN SEARCH OF THE PRICE

Once the associate price is set in the weekly meetings of Alcotexa, the actual prices begin to take shape both in Alexandria and in the world. The president of one of the public companies, who holds a Ph.D. in economics, explained the making of markets and prices when I met him in his office. The room had once served as the office of the owner of a global merchant house, one of the companies still active in the world cotton market. After I had explained my research project on the world cotton market to him, he replied: "[t]he main job of markets is to bring supply and demand together. Markets regulate trade and make prices." Drawing a large X shape in the air, he continued: "The price is the intersection of demand and supply."

> *Is this also how the market works in Egypt?*
> Oh no, we don't have supply and demand in Egypt. I think there is in America.
> *What does it mean to not have demand and supply in Egypt?*
> The market doesn't work the way a supply and demand graph works.
> Does it work this way in America?
> No! No. I didn't mean in the cotton market. Maybe other markets in America work this way. In reality, Americans do what we do. In September we come together and set a minimum price. We don't have a government who supports us, as is for Americans [*sic*]. So they [Americans] wait, they wait, and then they announce their prices to have a competitive edge.
> *Where is demand and supply here?*
> *Mish 'arif* [I don't know].

Another cotton merchant of a private trading company mentioned the problematic relationship between the United States and Egypt in terms of ELS cotton, as he showed me photographs of the old cotton bourse:

In Alcotexa we look at Pima,[4] and they [the U.S. merchants] look at us. I don't know who in the end makes the price. We do something and then they react. They do something and then we react. We declare our minimum price in September. . . . After we declare our price, they [the U.S. merchants] immediately decrease their price. It happens every year. But before doing that, both Americans and we look at world prices. Because if other cottons are cheaper than extralong staple, we know that we can't sell as much as we want. If the economy is bad, people buy cheaper garments. So we look at world prices.

What are these prices?

Looking at me and smiling, he showed me a faxed price report from Cotlook Ltd. and continued:

There is nothing called the world price. It does not exist. New York prices kept going down for more than a year until they reached the lowest ever, 30.00 c/lb last September. Then September 11 happened. It went up afterward. The low prices forced the USDA to subsidize cotton. For markets this is wrong. If the United States subsidizes cotton, what can we do? We lost the balance again; the freest market in the world is America, no? How can it be a free market when you support farmers and traders?

So if all subsidies stop, can we have a world market price?

You know, in reality, there is no world price. They are all index of this, index of that. Even if there was no government, we wouldn't have a world price. The government just moves the price up or down, it doesn't make it. I wish there was a world price so that we could sell and buy accordingly. Then we wouldn't have to work so hard. We spend all our time in search of the price.

So world prices help you find your price.

Yes, they help us. They help everyone, but they don't exist in reality.

What exists in reality?

[After a long pause] You know, bargaining, trying to learn what others know, what others want to do and don't want to do.

The president of one of the private companies in Egypt, who had been trained many decades ago in the Alexandria Futures Exchange of colonial times, explained the centrality of the associate prices and the way they prefigure world prosthetic prices, again by referring to "world prices that do not exist in reality," when I met him two weeks after I interviewed the merchant quoted above:

I don't look at Cotlook anymore; they totally rely on European merchant prices. I'll give you an example: I know that 2,000 bales are sold here, and the price was 69.00 c/lb. I look at them, the price is totally different.

[4] Pima and U.S. Pima are abbreviations for ELS cotton produced in the United States.

Getting information about ELS is very difficult. I see a price on Cotlook, and then I see other real prices. I don't understand. Contract prices are always different from posted prices. They don't represent the price, it is not realistic. I need another thing. Can you please find me a source? There is a webpage, seam.com. Where can I learn the real prices of U.S. Pima? Is Dunavant[5] giving prices? NYCE is covering the upland only!

For how long have you been a cotton merchant?

More then forty years now.

How come you don't know where to find the price?

[laughs] This is precisely the point. The price has to be made. You make it by reports, by strength, by meeting others. You also have to make your client feel that it is the best price. But it is not. That's why the real world price doesn't exist.

Do you really not look at Cotlook anymore?

No, I look at their prices everyday, you're right. There is nothing else.

Do you ever sell your ELS for a price less than the Alcotexa price?

At this point he stopped talking; his eyes locked with mine in a rather inquisitive manner. I felt the need to remind him that I would not reveal his real name in the book.

"But they would know anyway," he said. "We all know each other. Not only in Egypt, in the world." "Can they guess how you would answer my last question?" I asked in Arabic. Most Egyptian traders resisted my attempts to conduct interviews in Arabic; after greeting me in Arabic, they would immediately and without exception continue in English. Initially, I thought that it was my poor command of Arabic that made them speak English with me. Later, I realized that speaking English was more of a power performance than a practical choice. The choice of language was more related to the content of our conversations than to my command of a particular language. Hence, they would immediately start to speak Arabic when we changed the subject to something more interesting, more engaging, and less known.

Lowering my voice, and imitating how other traders talked about important things, I asked him this last question in Arabic. He answered in a hushed tone, also in Arabic:

Yes, they would guess the answer. But they wouldn't be happy to have it on paper.

What would it change?

If you were a cotton merchant, how would you feel if you read that others do not care for Alcotexa prices and sell their cotton for 98.00 c/lb, although Alcotexa's minimum price is 100 cents?

---

[5] Dunavant is the world's largest cotton merchant house.

How would you feel?
I would feel nothing. Because I know they do that.
Wa hadritak, ha-taʿmil nafs il-haga kaman *[And would you do the same thing, too]?*
Tabʿan [Of course].

The nature of pricing prosthetics changes as one moves from one market to another. This conclusion should not be confused with a culturalist position, suggesting that, as cultures change, the meaning of price changes. The changing nature of pricing prosthetics is neither an ideological nor a discursive matter. The argument is neither about how the price is understood differently in various cultural locations of the world, nor about how the meaning of the price changes as one moves from country to country. All market prices are prosthetic in nature; yet they are produced in specific mercantile platforms that are shaped by the history of their making and the everyday forms of power contestations in these locations. The rehearsal price realized in Izmir is different from the associate price of Alexandria not because they are understood differently. On the contrary, the logic of attending to the conditions of these prices is quite similar in almost all mercantile locations of the world. What is different is the ways in which these prices are made and deployed in everyday trade.

The world price of cotton, its indices, the rehearsal price of Izmir, and the associate price of Alexandria are all prices of different kinds, produced in different mercantile platforms, maintained every day in essentially political sites of markets. These sites change, expand, and contract, depending on the mercantile platforms on which traders operate. These multiple and dynamic boundaries of the market and their settings are technologies for making money in world trade.

Alcotexa's private merchants make associate prices by taking into account prices they do not trust. The world price is not a "real price," as merchants see it; yet it has to be deployed as a prosthesis. They do not necessarily respect the very associate price they make, for such a transgression of market boundaries is perceived precisely as the essence of trading. The boundaries are set in order to be challenged to create possibilities of making money.

However, not everyone is equal in this game of trade, barter, and exchange. Public companies cannot entertain similar transgressions of these multiple market boundaries, because regulations require them to abide by the laws of the markets. This paradoxical situation will soon force public companies into bankruptcy, although, most probably, advocates of free market reforms will still present them as uncompetitive establishments in capitalist markets.

THREE TRAITS OF TRADE

After the associate price is made by consulting the prosthetic prices created in different world market locations—from the rehearsal price of the IME to the Cotlook A Index—the merchants of Alexandria begin to make actual prices. Drawing on the associate price, these actual prices are made during lengthy negotiations and bargaining between trade partners. Trade in world cotton markets never takes place between anonymous sellers and buyers. It is an exchange relationship between sellers and buyers who almost always "know" each other. An anonymous international buyer or seller is a rarity.

In an Egyptian merchant house, the selling of cotton usually begins either by receiving a bid from a potential buyer, or by sending an offer to a client. This at the same time launches the actual and documentary circulations of commodities. If the house receives a bid, the trading manager should make up his mind before the bid expires. If the house sends a firm offer, the buyer has to reach a decision before the offer expires. This temporal framing of individual possibilities of transaction is crucial for limiting the otherwise unlimited realm of the market.

In order to be able to make sense of the price, the two parties of exchange depend on incessant researching and networking activities, taking significantly more time and energy than the trading decision and its execution itself. For Nagwa Waheed, the sales manager of a large public trading company, "trading never stops."

> [B]ecause our job requires constant attention to what is happening in the world. There is no *Eid* [major Muslim holiday] in Japan. When they want to buy, they call you any time. When I receive a call, I can't say, "Well, let me see what the price is." You have to give the price. So one has to be ready at all times.
>
> *How do you get ready?*
>
> I have a routine. I usually read the Egyptian prices. I look at market reports. I try to understand how international merchants put together their ideologies.
>
> *What do you mean by "ideology"?*
>
> You know, you want others to see the market as you see it, so that you can control what you don't know. If you can predict what others will do, you make money. I read reports to see how their ideology changes.
>
> *How do you see that?*
>
> First, I read the opening prices. Then I look at prospects, plantations, crop reports, futures prices, other spots, oil prices, and then put together an idea that guides my trading and prices.

Is this your personal ideology?
No. I don't propagate my own position. I don't write market reports.
Where do you find the prices?
I look at what everyone checks. I look at the Cotlook. Now, many people read
  Cotlook here, you know. I read the "week in brief" [a section of Cotlook's
  weekly reports]. I read the quotes. I also look at American Pima.
How do these prices guide you?
I make the price by looking at other prices, like the Pima. Now, they [the U.S.
  sellers] already set a price for Pima. As soon as we post our prices, they
  will decrease their price. This is how world trade is. We all look at each
  other. Americans look at us, we look at them. We have to know the prices
  abroad. We look at the Cotlook. It is a weekly. Alcotexa gets the daily
  quotations, too.

Waheed's everyday routine of research is not significantly different from
that of the other international and regional traders I discussed above.
They also rely on research in the wild, a term Callon uses to refer to
everyday research carried out by laymen. Similar to other merchants, she
also maintains a trading platform of capital, knowledge, and network.
She travels a lot, meets other traders, establishes new connections, has
endless dinners and lunches, and exchanges numerous gifts with other
merchants and clients. If she makes an offer, she always puts the price
a bit higher; if she receives a bid, she knows that the price is a bit lower
than the incipient actual price.

*After receiving a bid or sending an offer via fax or email, what is the next
  thing you do?*
It depends. If it is a good price, and prices are usually too good to be true, I
  can take it. But usually we call each other and continue bargaining over the
  phone.
Who can do the bargaining in the company?
Not many people. Usually me. Bargaining is an art. Not many people can
  do it. You have to be an actor, a good one, a convincing one. You need to
  know your position, your partner, your cotton, everything. You are not
  selling a piece of cloth. You are dealing with cotton perhaps produced by
  6,000 farmers. So you have to bargain well.

Three interesting themes appear in Waheed's understanding of the cotton market. First, like many of her colleagues in Turkey or the United
States, she refers to a vague category she colloquially locates as "other
prices." These other prices are prosthetic prices, produced in mercantile platforms through the constant maintenance work of "ideological"
production, to the making of supply and demand figures. She uses these
market prices as trading tools to make actual prices. The making of these
two prices, prosthetic and actual, belongs to two different worlds.

Second, every day she carries out research to be able to locate the actual price she will soon be making. For this, she relies on reports, their "ideologies," her experience, and networking. She has to maintain friendships to be able to call these "friends" later; she has to meet them frequently for conferences, dinners, and lunches. Networking is crucial for her decision-making. Yet networking does not merely consist of establishing connections with other people. It also means locating oneself within these connections, for in practice these networks always precede an individual in terms of presence.

Third, trading requires experience in bargaining and talent in persuasion. Markets rely on these traits of trade. Waheed's description of trading and the centrality of experience are similar to how Turkish cotton growers express their relationship with the merchants of Söke, or the "J. R.s," as some call them. They too underscore the importance of experience in buying and selling things and often complain about their lack of experience and power in comparison to the merchants with whom they deal.

Experience is an important matter among merchants themselves. One gains experience in either the family or the company. It is not a coincidence that all over the world cotton companies are usually family enterprises. In Egypt, too, the family has become an important aspect of trading. Before nationalization, almost all cotton trading companies were family-owned businesses. After nationalization, family ties became less important. However, in today's neoliberal times, family ties are making a comeback. In Egypt, half of the private cotton traders work with their relatives.

An actual price is set following the bargaining, but then Alcotexa still has to approve the trade before its circulation is launched. Anyone who trades with Egypt knows about this requirement. It is safe to assume that Alcotexa does not reject any trade in its meetings. The association only registers them. Waheed explained to me the trading practices immediately after bargaining as follows:

> Here in Egypt, without Alcotexa confirmation, no trade is possible. Moreover, the buyers should be registered. If you are a new buyer, you have to send an information letter to Alcotexa and pay ten percent of the total amount in advance before the cotton's shipment. But if you are known, usually everybody knows everyone else, there is no need for this.
> *What happens after you make a final deal?*
> After I get the bid and everything, I send the information to Alcotexa. They have weekly meetings on Sundays. We present all bids until Sunday at 11:00 a.m. Then, these twelve people come together and discuss all the bids, check whether there is a trade below the minimum price. After the meeting, they send their confirmation. I sign the contract and fedex it.

A few days later the contract comes back signed. I also receive shipping instructions from the buyer. He says something like: "I booked this vessel." I then give orders to my technical department, and then they do the rest. We contact the shipping company. They send the containers. Three people oversee the work in the port: one from my company, their controller, and an official from the port. Then I work to get the money. Old customers open for us a letter of credit. They have our bill of lading. In case of a problem, arbitration is carried out by Alcotexa. The association keeps the samples somewhere. If there is a problem, they look at the samples, compare them, and sort out the problem.

Cotton Comes to the Market

The way in which cotton trading decisions in Egypt are executed follows routines of documentary and actual commodity circulation similar to the ones I analyzed in chapter 2. Successful trading practice depends on experience in research, bargaining, and execution of the decisions, as well as maintaining a match between the documentary and actual circulation of commodities. However, the forging of this complex universe of trading is not enough, for merchants need to find cotton to trade. From where and how, then, does cotton come to these trading houses? I will examine the ways in which cotton is grown and sold by Egyptian farmers in greater detail in a later chapter. Here, I will show how private and public companies buy cotton and then prepare it for export through procedures such as *farfara*. In this way I will discuss the domestic conditions of market-making from the vantage point of trading companies; the same relations will appear radically different at a later point, when I will approach them from the Egyptian farmers' perspective.

Cotton is bought by trading houses either directly from farmers, usually in cotton sales rings called *halaqa*,[6] which are regulated by the Bank for Development and Agricultural Credit (PBDAC), or from small local traders who use their financial power to buy farmer's cotton. There are also three types of cooperatives—Land Reclamation Cooperatives, Credit Cooperatives, and Agrarian Reform Cooperatives—which irregularly enter the domestic market to buy cotton and then sell it to private or public trading companies.

There are nine different varieties of cotton currently grown in Egypt. Each variety is graded internally in thirteen subgrades, mostly based on

---

[6] A *halaqa* is a specific cotton ring, now organized by the Ministry of Agriculture and Land Reclamation. Cotton is bought and sold in these rings. For the history of *halaqa*, see Owen (1969, 218).

their staple length and cleanliness. To protect the specific characteristics and reputation of these varieties, the Egyptian government divides the country into nine different cotton-growing zones. As one moves from the south to the north, the quality of cotton increases. In the Nile Delta, the quality appreciates as one moves westward. The Cotton Arbitration and Testing General Organization (CATGO), supervised by the Ministry of Supply and Internal Trade, carries out the quality control and grading of these varieties.

Each cotton trading house maintains a domestic network of agents and regional and local offices to monitor, control, and interact with growers who cover the Egyptian landscape with a green sea of cotton every year. Now, there are more than 250 companies and individual domestic traders approved by the government-run Cotton and International Trade Holding Company. However, less than twenty percent of traders operating in the countryside are registered. In the locations where I carried out my field-work, I encountered only a handful of registered private individual traders. The registration ratio is positively correlated to the scale of operation.

Trading houses rely on their regional offices to buy cotton. In Egypt, all companies are assigned specific cotton rings by the Ministry of Agriculture and Land Reclamation (MALR). These rings (*halaqa*) are the location to which farmers bring their seed cotton for weighing, grading, and marketing. It is very unlikely that public companies would buy from informal small traders who illegally finance the farmers' production and then buy their clients' cotton. Public companies buy most of their cotton from MALR *halaqa*s, and the rest from the three cooperatives.

Registered and unregistered private individual traders almost without exception sell their cotton to private sector firms. The small traders' share in private merchant house purchases has been increasing since 1994. In 2000, private merchant houses covered eleven percent of their stocks from small private traders, thus providing a nest for illegality and informality in the Egyptian countryside. Half of the private merchant house cotton came from the *halaqa*s, and the rest from cooperatives.

There are two rounds of exchange before the private and public companies buy seed cotton. No reliable national statistics are available to make visible this first round of exchange in which the growers sell their produce to those who finance them in various forms. These "little helpers" exploit their competitive edge of being only sightly better off in monetary terms. Although their scale of operation is not large, the frequency of these trades makes these farmer-investors a major part of seed cotton marketing in Egypt. They do not operate as traders and usually disguise themselves as farmers. It is also not uncommon for them to be located in the networks of the cooperatives' marketing channels, thus using such means to their own advantage.

After the completion of this first round of exchange, the smallest and least powerful growers are alienated from the rest of the marketing rounds.[7] Statistically visible trading starts only after this primary marketing of cotton. In the following round of trading, private registered traders, public companies, and cooperatives become the major buyers of cotton. Another major difference between private and public companies becomes visible in this second round of trade. Public companies have to carry out internal checks and balances to ensure formalities, thus delaying payment at least for a while. Private merchants, however, always immediately pay in cash. They exploit this difference, understandably, by somewhat decreasing the price. Without exception, all farmers prefer to have a little less sooner, for they immediately need cash to pay the debt they incur during the growing of cotton.

Once the second round of exchange is over, regional offices of merchant houses claim the seed cotton and begin to process it for export. The town of Disuq, a provincial city along the Rashidiyyah branch of the Nile in the Kafr al-Sheikh governorate,[8] hosts one such regional office representing an Alexandria merchant house. I was sent to this office by the general manager of the company, as he explained to his regional director over the phone, "to study how Egyptians produce the best cotton in the world." He continued, again in Arabic, "He doesn't know Arabic, make sure that there is an English teacher around." He was one of the traders who never wanted to speak Arabic with me. I took a white Peugeot from the new bus station in Alexandria and went to the regional office early next morning.

The road to Disuq passes a small island on the Nile and reaches the busy center of the city after a one-hour trip. I had a quick breakfast of falafel, pickles, and mango juice. The restaurant's walls were covered with local election posters, each carrying the emblem of a local politician—a space shuttle, a watch, and a plane—meant to help illiterate voters locate their preferred candidate.

Before I found the office, the officials of the company, together with an English teacher ready to help, found me in the falafel place. To all of our surprise, we did not need the teacher, and he left. I spend the day in a ginning factory (*mahlag*) that was preparing a shipment for a Turkish merchant who happened to be one of the traders I had interviewed in Izmir six months earlier. The regional director was less surprised than I was. "The cotton world is a small one," he said. Contract workers unloaded cotton

---

[7] Almost all agricultural markets in the world draw on such a differentiated circulation regime. For the theoretical literature and empirical examples of differentiated systems of circulation, see Harriss-White (2008).

[8] Egypt is divided into twenty-six governorates (*muhafaza*).

bales and carried them to the ginning facility that partly operated on machines produced in 1881, the year when the British occupied Alexandria. Cotton graders then checked the grade of each variety by placing a large sample of cotton on a table and pressing on it with a glass framed by black wood. Only after such a literal enframing can the cotton be traded.

After enframing it, the graders sent the cotton to an enormous hall full of working gangs composed of women and men, girls and boys as young as eight years old. They were manually processing cotton with a technique called *farfara* to increase its quality. During this process, the air became full of miniscule flying naps, which the workers constantly inhale. The cleaned cotton then continued its journey to presses that produce a standard bale for the requested grade of cotton. Each bale then received a number and a stamp with an individual identification number, a lot number,[9] the variety of the cotton, the seller company's initials, and the weight. The bales then traveled via truck to Alexandria, from where they were shipped to the other side of the Mediterranean, to Izmir.

I visited three other regional centers with one public and two private merchant house regional offices and spent a total of ten days with the traders and officials. In al-Mansurah, a city along the Eastern branch of the Nile and the center of the governorate of Daqahliya, I was able to observe how the regional offices served as bridges between the headquarter offices in Alexandria and the countryside. Similarly, in a facility for cotton collection, treatment, and ginning sixty kilometers from Alexandria, I was able to observe how regional offices carry out research on the ground in order to monitor the growth of cotton and finance the farmers' production in case they cannot find money to spray pesticides or hire children to pick cotton worms from the plants.

In almost none of these locations was I permitted to talk to workers, whether they were children or not, without the presence of a company official. In one *farfara* facility in Mina al-Basal, Alexandria, I was not even allowed inside the building, although the company's general manager had sent me there. The guard resisted, as he was under orders not to admit any unauthorized personnel. "No journalist, no tourist," he added. The driver of the manager convinced him later, and he accompanied us into the large building which had once been owned by an international merchant before Nasser's nationalization of cotton companies.

Needless to say, I was not allowed to take photographs, but ended up taking more than I would have guessed. One of the main subcontractors hired for finding and overseeing workers came up to me as we walked into a huge *farfara* hall and introduced himself. It turned out that he was from a village I had visited for two weeks in 2001, Kamshish in the governorate

---

[9] Each bale is part of a lot containing eighty-eight bales.

of Munifiyah. He even knew the family who had hosted me. After asking me whether I was a Muslim and pleased to hear my response, he assigned himself as my tour guide. Both the manager's driver and the omnipotent guard were happy to watch me take photographs and talk to workers while their main contractor was around. He was in a position to find jobs for both the guard's and the driver's relatives, a crucial power in a world of unemployment.

In buildings such as this, working hours are long, especially in private company establishments where there are many illegal arrangements. All the workers are hired by gang leaders, reminiscent of the *elçis* or *dayıbaşıs* in Turkey. The *ra'is al-anfar*, as the gang leader is called in these facilities, usually hires workers with the help of his social networks. They receive a share of the workers' income for finding the job and overseeing their work. They also hire other overseers, depending on the scale of their services.

Workers typically earned 6 to 7 LE per day (then 1.30 to 1.52 USD). However, I was told by company officials that they were making at least 8 LE. I usually did not challenge these officials, since they were taking a great risk in granting me entry to these factories, for it is almost impossible for a researcher to enter them by obtaining a legal research permit from the government. One day, when I was told that the children I saw in the *mahlag* were not there to work, but "only playing around when their parents do the *farfara*," I asked a private company's regional director how much their parents were making per day. His answer located an even higher price, 10 LE. Then, I asked a rhetorical question and wondered aloud whether 1.50 USD already amounted to 10 LE.[10] He smiled, I smiled, and we did not talk more about salaries. He was among those asking me not to take pictures of the children, even though I reminded him that they were just "playing." "Others may confuse play with work," he told me as he reached for my camera.

The control of work changes according to the worker gang during *farfara*. *Farfara* is a lengthy and difficult job. Workers form circles around piles of cotton and clean the fibers, either by picking extraneous material by hand or by throwing it into the air. Doing this for hours needs concentration and great strength, psychological and physical. Especially children begin to drag their feet after a while and need incentives or punishment, as economists call them. Working harder is rarely rewarded, for the work is collective. Individual punishment in the form of insults and at times even physical violence is not infrequent. Incentives come in the form of games, such as singing songs or chanting slogans that praise hard work.

The control of adult labor operates on more subtle technologies of power. It is easier to put an adult to work, since he or she is well aware

---

[10] The official rate of exchange was 4.61 at the time of research.

Figure 8   Adult workers performing *farfara* in Egypt.

of the level of unemployment in Egypt. When one loses a job, it is difficult to find another. Moreover, since labor contractors know each other,
they tend not to hire "problem workers." Still, regardless of how docile
a worker is, he or she still can find avenues to resist exploitation, such as
slowing down the work or taking longer breaks. Labor contractors also
frequently block these avenues. Female worker gangs are controlled by
hired female overseers, and men control men.

Farfara is a crucial operation for both private and public trading houses.
Merchants increase the grade of cotton by blending different subgrades of
the same variety of cotton and cleaning the blend to make it more desirable for high-quality yarn production through this process. The reputation
of Egyptian cotton partially depends on *farfara*, because it significantly
increases the cleanliness and staple length uniformity (figure 8).

The regional centers of Egyptian merchant houses and their everyday
workings allow us to broaden the analysis of world markets, by giving us
the opportunity to study the making of markets in their multiple locations of encounter. These regional centers serve as the arm of Alexandria
merchants, with which they reach out to the countryside, buy cotton from
farmers, and sustain networks of communication, research, and control.
It is through these mechanisms that they can deploy the associate prices
and other prostheses of pricing effectively when it comes to cutting a
final deal on the actual price of cotton. They also use these centers to

increase the value of their cotton, by hiring workers, legally or not, to increase the crop's quality and, hence, its price. Finally, these centers serve as important research sites for merchants, because the everyday control of the countryside relies on knowing what is going on there. By providing the trade centers of Alexandria with information about the countryside, these regional centers also supply traders with tools to build stronger mercantile platforms.

CONCLUSION

An analysis of Egyptian cotton markets and the way in which global markets are made in their local sites of encounter in Egypt affirms the arguments of the previous chapters and carries them to another level. On the one hand, we can see that the global market is a derivative possibility, not the actual mercantile encounter itself. It is made by bringing together individual acts of trade, whether they take place in Alexandria or Izmir. The location of the global market is not geographical; it is documentary and technological. The global market and its prices are made in indices, reports, and market pictures. Traders deploy such a site of globality every day in order to govern local acts of trade. These individual acts of trade are then used by markets experts, researchers, and traders, and furnish a condition of possibility for the further making of global markets.

At the same time, the making, unmaking, and remaking of Egypt's cotton market and the ways it contributes to the making of global markets allow us to study the historical setting of major global experiments of economic restructuring. It was in Egypt that the first cotton futures were opened in a colonial context and connected to other imperial trade regimes. Alexandria was not a periphery of the global market; rather, it was its construction site. Yet, this site was constructed in the midst of war and ruin. The market and the nation were born at the same time in a colonial setting, and the market was saved and developed by an imperial occupation force. Nasser's reversal of the colonial legacy and his nationalization of the cotton trade brought an end to the influence of the Alexandria merchants vis-à-vis the farmers and native power elite.

The introduction and institutionalization of liberal economic policies under presidents Sadat and Mubarak, forged with the expertise of international financial institutions, aimed at reconstituting Egypt's centrality in world markets, by exploiting its competitive advantage. The reforms started with agriculture. In Egypt, commercial agriculture is synonymous with cotton-growing, for the country has the best in the world to offer, dominating the markets even in statist times at levels unprecedented in history. The results of these reforms were devastating even from the vantage point of trading regimes. Public Egyptian cotton traders lost their clients one by one as free market reforms were implemented in the country. The reforms aimed at keeping Egypt's doors open to the world. Yet, the more the doors were pushed open, the more Egypt's most competitive commodity lost ground in world trade.

The privatization of the cotton sector in 1994 began with the trauma of the Wahba case and forged a new regime of exchange in Alexandria. Private merchant houses institutionalized their dominance in trade within a few years and began to use their leverage in Alcotexa. Although a cotton exchange was opened, it has never been used. After all, traders know that it is not a mere exchange institution but their deliberative practices manifesting their interests and positions that make the price.

The market price is a prosthetic device in all locations of the market in cotton trade. Its making, however, is informed not by anonymous, unmediated forces of supply and demand, but within inherently political sites of encounter, whether in Izmir or Alexandria. If this is so, then the very nature of price realization should change as its sites of construction change.

An analysis of price realization in Alexandria confirms this conclusion. The private merchants of Alexandria come together every week to set the prosthetic price of Egyptian cotton; yet they do not take it as the actual price in their trade. The associate price is a tool they use to empower their position in trade in two ways. First, the associate price makes the market available for interaction. It is the beginning of trade, not its end result. It is produced in political sites of mercantile platforms. Second, it provides private merchants with tools to increase their competitiveness vis-à-vis public companies. For public companies, the associate price is a minimum actual price. For private merchants, it is just a prosthetic device. Private traders' private status makes it possible for them to use it in a more neoliberal fashion. In Egypt, too, we see that cotton trade takes place in a market process in which sites of exchange have multiple boundaries of formality and informality. These boundary-setting practices and their institutional sanctioning are technologies of power for those who can or cannot cross them.

After the market price is set, a new market appears where both public and private traders have to make an actual price. This new market resembles that of other traders abroad. Egyptian traders draw on the power of their mercantile platforms of capital, knowledge, and network. They need "arms" reaching to the countryside to find the best cotton. Their regional offices provide them with these networks. Moreover, they need to sustain networks abroad to be able to hold a rich client portfolio. They exchange gifts and letters, attend conferences, and host lunches and dinners.

Still, this is not sufficient. Only a handful of employees of the trading companies can actually trade cotton. To be able to trade, one has to have experience in carrying out research and making the actual price. The background of both the trader and his decision is crucial in making actual prices. The trader should be experienced in bargaining and at all times ready to talk about prices; for this reason, (s)he should at all time be informed. Traders also know that informing other traders is a way of affecting the market. One has to be selective and careful and devote a lot of attention to make the everyday market work.

This world of the cotton trade changes fundamentally as soon as one moves the vantage point to a different social location. Seen from the farmers' side, these mercantile platforms undergo a metamorphosis, and the mercantile prosthesis loses its meaning and even function. "The price" becomes something else, not easily fitting into the countryside's considerations. The market is seen in a radically different way, and the ways in which relations of exchange and production are enmeshed take a different form. Without bringing this new world of encounter into the picture, an analysis of the world cotton market is by definition incomplete, for without growers in the countryside, traders cannot trade anything, whether in cotton spots or options. The following two chapters will provide an analysis of the making of a global market from the vantage points of its other local makers: cotton farmers.

CHAPTER 5

Growing Cotton and Its Global Market in a Turkish Village

How can we understand the production and exchange processes of agricultural commodities from the vantage point of farmers? Prevailing scholarly literature addressing this question locates the answer by analyzing the effects of global market expansion on peasant political economy. The study of the countryside primarily draws on the register of peasant reaction to the developments unfolding around the village, such as world markets. Going beyond such a narrow perspective, this chapter analyzes the actual interaction between cotton fields and markets from the vantage point of Turkish peasants.

Early-twentieth-century approaches to farmers, especially those inspired by Marx, have viewed farmers as a transitory class doomed to disappear as a result of rapid industrialization and modernization. In the post–World War II period, scholars have expanded their focus to cover the economic motivations of the peasantry, farmers' modes of production, relations with the state and other classes, and their role in rural transformation and development (Bernstein 1977; Aydın, 1986; Bernstein et al. 1994). *Articulation theories* have looked at the ways in which farmers' surplus was extracted by urban actors (such as the state and capitalists); *persistence theses* have explained the survival strategies of farmers against the world-wide expansion of the market or capitalism; and *differentiation theses* have focused on the pace of proletariatization and internal variation among rural producers. In this vast literature, markets are considered outside factors that impact on the lives of farmers.[1]

Polanyi's Great Transformation has reinterpreted the meaning of markets, emphasizing the role of politics in their making (Polanyi 1944). Following Polanyi, researchers began to approach the countryside not only as a registrar of effects, but also as a site populated by at times dependent yet still autonomous agents. These researchers have argued that the study of exchange and production regimes requires the study of relations "embedded" in specific sociocultural settings. Furthermore, it is also by

---

[1] For a detailed discussion of this literature, see Sirman (1988); Bush (2002).

analyzing these specific contexts that larger social phenomena such as global markets can be understood (Arensberg, 1957; Bohannan and Dalton, 1965; Sahlins, 1972).

This chapter seeks to bridge the literature on the effects of market expansion on the countryside and that on the social study of the market, by investigating cotton growing and exchange in a Turkish village. It aims at depicting a universe of cotton production and exchange as they interact with each other, without holding one of them constant. By focusing on the production and trading practices in and around a village I will call Pamukköy, the largest cotton-growing village located in the Söke Plain in Western Turkey, the chapter will first document how the agents of production understand production and exchange processes and, second, how they enact this understanding in their fields and the cotton market.

Instead of analyzing the effect of market expansion on farming communities, the chapter focuses on an infrequently studied theme in the literature—that is, the ways in which farmers see the relationship between local production and global-regional exchange. It examines the interface between the field and the market, explaining farmers' engagement in the processes of exchange and production. The empirical discussion is organized in two parts. The first part depicts the ways in which farmers prepare their fields, mobilize their resources, hire labor, and create networks of exchange. The second part focuses on the moment of exchange—that is, the ways in which farmers encounter the market and the making of prices on the ground.

The first section opens the universe of power relations mobilized to grow cotton and the forms of negotiation among the various actors who interact on the field. In addition to presenting an account of cotton's growth, I will show that cotton production requires a considerable investment in research, expertise, labor, and networking. Yet almost none of the farmers perceive their work in such a way. For them, their job is a rather humble one with no skills required. However, once challenged, farmers have a tendency to change their position and assert their agency in terms of skill and dexterity. I seek to show that not recognizing any expertise in their own work is a frequently used rhetoric that empowers farmers. The first section concludes by describing how farmers have a dynamic way of bringing together various informal and flexible cooperatives to economize their resources and income. Still, farmers' innovative networking seems not to work in the cotton market.

In the second section, I will analyze the ways in which farmers encounter the cotton market as they sell their produce to private merchants or the cooperative. Farmers do not see the cooperative as a merchant. Because they have an organic relationship with the cooperative, its cotton purchase is seen as endogenous to their production process. In contrast, cotton traders and their offices are considered exogenous to the farmers' fields. As one farmer put it, "things happen there," referring to the trading tools and manners that traders produce and deploy to empower their position of bargaining in the market. Analyzing this relationship of market power, the chapter argues that prices should not be seen as a mere tool of exchange set by the supply and demand of cotton. Serving as a social and financial interface between the field and the market, the price is also a tool that merchants produce to deploy in the market. This tool—together with other specific ways of carrying out trade—limits the farmers' agency.

Through a detailed presentation and discussion of the ethnographic evidence, I will demonstrate that farmers and traders all have to mobilize various resources and tactics to acquire a degree of power in these two markets. These resources and tactics include what I call *market performances*, which are shaped through relations of power and people's positions in the labor and/or cotton markets. Thus, the amount of land one has, the degree of dispossession of a worker, the farmers' and workers' relations with labor gang leaders, the indebtedness of the farmer, the solidarity among merchants, and the power asymmetries between farmers and merchants at the moment of exchange all play a dynamic part in shaping local markets and their relation to global cotton exchange, always mediated through market performance.

Finally, I show that there is no single market price for cotton, as it is reflected in the index of world cotton prices. Rather, different price forms are experienced, produced, and deployed by farmers, merchants, the state, and the big players in the world market. The chapter concludes by demonstrating that Pamukköy farmers see the market neither as a place where the price is set, nor as a mere location of commodity exchange. The market is a power field where farmers encounter the realization of price as relatively passive agents of trade. It is in these relations of power that the markets are made in the simultaneous processes of exchange and production of commodities, their translations, research results, and struggles between farmers, children, overseers, graders, traders, pests, and all other agents who want to use the cotton for satisfying their own needs.

FIELD PREPARATION AND SOWING IN PAMUKKÖY

Mehmet Aydın woke up before 4:30 a.m. on June 8, 2001, in his two-bedroom house in Pamukköy to get ready to sow cotton. In fifteen minutes, I was sitting on the wheel-cover of his tractor on the way to his 22 decares of land. At dawn, the village was twinkling with the lights of tractors and houses. The road was congested with traffic, and the air was full of the voices of men greeting each other, women shouting to their children, dogs barking to strangers, donkeys braying, and engines sputtering. We were carrying 250 kilograms of cotton seed he had bought from a local merchant in Sarı, the closest municipal center. It was going to be a late sowing, for he had grown barley before cotton and harvested it only a couple of days ago. Unlike more than half of the households of Pamukköy, he had chosen not to start sowing cotton sometime between late April and end of May. Instead, he had taken the risk of growing barley to use it as animal fodder.

Cotton reaches maturity after approximately five months if provided with a hot, sunny, and dry climate. The leaves of the plant, like sunflowers, follow the sun during the day to accumulate as much energy as possible. The Aegean region's climate gives farmers and cotton a little more than six and a half months of good weather. Mehmet was using the last five months of this good weather to grow his cotton. Such a decision bore great risk. It delayed the cotton harvest by at least four weeks, making it more likely to rain during the harvest. Rain decreases the quality of cotton fibers, making them wet and dirty and creating rain spots on the lint. Furthermore, it makes it more costly to pick the cotton, because, on the one hand, wet soil decreases the speed of the workers and, on the other hand, rainwater increases the weight of cotton, thus increasing the cost of the workers' daily wages. The daily wage that farmers pay to workers is a function of the weight of the cotton that the workers pick.

Mehmet's land was three kilometers away from the village. Compared to other cotton growers, he considered himself lucky for a number of reasons. His land, located next to the Büyük Menderes (Meander) River, was one piece and not scattered around the village. Furthermore, it was close to water, decreasing the cost of irrigation. Finally, it was not far from the village, which made it easier to inspect the growth of the cotton.

Slightly more than ten percent of Turkey's total production comes from the Söke Plain, Turkey's second-largest cotton-growing plain.[2] Located in the province of Aydın, the plain is in the administrative boundaries of the town of Söke, an agro-industrial city 120 km west of Izmir. Cotton is the single most important cash crop of the plain. Looking down from the hills of the Samsun Mountains in August, the plain looks like a green sea of cotton, encircled by Lake Bafa, the Beşparmak Mountains, and the Aegean Sea. Around 5,000 farmers grow cotton in the plain and live in the villages and towns encircling this green sea, which provides cash revenue not only to cotton growers, but also to thousands of migrant agricultural workers who arrive in the plain every year to work in the fields.

---

[2] For more information regarding cotton production in Turkey, see Özüdoğru (2006).

We reached Mehmet's field after a fifteen-minute ride and found his 31-year-old son Enver inspecting the land. Following a short greeting, we unloaded the cotton seed sacks and emptied them into the four containers placed on top of the sowing machine. This was the beginning of a long work period that would end with the selling of the family's cotton in October, for a price only slightly more than the family's cost of production.

Like the other families of the village, the Aydın family would follow six stages of growing cotton, based on the steps of the plant's bioeconomic life cycle of growth and marketing: field preparation, sowing, hoeing and selection, watering, harvesting, and, finally, marketing. In each of these stages, new struggles would be waged among growers, workers, traders, insects, the cotton plant, and the natural environment.

Field preparation happens nearly the entire time while the field is empty. How Pamukköy farmers attend to their field directly affects their yield. This is why the first stage of a growing year almost coincides with the last stage of the previous cotton year. Before sowing starts, the soil has to be aerated to enhance its productivity. After that, growers apply fertilizers and mix them with the subsoil and the upper crust of the land by ploughing the field, mostly with the help of tractors. Finally, the land has to be rolled by driving a heavy roller over the field, so that the soil is sealed to prevent the loss of nutrients and water.

Almost none of the cotton-growing households in the village hire workers or drivers to carry out the sowing. There are 287 households in Pamukköy. However, only 257 of them spend all of their time in the village. Thirty households divide their time between the city and the village, creating a category which makes visible the problematic nature of assuming a clear-cut boundary between city and countryside. All but seven of the households that permanently reside in the village grow cotton and consider it their major cash income.

In 1981 Pamukköy had around 1,700 inhabitants. The implementation of neoliberal reforms in the early 1980s increased migration from the village to cities, thus decreasing its population to 734 by November of 2001. The 250 households of Pamukköy own 2,495 decares of land, an average land size of about ten decares per household. Of the households, seventy-one percent own land in the village. Half of the remaining households rent land for cotton production, usually no more than five decares. The rest do not grow cotton, but have household members who work in cotton-related jobs; they work in others' fields and drive their tractors. Those who do not reside in the village own fourteen percent of the village land. Farmers who reside in Pamukköy use almost all of this land in exchange for either rent or cotton. Land use patterns follow land distribution patterns in the village.

Field preparation and sowing are not the most labor-intensive stages of cotton cultivation. Using a tractor, two farmers can complete these two stages without external help. Only three percent of cotton growers in Pamukköy hire external labor for these two stages; the rest use labor barter and unpaid household labor. Two men, usually relatives, come together, work in each other's land, and exchange their labor power. Alternatively, if there are two mature men in the immediate family, like Mehmet and Enver of the Aydın family, field preparation is carried out solely by household labor. In large landowners' fields, either seasonal or full-time workers do the presowing preparations.

The successful germination of the plant signals the beginning of a series of activities to be carried out in the field: mechanical and manual hoeing. These activities comprise the secondmost labor-intensive stage of cotton cultivation after harvesting and have to be finished by the beginning of irrigation, roughly six weeks following the appearance of the first shoots.

MECHANICAL AND MANUAL HOEING

At 6:00 a.m. on June 19 Mehmet and I arrived at his field for mechanical hoeing. The depth of the hoe had to be fine-tuned according to the field's leveling and the cotton's height. The four sets of steel flat spoons of the hoe had to aerate the soil, while at the same time neither cutting nor burying the fragile plant. The hoeing was completed at around 3:00 p.m. It took twenty minutes to return home for a short rest.

Over dinner, I asked about the work day. "This is not real work," Mehmet said. "We are working just with our muscles. What we do does not require mental work. It is routine, all the same. We don't need to learn anything, nor use our brains." I challenged him by reading him the notes I had taken, especially the part on why I thought that it required expertise and years of training to grow cotton. Combing his gray mustache with his fingers, he said: "We're accustomed to see it that way. Besides, it is shameful for one to present himself as someone important in a praiseful manner." This was quite a contrast to the way merchants and traders marketed their importance in the world of cotton exchange.

After the machine hoeing, the time had come in Pamukköy to begin spending cash, especially for hiring the workers Mehmet needed for hand-hoeing the cotton. This expenditure is the secondmost costly procedure after the harvest itself. Exactly two weeks after we sowed the cotton Mehmet hired twelve women workers to carry out the delicate process of aerating the soil by using a hand hoe, around each plant, one by one. This process weeds out two-thirds of the cotton, while cleaning up the weeds in and around the rows. Tractors help both farmers and pests. The furrows that tractors leave behind help pests to reach the roots of the plant more easily. The hand hoers therefore also have to disrupt the lines left behind by the tractors' huge tires.

Like many other forms of work, hoeing is determined by the gender of the village work force. Hoeing on others' fields is considered a woman's job. It is a sign of poverty and weakness for Pamukköy's men to cover their heads and go hoeing for money. For Central Anatolian and Kurdish men of the southeast, who migrate to the Söke Plain to work, hoeing is acceptable, since they are already known as poor and, thus, weak.

Two men worked as *dayıbaşı* (labor gang leaders) in the village, organizing gangs of female and male laborers for those who exchanged money for labor. Children of the village do not work in the fields. The youngest child I saw working was a fifteen-year-old girl from a very poor family. Yet, Pamukköy farmers do not have strong objections to putting Kurdish child laborers to work. "It is their business," one cotton farmer told me as I asked him the reason why he employed children. Finding workers for others is done informally, because gang leaders do not pay taxes. Neither of the two gang leaders from the village owned land in the village. Their power stems from the networks they forge among those who hire labor and those who sell it. Since those who hire are men and those who sell are women, wives of gang leaders play a role as central as that of their husbands.

The hoeing can be divided into two main stages. At the beginning and end of the hoeing season, the number of fields to be hoed is limited; thus, work opportunities are limited as well. It is critical for workers to find a job in the village during these days, for they prefer to work as much as possible to earn cash to grow cotton in their own small fields. They have to sustain a working relationship with the gang leaders, and the gang leaders have to forge good networks with the employers, so that they can acquire either money or other favors from them when needed. Both gang leaders and farmers prefer the poorest and least powerful female workers. The poorest workers need the work the most.

However, the real reason for the preference to hire the neediest has nothing to do with benevolence. The poorest cannot refuse work when needed. They are more flexible in terms of the duration and conditions of work. They do not have anything to lose but time during these rare days of work. Both the poorest and the better-off make 50 cents per hour; yet, for the poor, the 50 cents are more valuable. When field owners ask workers to continue hoeing for a couple of hours after 3:30, the usual time to stop work in the afternoon, poor workers rarely decline. Paradoxically, the immediate reason for their compliance is not their need for cash, but their fear of losing work opportunities in the future if they decline. They are always willing to give up the additional payment to be able to stop work on time, because there are many more tasks to be done before going to sleep around 10:00 p.m.

The workers bring sacks with them to carry the grass and other weeds that they find around the fields, to be used as feed for their animals. For collecting grass and weeds, they need additional time. They also have to work their own fields, usually not more than three decares, which also requires time. Moreover, they have to cook, serve the food, do the dishes, look after the kids, take care of the animal(s), do some hand work such as mending clothes, sewing, and knitting, while keeping an eye on the television and then prepare the beds. These tasks need more than six and a half hours, and the additional time spent in others' fields steals time away from their sleep, thus making the next day's work harder.

The 50 cents earned after 3:30 p.m. is thus less valuable than those earned earlier. Yet, they cannot refuse, since the marginal loss they choose to make may result in punishment by the field owner or gang leader. They might not be hired the next time. This is why the field owners who want to employ the best workers—that is, the neediest and least powerful—treat the gang leader well, mostly in monetary terms. In return, they get the poorest workers. And the poorest treat the gang leader's wife well to make sure that they get a place among the women who hoe the fields. Favors mostly take the form of bartering labor when workers cannot find employment in the winter, or of giving the gang leader's wife a hand-made gift that can be exchanged or bartered later.

A couple of days before the field was ready to be hoed by hand, Mehmet went to see one of the gang leaders, a young man from a rather poor family in the village, for help to put together a gang of workers. On the day of hoeing, he drove his tractor to the end of the village and then made a U-turn to collect the twelve women workers from the minibus stops on the road. They each carried a bag with their lunch, either fastened to the wood handles of their steel hoes or placed in wickerwork baskets. It was a quarter to five when Mehmet reached the coffeehouse to meet the gang leader who would find workers for him. I watched seven tractors pass in front of us, all towing trailers full of workers. Only one of them were men among the workers. Women's heads were covered with orange and white turbans, protecting them from the cold in the morning and the sun during the day. The gang leader did not show up. Mehmet called him on his cell phone. There was no answer, and we left. Looking at the workers looking at us, he said: "There was a misunderstanding." He was not given the workers he wanted; they were all from families who had land in the village, workers who did not urgently need the work. I would better appreciate Mehmet's concerned look by the end of the hoeing day, around 3:30 p.m.

As we approached the harvest, calculated misunderstandings in the village and the greater region increased in frequency. The next day, we learned that, after receiving a call from the city, the gang leader had left for a large landowner's field, rearranging the entire gang who worked for him and taking the poorest with him. The large landowners pay one daily wage extra to the gang leader for every fifteen workers he finds for them. However, he would be paid less in the village, losing one extra wage for every twelve workers. Since the large landlords hire as many as 120 workers, the gang leader's income increases tenfold.

We reached the field and parked the tractor under a mulberry tree. The work started at 5:30 a.m. sharp. The workers formed a row in the middle of the field, each quickly hoeing one cotton line as the sun rose slowly. They each hoed until the edge of the field, then walked slowly back to the middle and continued the other way. Walking a little before each half-row helped their backs rest, for they would spend hours hunched over. The hoe is small, yet its weight increases as one uses it, cutting three to four shoots, then digging gently three to four times around the fifth, chopping the weeds surrounding it, mixing the weed and dead cotton with the soil, and taking a step forward only to begin the same operation again.

A few hours before the end of the work day, the workers had not even finished two-thirds of the field. Mehmet was silent and looked anxious. "It is not going to be done," he said and silently accused the workers of hoeing slowly. He walked toward the row of working women. They stopped as we approached them. "It is almost 2:30, let's work a bit faster and finish our work," he said. The younger ones remained silent. An older woman, gesturing at the field with her hand, replied: "This is not going to finish, there is too much work. We have to leave anyway." The others' silence meant approval. To my surprise, Elif did not support her father and instead toyed with her hoe, implicitly supporting the workers. Mehmet then offered an additional eighty cents on top of their daily wage if they finished the work. They declined and returned to the work, then stopped at 3:30 p.m. sharp.

We left the field unfinished, giving the workers a lift back to the village. Mehmet had to hire six more workers to continue hoeing the following day. He was frustrated. "They have animals, they are wage workers, they are landowners, and they are everything. Nobody knows what they really are," he said over dinner, referring to the workers he had hired, his fellow village women. "Are they really workers? A worker is the one who works whenever you pay! These say 'no, we'll work in our fields, cut our grass, and hoe our cotton.'" He then accused the gang leader of not "giving" him really "hungry workers." "The ones you saw today," he continued, "are the ones with full bellies." This is why he was not happy to have workers who can decide when and where to work, those who were more or less in a condition similar to his.

The labor market—that is, the exchange of labor in return for wages— is enacted on the farmers' fields in Pamukköy. Cotton growers like Mehmet and agricultural workers from the village, such as the women who worked on his land, can negotiate the terms of exchange on a relatively equal footing, if not in a totally symmetrical relationship of power. The workers of Pamukköy do not bow before Mehmet's demands for longer hours or more intense work in return for the meager wages they make, because of their relative strength in the labor market. This semblance of market strength derives from the fact that they are not indebted to Mehmet and own at least some land, even if very little.

IRRIGATION

After hoeing finished on June 23, Mehmet spent thirty-three days on the field, carrying out various tasks, from spraying pesticides and killing insects and other creatures on the cotton and the field, to applying various fertilizers. He did not hire any workers, nor did he want help from others until the time for the second hoeing came on August 3. For this, he hired seven woman workers, again from the village. He spent the entire time overseeing the workers as they wove through row after row. The workers aerated the soil around the fragile cotton plants, carefully protected from small insects with big appetites and unruly weeds of no commercial value. Only the cotton has the right to life on the farmer's land. After the second hoeing, the field was ready for irrigation, perhaps the most difficult part of the long months of work. Once the watering starts, growers cannot take a break until it is completed. Irrigation can take as long as two days of nearly continuous work.

We left my house to pick up another farmer whom Mehmet had hired to work in the field. Süleyman was twenty-nine years old, my age then, yet looked older. He did not own any land or olive trees. He rented "a corner," as he called the tiny two decares, and worked it with his wife. He did not pay rent in cash, but bartered his and his wife's labor with the man who leased him the corner. Süleyman was born into poverty and a life of hard work. He would make sixty cents an hour and hope to save enough to buy the corner, those two decares of land. "I sometimes have a dream. I wake up happier and want to work more. One day, God willing, I'll own that land (the two decares). We save whatever we make," he said, as we rode down the hill toward the field, "a huge twenty-two decares," according to Süleyman, and a tiny piece for Enver, Mehmet's son. Mehmet would not be able to buy any land that year or in the next seven years. Instead, he would sell some land in order to pay his debts.

As we reached the field, Mehmet drove the tractor backward toward the water. Süleyman unwound a large plastic hose into the field. He connected it to a water pump, then connected the pump to the tractor with a drive belt. Once they started the engine, the tractor supplied power to the pump, and the pump supplied water to the field. The field was divided into many smaller plots, creating a grid of one-meter-high partitions. Each small pool would be filled with water, so that the plant could grow quickly and produce more fibers. One imagines watering to be less challenging than hoeing or hand picking. After all, one fills the land with water and then waits, or perhaps even leaves for the village. "Land is very fragile," Süleyman explained as he worked. One needs to continue leveling, even on plots that are machine leveled, a process carried out with huge tractors and heavy equipment to flatten the land surface so that the soil's upper crust has an even height. "You have to carry a bit of soil from here to there, a bit of soil from there to here," he continued, resting his back by leaning against the wood handle of a tall shovel.

The work on Mehmet's land was completed in twenty hours. Süleyman earned twelve dollars. We barely slept that night. The field had to be overseen, but one cannot oversee a field when it is dark. One has to walk around in the field, listen to the sound of feet sinking into the soft soil, sense whether the water is enough or not, touch the cotton, smell it. The field was not left alone until the next watering on September 6, 2001. However, the work in between was not limited to inspection. Each round of watering takes less and less time as the soil absorbs more and more water. Two days were spent cutting wood from the bushes around the river, wood that would be used by the Kurdish workers who would soon arrive from northern Turkey, where they worked in the hazelnut harvest in the Black Sea region. If the farmers do not cut wood, they need to buy it in order to supply the workers with fuel for heating water and cooking. Three days were spent inspecting the animals in the upland pastures and then selling a few in order to raise cash. The water tanker needed repairs, so that the workers could use it around their tents. New weeds that had fed on the fertilizers had to be killed and recycled back into the soil. The list of tasks was long. In short, without exception, farmers have seven-day work weeks until the few weeks following the harvest, when their anxiety is replaced by a short-lived period of joy.

The Harvest

After months of hard work, networking, raising cash, borrowing money, killing insects, spraying weeds, cutting wood, selling cows, giving gifts, cleaning excrement, and driving the tractor, the time had come in Pamukköy to get ready for the harvest between late September and mid-November. The selling of the cotton following the harvest would be the only major cash revenue for Pamukköy farmers. The harvest is the most labor-intensive part of the entire cotton-growing process. The way in which the harvest is organized follows the same logic employed during the hoeing. Three different groups of farmers deploy three distinct ways of concluding their individual growing season.

First, those who have a large enough supply of labor in their households and relatively little land to work on by and large draw on nonmonetary forms of labor exchange during the harvest. It is safe to assume that a family can rely on household labor if it has less than two decares of land per working household member. Even in these cases, these families usually borrow labor from others. However, a land/household member ratio above that requires some sort of monetary or nonmonetary labor exchange in the village. Second, those families who own more than two decares per working household member, but do not have enough money to hire laborers from either the village or abroad, tend to employ labor-pooling. A few families come together to work in each other's land. Farmers use complex methods of labor control in such arrangements.

Kasım, a thirty-year-old farmer who has six decares of land and one small child, organizes a labor-pooling program with three other families:

> You know no one works in the other's field as if it's his own. They won't work the same way as you just let the villagers work, with no control. Because what we do is difficult work. Under a burning sun we pick cotton. One is dirty all the time, covered with dust and earth. Your back hurts a lot. Spending hours bent over the land doing small things is difficult. And if these small things do not belong to you, you don't want to do them. So we control each other. If my wife and I work for our cousins' land and pick one hundred and seventy kilos of cotton a day, and if our cousins pick only one hundred and fifty in our field, it is a problem. So we sort out the difference with money in the end. The more you pick, the more you earn.

Ödek is the local term for these arrangements. Families of different sizes come together to pool their resources. Because all have different capacities to contribute to the pool, the surplus or shortage is covered by cash. In other words, the difference between individual contributions is accounted for by drawing on wages charged for the same kind of work performed for money. These complex cooperatives are a frequently used form of labor-pooling arrangement in many developing countries where the majority of farmers rely on unpaid domestic labor for survival.[3] Their flexibility is striking in the sense that these informal cooperatives can form a workshop in a couple of hours and dissolve it even more quickly.

[3] For empirical examples and a discussion of this literature, see Abdel-Aal and Reem (1999); Toth (1999).

The final group of farmers depends solely on hired labor. Compared to the first and second groups, these farmers use less complex means of labor control in the field. Workers are paid according to the weight of cotton they pick. The poverty of workers and their lack of union power facilitate labor control for those who have enough means to hire them. If a worker loses her job, she cannot make it to the next harvest without borrowing money.

The speed of picking cotton depends on dexterity, determination, and wealth. Those who work on their own fields can work a bit more slowly, without exhausting themselves too much. Those who work for friends and relatives can choose not to enter a field when it rains, for the mud makes it very difficult to move in the field. The neediest and most impoverished are the ones who find themselves working under any conditions. And they are mostly Kurdish seasonal migrant workers.

A family of four working members can finish hand-picking their cotton in two months or less if their field does not exceed twenty decares. With four seasonal workers, the same amount of land can be hand-picked in twelve to fifteen working days. However, since there has to be a waiting period between each round of picking, which is called a "hand" (el), these workers are employed on several fields simultaneously. It is safe to assume that, on average, workers can pick eighty-five kilograms of seed cotton per day. In two months' time, this equals more than five tons of cotton. Hand picking is usually carried out three times. The third picking becomes costly for large farms that employ paid labor. Compared to those closer to the upper parts of the plant, the cotton balls closer to the root mature faster, because their lint dries earlier. Farmers tend to wait a week or more after the first hand, depending on the weather conditions, before starting the second. Only those who do not hire labor perform the third, for the amount that can be picked progressively decreases as one reaches the last hand.[4]

The organization of work during the harvest is very similar in Kurdish and Turkish work gangs. The work starts early, right after dawn and continues until before dusk. Workers quickly pick the cotton as they bend over the cotton plant and fill the sacks fastened around their waists. Husbands and wives usually fill the same sack and get paid collectively. Their children, not older than fifteen, are usually included in these small cooperatives. Turkish women, however, refuse to throw their cotton into their husbands' sacks, since, as one of them explained during the harvest, "men tend to be lazy and hide behind the joint sack." Kurdish, Arab, and Turkish workers hardly ever work together in the same field. If they do on a rare occasion, they always work in ethnically homogenous gangs.

---

[4] Machine picking is also carried out in the Söke Plain and may completely replace hand picking in less than a decade.

Workers pick the cotton and fill the balls into jute sacks. When the sacks are full, they are brought to a corner of the field, where either the farmer or someone older who can no longer pick cotton weighs and registers them under the worker's name. After unloading the sack, the worker returns to his row, for they cannot leave a row of cotton until it is all picked. The cotton is mixed with the other workers' harvests, pooled, and pressed into large jute sacks. These bales of seed cotton are then brought and sold either to the cooperative's buying centers or to private traders. The moment of pressing the cotton into the sacks is the last time that farmers see their cotton on the field.

THE MARKET: EXCHANGING COTTON IN PAMUKKÖY

The end of the harvest marks the last stage of the cotton's life cycle in villages like Pamukköy. Farmers sell their entire crop before the last day of October. There are two main buyers of cotton in the plain: the agricultural sales cooperative (TARİŞ) and private merchants who also own ginning factories. Since cotton has to be ginned before it can be sold in the institutionalized market settings—such as the cotton trading pit of the Izmir Mercantile Exchange (IME)—a vast majority of farmers (except for a few large landowners) are excluded from lint markets. For farmers like those of Pamukköy, the exchange of their cotton takes place outside the exchange building. It is still possible to keep their seed cotton and sell it to a trader later, but this possibility is realized only in a few marginal instances.

There are many reasons for the immediate selling of the crop. The primary reason is that growing cotton requires farmers to borrow heavily, thus creating an urgent need for cash after the harvest. Farmers who own more land than twenty decares hire labor and pay the daily wages in cash, usually by borrowing. The farmers all have different means of raising the money. Ibrahim, a farmer owning eighteen decares of land, borrowed money from a merchant who had a ginning factory in Söke. Although the terms were similar, he chose not to borrow from the state-owned Agricultural Bank (*Ziraat Bankası*) for several reasons. First, the bank required the farmer to have land under his name as collateral. Ibrahim's land was not registered under his name. He owned the land, yet the land was formally registered as village property. Secondly, banks use formal written means of communication, visible to everyone. The letters sent to the villagers can be seen by anyone who frequents the coffeehouse; the recipient of the letter will become the topic of conversation later in the day. To be known as someone who does not have the financial resources to grow cotton is shameful for many farmers. An indebted farmer's status declines in the village (figure 9).

Figure 9   The author (third from right) and farmers in the coffeehouse.

Informal bankers generally apply high interest rates, at least five percent higher than bank rates. They manage to buy their clients' cotton for
less money, thus contributing to the temporary depression of prices during and immediately after the harvest. Moreover, when it comes to buying the cotton from the indebted farmer, it is not uncommon for them to
overweigh the produce and downgrade the ginning outturn of the cotton.
Farmers cannot resist selling their cotton to merchants, for they always
sign a contract with these cotton-money merchants to pay their debt
back on October 31, immediately following the harvest. Without financial backing, it is not possible for growers to keep their crop until the time
comes to sell it under relatively better terms. The abundance of cotton
and the urgent need for cash depress the prices between late September
and early November. It would not make any difference if they chose to
sell to TARİŞ, since the cooperative pays the price of the day when cotton
farmers bring their crop.

THE TRADERS' PRICE

An analysis of monthly cotton prices makes visible the large price differential between prices in October and in other months. In the eleven years
between September 1993 and August 2004, the average of the Cotlook

A Index, one of the prosthetic prices representing world market price analyzed in chapter 1, was 66.78 c/lb. The average of October prices was 63.78 c/lb. This is a deviation of exactly 300 points, a difference vast enough for the New York Board of Trade (NYBOT) to formally enforce a halt in trading, because in the globally recognized cotton futures market of NYBOT a 300 cent deviation in a single trading session is an institutionally recognized sign of market crisis.

The Cotlook A Index represents the price deviation only to a limited extent, possibly under-representing the variance, for it incorporates the traders' perceptions of the price. The prices as they are shaped in the Izmir Mercantile Exchange reveal a more alarming difference. The average for October prices between 1993 and 2004, including the price of 2001, is a mere 65.23 c/lb. The average price for all other months is 73.19 c/lb, making a vast difference of 796 points. This is approximately eight cents for each pound of cotton, an amount more than twice the difference on the NYBOT, enough to call a market crisis if it happened in the world of merchants.

Farmers are excluded from lint markets because they do not have warehouses to store their cotton, the financial means to insure it, the means to follow prices on a daily basis, or the political power to participate in the making of prosthetic prices. These prices belong to the world of traders, merchants, brokers, and a few large landowners. To give an example, as discussed in chapter 3 cotton prices in the Izmir Mercantile Exchange are produced in three main forms in four different market places. Each of these price forms is produced in specific market geographies, almost all of which are designed to keep the farmers outside the exchange. The market price of the Izmir Mercantile Exchange is a price indicator used to set individual prices; the pit trading price is a pricing tool that merchants produce in order to probe the market to see whether it is bullish or bearish; and postpit prices are the actual prices of cotton exchanged in the market, but because they are not posted, no one has certain knowledge of them. In short, the market as it takes shape in Izmir has multiple prices that work as prosthetic devices used by traders to pursue their mercantile interests.

Apart from the production and deployment of various price forms, traders also affect the making of prices by negotiating each year's supply and demand estimates. These estimates are more effective in creating prices than their real levels, for the actual levels are known only after all the cotton is bought and sold on the market in late October. In other words, in actual markets hypothetical supply and demand figures affect prices, not their actual levels. As a result, the meetings in which the estimates of the year's supply and demand figures are set are formative of the actual prices.

Three main groups with three diverse motivations—merchants, the TARİŞ cooperative, and government representatives—attend the meeting of the Permanent Working Group on Cotton where supply and demand are estimated each year. Merchants dominate the meeting as the hosts of the caucus; the meeting takes place in the Exchange run by the traders. Merchants lead the meeting in terms of numbers, too, for they attend all together, creating the absolute majority in the meeting room. They have an interest in depressing prices, because lower prices make it possible for them to trade larger volumes. As a result, they do their best to prevent the meeting from producing an underestimated production level, since a forecast of decreasing supply pushes up prices. The cooperative representatives have a contrasting motivation. Obviously, they benefit more from increasing prices, since higher prices mean a higher profit margin for the cooperative, the largest cotton seller in Izmir. Thus, they have an interest in preventing an overestimation of the production level, because guessing a higher supply would depress prices. The government representatives, however, do not have the same interest in price levels as the previous two groups. Their main purpose is to note the cotton supply levels as accurately as possible in order to inform the Minister of Agriculture.

My fieldwork at the IME suggests that merchants have a larger say in these estimates. Every year, traders manage to have the meeting produce an estimate higher than the actual levels and, thus, successfully depress prices before the harvest. These price forms disappear as the traders approach the countryside. Price as a prosthetic device does not play any role in the way farmers attend to the conditions of exchanging their produce. Very few—that is, those who cultivate cotton on large farms (less than one percent of Söke Plain cotton farmers and none of the Pamukköy growers)—follow the prices of the Izmir Mercantile Exchange and other prosthetic prices. For the vast majority of farmers, market prostheses or prices as device do not mean much, for a number of reasons:

First, the terms "merchant" and "trader" are used only in the singular form and in a pejorative sense. Traders are not trusted in the countryside. They are considered money lenders. Frequently, they are thought to protect the yarn producers' and their own interests. Therefore, any price in any form associated with merchant houses or their organizations is regarded with suspicion, as just another tool used to get the farmer's produce. The price is thought to be a mercantile tool in the countryside.

Second, a great majority of the cotton farmers are either locked into relations of debt with the merchants, or pledged into selling their cotton to their cooperative TARİŞ, for this is the only way they can get the credit they need to continue production. TARİŞ can extend indirect credits—such as supplying farmers with fertilizer, seed or pesticide—during the planting season and deduct the cost of these when the farmers sell their produce back to the cooperative.

If the merchants depress the prices, they can buy more cotton and sell for less. Not only does the markup make a difference, but when the cotton price is depressed, more and more yarn factories switch from cheap, oil-based polyester inputs to cotton; they buy more cotton and thus contribute more to the merchants' income. Finally, as the price decreases in the countryside, merchants need less capital to purchase the commodity, so their carryover increases in real terms. Paradoxically, the reason for the increase in merchants' income can lead to the eventual loss of all profit. The more they depress prices, the more difficult it becomes for small farmers to grow cotton—not only because of the decreasing contribution of cotton to their income, but also because the farmers are selling their land to pay off their debt, thus losing the chance to grow cotton altogether. If the process of being indebted continues for two more decades, the land will be consolidated in fewer hands and prosthetic prices may become more relevant in the countryside, not because the farmers will have understood how to use derivative markets, but because no small farmers will be left.

THE FARMERS' PRICE

The cotton price for a farmer is never the formal posted price. For them, formal prices—whether posted by merchant houses or by TARİŞ—are only indicative of what they can get for their cotton. "The price is what I carry in my pocket after I sell my crop," said Numan, a cotton-grower who had to sell his cotton to a private merchant. He borrowed cash to be able to continue producing cotton. He did not use formal means to raise the money, for the reasons explained above. Instead, he approached a ginning factory owner, received his money in less than an hour, and made a deal to "give" his cotton to this private trader, settling the difference after the debt had been deducted.

As we discussed the market over dinner in his house, he gently shook his head toward the door for his sons to leave and lowered his voice as if to reveal a secret, a common way of talking about power relations in Pamukköy. He explained how the price that farmers receive is always lower than the price they are offered:

> Even if a farmer sells to the cooperative, the price he ends up getting is lower than what he accepted. They deduct this, they deduct that. The government used to announce the minimum prices. No more. We have only the market. But even then, the price we used to get was lower than the announced price. If one

sells the cotton to traders, the price will be even lower. *They get our cotton by doing things* (emphasis added).

The "things they do" begin with illegally lending money, yet creating a legal context for it. When Numan went to the ginning factory owner Hüseyin to borrow money, the trader told him that he had some bank credit he did not need at the time, and "since he liked Numan a lot," he offered Numan the money to use. The interest rate he applied was even one point lower than the private banks' rate. Hüseyin presented himself as a person doing a favor to Numan by using his network of "friends" at the bank. He sold his money, but pretended that he served as an intermediary between the bank and the farmer. "Usually, they never give money directly to us. We go and get it from the bank. It looks as if the bank gives us the money," continued Numan, again in a hushed tone. He would stop talking when his wife entered the room.

> I know that it doesn't come from the bank. He [the money lender] sends a note to his friends in the bank, authorizes me to withdraw money from his account, and it is his money that I get. Other villagers don't know. They think it is the bank that gives them the money and that the *fabrikacı* [the ginning factory owner] is the intermediary. When there is a bank, there is paperwork, the state is involved, courts, etc. They send letters and stuff. Everybody knows that you borrow money in the village, so other villagers don't want to work with you. You cannot even treat someone to a cup of tea if they know. They make fun of you in the coffeehouse.
>
> *What else happens before you get his money from the bank?*
>
> You know, the first thing he [the merchant] asks is not the amount of money we need, but the amount of field we have. Because he will not get the cash back, he will ask for my cotton instead. He says, "I'll also help you sell your cotton." I know how to sell my cotton. How exactly is he going to help me other than buying it?
>
> *What is the price he offered you?*
>
> It is always whatever TARİŞ announces. This is usually the deal. You cannot have a farmer sell his crop in advance without having TARİŞ's price. The merchant also offers the TARİŞ price. But the amount he pays is always lower. For example, when you bring your cotton, he never likes it. His face becomes sour as he looks at it. I feel bad, a bit ashamed. He makes us feel that way. It happens all the time.
>
> *Can you explain a bit more?*
>
> I go to his factory with the cotton, he looks at me like this [he shows a face simultaneously angry and sad]. I feel bad. After all, this is my months of work. You feel bad when one looks down upon it. Then he gins a few samples. The ginning outturn is everything in cotton. If the cotton has more seeds, it has less lint. So the money I get goes down if the outturn

decreases. The merchants always mess with these roller gins. They fix their scissors so that they pick a little bit less lint. So they pay less. They also play with their scales. Farmers' cotton always weighs less. They make money in this way too.

A former ginning factory owner confirmed Numan's description of how the cotton is sold in the market. We had dinner in Izmir three months after I had talked to Numan. He contradicted Numan only when he said that the merchant usually offers less than the price TARİŞ would announce during the harvest:

> This business of debt is making the rich richer, the poor poorer. But what can farmers really do? The Agricultural Bank does not give credit anymore. The cooperative's bank is taken away. Farmers are left alone. Their lives are full of unexpected turns. They need money, and usually very rapidly. Who has money? The ginners. They don't like the poorest farmers. They don't like the richest farmers. The poor have nothing to lose; the rich have power to resist. They want the middle farmers who produce enough, yet don't have money to finance themselves. These farmers also need them, because they want to borrow fast, and they want to borrow it secretly. Ginners keep it secret, and sometimes the farmers lose their land secretly if they cannot pay the debt.

Not all farmers are indebted, yet they still work with private traders. Scales and sampling roller gins usually are more balanced when it comes to working with farmers who are not indebted.

In discussing how the farmers' prices are formed, one needs to mention the performances put on by traders, which weigh heavily against the farmers. Selami, who with his wife owned fifteen decares and rented five more decares, wanted to sell his cotton to a private trader. He had inherited money the previous year and had better financial resources. He talked to a few ginners before the harvest about his intention to sell. "Initially all of them thought that I wanted to borrow money. They were nice to me, wanting to help me like a father. One of them even told me that I should consider him as a father, although it was the first time in his life that he met me." Selami and I were sitting in a coffeehouse in Söke. I asked him whether the ginners' manners had changed once they learned that he did not want to borrow money. He replied:

> No, not much. They were still nice. But they changed after I brought them samples of my cotton after the harvest. They looked at it, didn't like it, yet still wanted to buy it. They are real actors. Like those on TV. They are real *Ceyars* [J.R.'s].
> *What do they do?*
> Difficult to tell. The one to whom I gave my cotton was a short fellow. But he used to look at me as though he was taller. You see, compared to him, I am

a bigger, stronger, and taller guy, but I feel small when I am in his office. He has a large desk, a picture of Atatürk, awards he got. I can't quite express myself. Something happens when I am there.
What happens?
I don't know. They know how to bargain, to sell and buy things. We sell only once every year. In one day, he does it more than I do in my entire life.
[. . .] *You don't have to sell to him, do you? You can sell your cotton to someone else until you get the price you want.*
No, it doesn't work that way. You can't sell it to others, not always. They don't like smart ones like me. They call each other, they make sure that they don't pay more than TARİŞ. They stick together. Even if they don't stand together, they do it the same way. They are all J. R.'s knowing how to bargain. They look as if they don't like your cotton, they don't want it, so that you feel happy if they buy your cotton in the end.

The "it" he refers to is the market experience. When a rich trader and a poor farmer come together within an exchange context, as in any other context where the powerful and the powerless meet, the latter finds himself in a field of power that works against him. A trader tends to speak the language better, can articulate his position better, and uses an idiom farmers are accustomed to hearing only on TV. Traders are experienced in buying and selling. They perform better, not only because they are more skilled, but also because their financial power backs them with a cushion in case they do not win the bargaining. This is hardly the case for farmers like Selami. He cannot continue driving his tractor around the plain to find a buyer, show his samples, and expect to gain a good bargaining position. The amount he hoped to sell is little compared to the amount the traders buy everyday. Selami knew that he was less experienced. He was aware of the power field of bargaining. Like many other farmers, he knew that the trader performs in a certain way, much like an actor:

> *But Selami, you seem to know that they are only acting, like J. R. himself.*
> Yes, we know that, but it doesn't help.

Knowing that trading performances are only an act does not help the Pamukköy farmers. The urgency they feel to sell their produce in order to pay their debt dominates the farmers' motivations in the marketplace. They cannot get their cotton ginned and wait for the best opportunity to sell their commodity. They cannot produce and deploy various prices to empower their trading position, for they do not have one. They cannot travel with their cotton between various potential buyers, nor can they shop around to find the best merchant. The market as seen by Pamukköy farmers is not a neutral place where supply and demand set the price. It is a power field where the traders' various performances and the farmers' indebtedness make the farmers relatively powerless agents of the exchange relationship that turns their cotton into money. This conclusion suggests a rethinking of the relationship between the field and the market.

CONCLUSION

The prevailing focus in the analysis of the global countryside seeks to register the effects of the expanding market on peasant livelihood and to explain the persistence or disappearance of farmers' modes of survival. This macro perspective assumes the presence of the market without explaining what it is and how it works in reality. In contrast, this chapter has analyzed the interaction between the processes of agricultural production and exchange, and how markets work on the ground, through an ethnographic investigation of cotton production and exchange in western Turkey.

In the first part of the chapter, I discussed the relations that farmers mobilize in order to produce cotton. Depending on their financial power, farmers mobilize different resources and networks. As the ratio of land size to adult household member increases, farmers tend to depend more on paid labor. In Pamukköy, a family that has two decares of land per family member can carry out all of the field work without hiring external labor. Yet the farmers with the smallest landholdings choose to bring together informal labor-pooling cooperatives, work in each others' fields, and economize on their resources, only minimally deploying money in the labor exchange. As farm size increases, growers depend more on monetary relations of exchange; thus, the contact between the labor market and the field becomes more frequent.

Independent of farm size, cotton production requires investment in research, expertise, labor, and networking. Farmers continuously carry out research to increase their yield, find cheaper labor resources and locate easier and more effective techniques of cotton-growing. They even earmark parts of their fields to test the performance of a new seed or growing technique. Their profession requires years of learning and observation. Interestingly, the farmers of Pamukköy do not regard farming as a skilled profession. Many see themselves as simple peasants who just watch the land: "We are working just with our muscles. What we do does not require mental work," as one farmer says.

Yet, once challenged, farmers have a tendency to change their position and assert their agency through various skills and performances. A performance of humbleness and poverty is a frequently used tactic in the countryside. Such a performance empowers farmers as they negotiate the terms of labor-pooling, networking, finding cash, and hiring labor during the production process. Farmers see their fields as a space in which they can assert active agency. Farmers know that they cannot control all the parameters that affect cotton growing. They are aware of the risks— it may rain too much, or not at all; the workers may not come to pick the cotton, or pick it badly; and so on. Nevertheless, they regard themselves as active agents of the political economic universe that surrounds them on the field.

Such a feeling of agency vanishes rapidly once farmers begin to consider the place of the cotton market in their lives. Although farmers engage in many exchange processes as they buy inputs and labor, they often do not regard such encounters as a market relationship; rather, they express these exchanges through an idiom of relationship of solidarity. For farmers, the place of the market is the trader's office, usually located in a ginning factory owned by the merchant himself. Contact with the market is composed of bargaining and agreeing on a price.

Three factors prefigure the bargaining prior to the farmers' visit to the traders' offices. First, the previous relationship between the trader and the farmer has a strong effect on the terms of negotiation. If the farmer owes money to the trader, he has to pay it back, usually before October 31. Traders informally cooperate not to buy from a farmer if he is indebted to another trader. Farmers have to sell their cotton to the trader from whom they borrow. In this context, farmers are at the mercy of the traders. According to my calculations, in 2001 the Pamukköy farmers who borrowed from private traders sold their cotton for a price eleven percent less than farmers who borrowed from family members or the cooperative.

The second factor that prefigures bargaining is related to the specific processes that take place in the Izmir Mercantile Exchange, the central merchant organization and hub of cotton trade in the country. All traders active in the Söke Plain have representatives in the Exchange. Well before the cotton hits the market, traders begin to work on preparing the ground for bargaining. As discussed in chapter 3, various prosthetic prices are probed and produced during pit and postpit trading. Also, traders work hard to affect the market process. For instance, they lobby agricultural engineers, statisticians, researchers, government officials, and cooperative representatives to influence their perception of the coming harvest. The traders' objective is to produce an estimate that foresees a high yield and low production costs. In caucuses dominated by traders, such as the Permanent Working Group on Cotton, the very supply of cotton is determined even before farmers harvest their crop. These estimates are always lower than the actual levels, which are yet to be known.

The third factor that affects the bargaining in the market is related to the trading performances and politics that merchants forge on the ground. According to the Pamukköy farmers and many traders I inter-viewed, traders look down upon the farmers' produce to strengthen their trading position. Furthermore, merchants cooperate to ensure that they fix their sellers even before the harvest. All cotton buyers in the plain, with the exception of a few, lend money to farmers, then buy the farmers' cotton and settle the difference. They refuse to buy the cotton of a farmer who has borrowed from another trader.

As a result of these three factors, the farmers of Pamukköy see the market neither as a place where the price is set, nor as a mere location of commodity exchange. My research suggests that the market is a power field where farmers encounter the production of price as relatively pas-sive agents of trade. The market price that farmers encounter in traders' offices is produced prior to the moment of exchange. Merchants spend much time in building networks to affect the price levels, while farmers enter into these locations of exchange from a different space where they must spend all available time growing cotton, hiring or pooling labor in cooperatives, hoeing their fields, or picking their cotton. Farmers do not have the time to carry out market politics. They cannot maintain markets and grow cotton at the same time, for market exchange draws on con-crete forms of production, performance, and maintenance.

The price that serves as the interface between the field and the market can be regarded as a summary of all the power contestations that take place before and during the moment of exchange. Studies of rural rela-tions of exchange and production should take into account the specific nature of price-making on the ground. Furthermore, without consider-ing the asymmetries in the way prices are produced, any study of ex-change and production relations would be incomplete. Treating prices as things that are set in the market is itself a political investment in shaping markets. Prices are not set through actual demand and supply; they are produced as prostheses to be used by a select group of market partici-pants only. Without attending to these, scholarly research on agricultural production and commodity markets risks being a formative part of the political economic universe it studies.

The Pamukköy farmers see the markets and fields not as places of neu-trality where supply and demand meet each other to set a price. Instead, these are power fields where various trading performances take place. The farmers' capacity to improvise and exploit these performances in the field increases together with their land size. Yet, for most of the cot-ton farmers living in the largest cotton-growing village of the Söke Plain, such relative autonomy vanishes as they leave their fields and enter the cotton market. The market makes the growers relatively powerless agents within the exchange relationship.

In conclusion, understanding economic activities in the countryside requires situating them in fields of power where a web of asymmetrical relations are forged and maintained by a multiplicity of actors. These actors operate in a cascading relationship of domination, resistance, and negotiation, structured in an essentially political topography of encounter. Such a political context can only be understood if one pays ethnographic attention to the specific predicaments of different actors involved in commodity markets.

CHAPTER 6

Cotton Fields of Power in Rural Egypt

EGYPT CONSTITUTES AN EXEMPLARY case reflecting the three main global transformations of modernity: it was colonized and restructured by the British; its independence following the Free Officers' Coup brought with it so-called socialist planning; and its "opening to the world" (*infitah*) and, later, embracing of neoliberalism made it a center of attention for free market reform. The country became one of the world's forerunners of neoliberal market reforms, to an extent that even the IMF praised its determination to restructure the economy and participate in global markets as "an achievement that has few parallels."[1]

Neoliberalism, the last of these global experiments, came with an interesting twist. During colonial and postwar developmentalist times, the state was identified as the main agent of development in the countryside. Under neoliberalism, however, it was believed that the countryside could take off only if farmers were left alone, so that the market could do its job. Rural Egypt has become a playground for neoliberal experts, not only because of a policy choice, but because of the relative political weakness of farming communities. This was not a scientific choice, but a political outcome. Historically, Third World farmers have been the most under-represented class in politics. Solutions to the problems of the country-side all over the post-1980 Third World were formulated along the same lines: it was claimed that the state had intervened too much in relations of exchange and production, thus upsetting the balance of a working free market. Public enterprises were not efficient and had to be sold. The government had to be rolled back to its main functions—that is, overseeing a well-working market and providing it with the necessary institutional environment to ensure its balance. Almost all recipes for economic take-off praised flexibility and adaptation to changing conditions. Paradoxically, these approaches offered the same set of policies in an inflexible way, advising and even forcing governments to apply them globally.

The neoliberal prescription for the largest single sector of the world, agriculture, was to stop the government's manipulation of input prices, such as fertilizers, pesticides, and seeds; to make all factors of production

[1] Cited in Dana (2000).

a commodity in the free market; to abolish the setting of floor prices; to allow banks to set their own interest rates in order to ensure a free credit market; to discontinue government manipulation of agricultural cooperatives and make the latter a part of the free market; and to open the domestic market to the world in order to ensure a competitive environment and efficiency in production and marketing. It was expected that, once deregulation became the norm and private enterprise the form, farmers and traders would move toward the market, which in turn would promise an increase in both agricultural exports and economic growth.

More than a quarter of a century has passed since the economic prescriptions of neoliberal experts first guided Egyptian policy-makers. We are now in a better position to observe the outcome of these experiments. Contrary to neoliberal expectations, recent scholarship has shown that, rather than moving toward the market, farmers have favored increased self-provisioning and protection from neoliberal policies once economies took successful steps toward free market reforms (Mitchell 1998; Abdel-Aal and Reem 1999; Abdel-Aal and Saad 1999; Bush 1999).

The results of these reforms in Egypt's agriculture can be summarized as follows: the prices of all agricultural inputs have increased without a subsequent increase in farm income, while almost all economic subsidies for farmers have decreased (Bush 2002). These developments took place while real wages in the agricultural sector declined (Abou-Zeid 1997). The liberalization of the market for agricultural inputs has created private monopolies that tend to reverse the depressed price regimes, which has resulted in a decreased use of fertilizers (Mitchell 1998; Toth and Elyachar 2001). Especially Law 96 of 1992, which introduced a free market in real estate, reversed Nasser's reforms in the countryside. The price of land and average land size has increased, contributing to the increasing population of landless farmers (Fergany 2002; LCHR 2002; Saad 2002; LCHR 2005). The privatization of credit and the decreasing financial power of farmers have also resulted in a proliferation of private money lenders in the countryside, thus contributing to the further informalization of credit relations. The combined effect of these outcomes on the farmers' income has been phenomenally depressing. In only two years, between 1997 and 1999, the farmers' income decreased by thirty-three percent (Haddad and Ahmed 2000).

These reforms were passed without much democratic participation or discussion. In some cases, the government did not even inform farming communities about the transformations they were about to undergo. In 1995, Abdel-Aal found that less than a quarter of tenant farmers knew that they were going to lose their tenancy rights, and that the land rent was to be fixed at seven times the amount of the land tax. After this temporary measure, the rents were left unregulated.[2]

These reforms were carried out with the stated objective of connecting Egyptian farmers to the globalizing world, thus integrating them into world markets. This would ensure increasing efficiency in Egyptian agriculture. World Bank experts believed that cotton farmers would be the first rural population to benefit from becoming a part of the global cotton market. In this chapter, we will see what this integration means for cotton farmers, and how world markets are made and maintained from the vantage point of farmers with a postcolonial background.

Cotton Is Disappearing in Egypt

Perhaps the most telling example of the failure of neoliberal reforms is the phenomenal decrease of cotton production in Egypt. It was believed that Egypt would become an agricultural export giant, if the country only reformed its agriculture. In 2001, a decade after Egypt had lost its market to U.S. Pima cotton, the World Bank reported that "Egypt has considerable potential to expand cotton exports, particularly of high-quality ELS varieties. In order to achieve this, one of the most pressing challenges for Egyptian cotton sector reforms is the need to liberalize the seed market" (World Bank 2001).

The decrease in Egyptian cotton production has been unmatched in history. Chapter 4 has outlined how Egypt lost its market share to U.S. corporations as a result of neoliberal market reforms. The larger the number of free market policies adopted, the fewer farmers produced cotton. It was believed that the comparative advantage of Egyptian cotton would create incentives for farmers to produce more, given that cotton has been Egypt's second most important source of foreign exchange revenue after petroleum and is considered the world's best extralong- and long-staple cotton in the world. The decrease in the area of cotton production is extensive: in 2008, the area of production was less than a quarter of the acreage in 1930.

While Egyptian cotton lost its hegemonic share in world markets, around 25,000 cotton-growing companies in the United States increased their production and share in the world trade under the wings of the U.S. government. The World Bank, the foremost institution preaching neoliberalism in Egypt, reported that between 1996–97 and 2001–2 these U.S. companies received a total of USD 13,343,000,000,[3] as direct and

---

[2] Cited in Saad (2002).
[3] This amount was more than the Egyptian national reserves in 2001.

indirect subsidies in the form of Loan Deficiency Payments, Marketing Loan Gains, Forfeitures, Production Flexibility Contracts, Market Loss Assistance, Insurance, and Step-2 payments (Baffes 2004c). When one considers the scale of subsidies in terms of their share in world prosthetic prices, the results look even more alarming. In the same period, the average subsidy that U.S. companies received per kilogram of cotton was 48.16 percent of the Cotlook A Index, the prosthetic price commonly referred to as the world price of cotton. In the 2001–2 season, this ratio reached a record-breaking eighty-nine percent of the A Index.

It would be misleading to argue that the only beneficiaries of these subsidies are cotton-growing companies. Sustaining cotton growth has two important indirect effects on U.S. financial markets and traders. On the one hand, almost all agricultural land in the United States is registered as collateral for credit. The U.S. cotton sector is among the least efficient in the world and would shrink considerably, if not disappear altogether, if neoliberal reforms also reached the U.S. countryside. Such a development would collapse the worth of agricultural land and thus indirectly affect banks. For this reason, banks in the United States also contributed financially to the lobbying of the U.S. government to pass the last Farm Bill of 2002, which remained effective until 2008.

Second, in the absence of cotton-growing, one of the most lucrative financial instruments might disappear, the cotton futures and option market of the New York Board of Trade (NYBOT). Although one does not need to own cotton in order to trade in these markets—almost all contracts are closed as cash settlements before their maturation—one still needs cotton. Information regarding the growth and trade of cotton is the main mercantile tool of price realization in these markets.

AN ILLEGAL ALIEN IN THE EGYPTIAN COUNTRYSIDE

Another clear sign of the failure of neoliberal reforms becomes visible when one considers the level of violence and insecurity that the reforms introduced to the Egyptian countryside. Egypt has been governed under formal martial law since the assassination of Sadat in 1981, even though one can feel this neither in tourist venues, nor in Cairo's upscale neighborhoods of Zamalek or Ma'adi. As soon as one leaves the main tourist sites and the roads connecting them, another Egypt slowly begins to appear.

By law, foreigners are not allowed to leave the tourist sites and main highways without the approval of the Ministry of the Interior. Even if foreign nationals have government approval, they cannot stay in the countryside for more than a week. If the stay exceeds this time limit, the host and the guest are required by law to visit the nearest police or military center to register and to explain the nature of their relationship. However, no one carries out this registration process. When registration does occur, it arouses much attention and suspicion.

In 2000, my host and I did not want to register. I was visiting Kamshish, the first village I had ever visited in Egypt, for the second time. Its revolutionary social history was of great interest to me as a young and engaged graduate student. The Maoist past of Pamukköy, I thought, would present an interesting contrast to that of Kamshish. I stayed in Kamshish for two weeks that summer, hosted by a corn farmer I had met in Cairo.

All the major roads of Egypt have frequent military checkpoints. The entry and exit points of all large and mid-size villages are monitored by similar checkpoints, giving the impression that the country is under military occupation. Noticing my host's uneasiness as we took a minibus from Cairo to Shebin al-Kom, I felt that I needed to turn my face away from the soldiers as their eyes scanned us. I rarely passed as an Egyptian. To my surprise, many Egyptians thought I was from East Asia, sometimes from China, frequently from Japan. As my time in the village extended, my host's uneasiness about my presence increased. One day he told me that it was necessary to make up a story for the police in case we were arrested. Shocked and uneasy, I listened to him. "You should never say that you are doing research with farmers," he said. Instead, I should say that my grandfather was from the village and that I had come to visit the place where he had spent his childhood. According to Mohammad's story, I was learning about my Muslim background. We even rehearsed. "Use some *fusha* [Classical Qur'anic Arabic, in contrast to the local, more colloquial dialect]," he said, "they'll like that."

Two days after rehearsing my new story, I left Kamshish for good, deciding not to carry out research there.[4] A month after I had left, Mohammad told me over the phone that a group of bullies, hired by an absentee landlord who wanted to evict his tenants, had badly beaten four tenant farmers. One of them had remained in intensive care in Shebin al-Kom for a week. The farmers did not leave the land, nor was their rent increased.

This incident in Kamshish was only one example of the spread of violence throughout rural Egypt. In only six years, between 1996 and 2002, 119 farmers lost their lives, 846 were hospitalized, and 1,409 arrested as a result of clashes and land disputes incited by Law 96 of 1992 (LCHR 2002). The carrying out of research in such a setting is not something the Egyptian government endorses. Even for Egyptian researchers, it

---

[4] A colleague in Cairo, Reem Saad, helped me make this decision. It was Reem who advised me that the past of the village of Kamshish would create problems for my research.

became a difficult task. For non-Egyptians, however, doing research in the countryside necessitates mastering the shifting boundaries between formality and informality. Compared to the research I conducted in rural Turkey, the research I did in rural Egypt was more limited and scattered. I had to conduct research in two villages, taking short breaks of a few days between my alternating extended stays in the villages of Kafr Gaffar and 'Izbet Sabri.

While my host in Kamshish had been anxious, probably because of the role that the village had played in Egyptian political history, my hosts in the villages of Kafr Gaffar and 'Izbet Sabri were not worried. One of them had an uncle in the police station who came to fetch me from the make-shift minibus stop on the road that connected Faqus in Sharqiyyah to Cairo. He wanted to move to the United States, and after I had stayed for two months in 'Izbet Sabri, a very small village of sixty households, he asked me if I could help him receive a visa from the embassy. "I am a legal alien both in the United States and Egypt," I replied, "I can't do much, but yes, I'll do my best to help." And I helped, as much as I could.

Compared to my stay in Kamshish, my presence was felt even less in the second fieldwork site, Kafr Gaffar, a village of 5,600 people. A rural development project there had already been carrying out research for a year. With the project manager's consent, I passed as just another researcher. My initial hosts, who were not farmers, were well-connected in the village. They provided me with an environment and connections that made my stay simultaneously legitimate and productive. The reach of the state is always limited in the provinces, and where it does reach, it is through the mediation of local constellations of power. In both villages, it was the very representatives of the state that made it possible for me to stay and conduct my research; yet the state also tried to present the countryside only in a certain way.

GROWING COTTON IN THE FIELDS OF KAFR GAFFAR AND 'IZBET SABRI

For growers and merchants, cotton is the foremost cash crop in Egypt. As the second most important export commodity after oil, cotton used to contribute to the country's foreign exchange revenues more than all other agricultural exports combined.[5]

---

[5] Source: FAO. Noncotton exports include the following: milled paddy rice, potatoes, molasses, oranges, vegetables, dehydrated vegetables, frozen beans, dry seeds, fruit, spores, tea, essential oils, flax fiber, cheese made from whole cows' milk, hydrogenated oils, centrifugal and raw sugar, and prepared vegetables.

There are two main cultivation seasons in Egypt, roughly identified as winter and summer. Between April and the last week of October, rice, maize, and cotton dominate the cropping patterns. From early November to late March, the fields are allocated to wheat, *fool*,[6] barley, and *berseem*.[7] In Upper Egypt, cotton cultivation starts in March. In Lower Egypt, because the sunlight reaches the soil at a higher angle, farmers prepare their fields for planting between late March and early April. Ahmad, a thirty-year-old cotton farmer from 'Izbet Sabri, shares two acres of land with his two brothers. He is among the vast majority of small farmers in Egypt. Almost ninety percent of agricultural land in Egypt is in holdings of less than five acres. Larger plots of fifty or more acres represent around two percent (Abdel Aal 2002).

The best time for sowing cotton to ensure the highest yield is in the first two weeks of April. The best yields are achieved if the seeds are planted after the first cutting of *berseem*: keeping the crop in the field longer decreases the nutritional content of the soil and results in missing the best time to sow.

Ahmad and his brothers were more concerned about their three water buffalos (*gamoosa*). The *berseem* used for feeding the animals had to stay on the field a bit longer to allow for a final cut, until the field was to be prepared for cotton. Similar to Mehmet from Pamukköy, Ahmad chose to start planting slightly later in order to have enough fodder to feed his family's water buffalos with the home-grown crop. Yet, the risk he takes is minimal compared to Pamukköy farmers who sow late, because it almost never rains during harvest in Egypt. For both Ahmad and Mehmet, the main motivation is to avoid relations that entail monetary exchange.

The principal work periods of growing cotton in Egypt and Turkey are the same. They follow the main pattern of the six stages of growth, each paralleling the crop's life cycle of maturing and marketing: (1) field preparation, (2) sowing, (3) hoeing and thinning, (4) watering, (5) harvesting, and (6) marketing. However, in each of these stages, Egyptian farmers differ greatly from their Turkish colleagues in the ways in which they attend to the conditions of cotton cultivation.

Farmers either harvest *berseem* to use it later as animal fodder or let the animals graze on the field so that the natural fertilizer that the *gamoosas* produce directly reaches the soil. The field is prepared for sowing cotton immediately after this process. Field preparation consists of freshening up the soil by plowing it to increase its productivity. The remainders of

---

[6] *Ful*, or broad beans, is the main ingredient of a very popular Egyptian dish, mostly consumed by the lower and middle classes.

[7] *Berseem*, Egyptian clover or *Trofolium Alexandrina*, is a protein-rich animal fodder. Sugar cane is also a major crop of the country. It is mostly cultivated in Upper Egypt.

the previous crop are mixed with the soil and the fertilizers in order to help the soil to recover. Plowing of the soil is followed by application of a heavy roller onto the surface in order to seal the field, until it is broken again by the tool called *mazraʿa* to sow the seeds. These preparations are usually carried out with the help of a rented tractor. In Egypt, this stage is usually the last one that relies on the usage of tractors. Afterward, cotton farmers use tractors less frequently, or even not at all, if they are small cultivators. Unlike that in Pamukköy, the soil in Kafr Gaffar is irrigated before sowing, in order reach a certain level of moisture and to process the fertilizers previously applied. In Ahmad's field, ten days after watering the land was readied for sowing by leveling its surface. Ahmad and his younger brother used a mule to tow a heavy metal roller. Together, they sealed the soil until the time came to break it again during planting.

In comparison to Turkey, in Egypt tractors are used less frequently in cotton cultivation, and even more infrequently in smaller villages. In ʿIzbet Ramzi, none of the sixty cotton-growing households use a tractor to plant cotton. In Kafr Gaffar, larger landowners will occasionally use tractors and sometimes lend them to farmers in exchange for money or services. Yet, because in both villages the plots can be as small as a few *qirats*,[8] using a tractor is not necessarily the best agricultural technique. Because of having to make frequent turns on the edges of the fields, the enormous tractor tires damage the fragile and rich soil. The damage reaches such an extent that, in smaller plots, it can amount to as much as ten percent of the field, disallowing the growth of cotton in these "injured" locations, as a farmer put it. Animals do not injure the soil. On the contrary, their gentle steps are good for the soil's productivity, for they hoe it naturally as the animals move over the land.

Another reason for avoiding mechanical sowing is the low agricultural wages in the countryside. In Egypt, cotton is sown by children, young men, and women. Either they or their parents borrow small amounts from labor contractors, like so many agricultural workers in Egypt and Turkey, and then pay back the debt as services. This form of financing comes with a price tag of depressed wages, and in some instances no wage at all.

In Kafr Gaffar and ʿIzbet Sabri, cotton farmers do not buy seeds from private dealers. Because the planting regions of different cotton varieties are fixed by the government to prevent the mixing of different types of cotton, the seeds are distributed by an agricultural cooperative under government control. In Kafr Gaffar, the cooperative is located in the village, but the farmers of ʿIzbet Ramzi have to visit the neighboring village to buy the seeds.

---

[8] One *qirat* is 175 square meters or 1/24 of an acre.

Before the sowing begins, ridging is carried out with the help of tractors. The surface of these ridges is then flattened with hand hoes. Between the ridges, furrows are made to help the even distribution of water during the irrigation. This operation effectively allows farmers to divide their fields into smaller portions of land, usually by using a furrow pulled by an animal, thus increasing their capacity to intervene in the growth process of the plant. Each field is divided by taller ridges into several *fardas*, and then each *farda* is further divided into smaller *hawwal*s containing around ten rows each.

So Your Egyptians Are Kurds, No?

Once the seeds are bought and the field is prepared, farmers organize the work gangs for sowing. Before the sowing starts, either the person who owns the land, or the person hired by the landowner makes sure that the children and adult workers carefully sow in straight lines, around 75 centimeters apart from each other. This means that each acre is planted with 55 kilograms of seeds.

If the labor is hired, the person who supplies the landowner with workers is subcontracted to control them. If the labor is organized by village-based informal cooperatives, the farmer himself takes care of labor control. The *zimiil* in Egypt operates in a complex labor-sharing arrangement reminiscent of the *ödek* in Western Turkey. Farmers bring together their labor resources to avoid monetary exchange relations. If a household extends more services to another in terms of daily work, household members settle the difference with various objects of exchange, such as fertilizer, money, or even chickens.

Once the field is ready, the seeds bought, and the workers hired, sowing starts at dawn. Boys and girls are usually brought to the field at a very young age and learn to work there. Imitating their parents or elder relatives, they cultivate both an expertise in production and a capacity for discipline. In the countryside, it is almost impossible to find a person who does not know how to use a *mazra'a*, the tool used to sow cotton seeds. With this small instrument, workers dig a four-centimeter-deep hole in the mildly flattened top of the ridge and then place the seeds in the front part of it while holding the *mazra'a*'s wood handle. Then they send the seeds into the soil, covering the hole with the soil they have previously dug by pulling the tool out of the ridge. After finishing, the workers move about 15 centimeters further, taking one small step forward, and measure the next planting location on the ridge by using the *mazra'a* as a ruler. They repeat this process hundreds of times. As in Turkey, farmers plant more seeds than required, in order to allow them to select the most powerful shoots during the thinning process.

I met Ragab, an eight-year-old worker, during a break in Ahmad's field on the first day of sowing. He did not have a conception of work, wage, and production as older workers knew them. Working was "going to the field" for him, a part of his life, not a job to be carried out for a living. He did not even have a conception of a labor market in which his labor is exchanged for money or favors. He was one of Ahmad's many nephews, who had been enrolled in primary school but dropped out immediately. As he reached with a thin loaf of bread into the green plastic cup full of *ful* during lunch, he asked me if we also ate beans in New York. "Yes," I said, "But not as much as you do." His father was with us, somewhat uneasy about putting his son to work. I did not ask him any question, but he told me that "Ragab was just hanging out with his parents, because he is so small, he could not stay at home alone."

I did not challenge him. He was trying to conceal the unbearable economic conditions that his family faced. Having finished his lunch, Ragab began running around the field, chasing one of his cousins. "Look, he plays everyday [*shuf, beyil'ab kull youm, ba'a*]," the father said, pointing to the children. Ahmad, Ragab's uncle, later explained to me at night over a cup of tea that in his youth his parents did not put him to work. "It was better, we used to play. I went to school, a few years only. I can still read. Now children are working all the time. We say they are lucky if they find work."

> *At what age do they start working?*
> I don't know. They come with us to the fields. One day they hold the *mazra'a* or a hoe. You show them how. If they work well, you say good things. They like to be praised, so they learn faster.
> *Do they earn wages?*
> Yes, but later. When they are young, they are a part of the *zimiil*. Their family arranges the work. How is it in Turkey?
> *Children work in Turkey, too, but a bit later. In the East, children begin work earlier, like here. They also move to Western Turkey, where Pamukköy is, like tarahil workers here. Kurdish children start work at least five years earlier than Turkish ones.*
> So your Egyptians are Kurds, no?

The sowing of cotton in both villages is carried out in the same way. 'Izbet Sabri farmers grew Giza 85 in 2002, whereas Kafr Gaffar farmers sowed Giza 89. Both of these varieties are long-staple cottons. Yet, other things being equal, the former receives a higher premium for its slightly better quality.

In the three weeks following the sowing, the cotton-growing families of Kafr Gaffar and 'Izbet Sabri watered their fields, inspected the growth of the crop, and finally thinned the cotton to sort out the weak and slowly growing plants. Said's family is one of the farming families in Kafr Gaffar that carry out almost everything alone, without hiring workers for their three acres of land; they practice labor-pooling with their extended families. They use a small corner of their field for growing vegetables for household use, while the rest is for cotton. Three weeks after they sowed the cotton, following almost the exact techniques Ahmad's family used, Said, his wife, their three children, and his two brothers and their wives and children, came together to start thinning the cotton, uprooting the relatively weaker shoots whose fragile stems turned the working men and women's hands black.

The first thinning requires uprooting one out of every three shoots. Then, according to the specific growth pattern of the crop, the second thinning may remove up to half of the remaining shoots, while recycling the destroyed plants as fertilizer for the rest. The cotton continues to grow as farmers work relentlessly to survive. The revenue from selling the crop constitutes virtually the only major cash earnings for the cotton-growing families. Similar to other investments, it requires gathering resources from a variety of locations: from children's bodies to networks of friendship and family, from forging partnerships with poorer and richer farmers to continuing research to increase family revenues.

THE STRUGGLE TO SURVIVE: FARMERS, ANIMALS, AND STOCK

How can one make sense of this complex world of partnership and economic engagement in the countryside? The patterns of the farmers' economic engagements defy any predetermined logic of encounter. It is possible to locate these activities neither as capitalist agricultural production, nor as subsistence-oriented cultivation, without privileging a vantage point and then making it a criterion for imposing a predetermined theoretical order of things over the countryside. The cash-raising activities of farmers present a clear illustrative example of this situation which locates farmers, much like traders in Memphis or Faqus, in a simultaneous engagement in relations of production and exchange in which all the actors of cotton growth and circulation deploy heterogeneous strategies of money-making or surviving, by constantly transgressing the invisible border between formality and informality.

Gamal's family owns twenty *qirat* of land half a kilometer south of 'Izbet Sabri. Like the great majority of Egyptian farmers, the family does not have a legal title to that land. After Nasser's land reforms, the village land was divided into smaller portions and then leased to farmers in exchange for an affordable rent. Gamal's father, a strong supporter of Nasser, received around two acres of land from the estate of the land-owner who owned the entire village, including all the land and the houses built on it. Because the rent was pegged to the land tax and the land tax to the government's mercy, the land informally became the property of Gamal's father. The rent payments were small and the tenants many, so after a decade the original owner ceased to collect remuneration. Conse-quently, after his death in the 1980s, the heirs of his property were un-aware of the land's precise location.

Four decades are long enough for the entire landscape within the ad-ministrative borders of a village (*zimam*) to undergo significant change. The plots allocated to local farmers changed hands periodically during the lifetime of the generation that secured its access. Since these deals were alienable, the farmers' children grew up laboring on the land they were to inherit later. Gamal now owns a portion of the plot that his late father bequeathed to him. During the implementation of the reforms, the government required all farmers to eliminate the boundary-setting high ridges between smaller plots in order to increase land productivity. Be-cause the boundary of Gamal's inherited land intersected with the field he currently owns, he exchanged half of it with his field neighbor. When the restrictions on constructing ridges between fields were relaxed during the launching of free market reforms, the old boundaries changed again. The invisible titles to land in the Egyptian countryside are too mobile to be observed if one follows the logics of formality. Thus, imposition of a formal order that does not recognize the rich relationship between the land and the farmers does not merely mean misunderstanding the coun-tryside's complexity, but also neglecting the political choice of resource distribution.

The land use patterns can form more than eleven possible combina-tions of different access types in 'Izbet Sabri. Had I continued to fol-low these different arrangements, I might have spent my entire time there assembling 'Izbet Sabri's "tenancy web," as Abdel-Aal calls it.[9] After interviewing the fifteenth household of the sixty-household village I dis-continued my research on the tenancy web.

In 1994, this rich tenancy web, whose flexibility contributed to the survival strategies of farmers like Gamal, was interrupted by the single largest measure ever taken by the government since the nationalization of the 1960s. The introduction of a free market in real estate effectively

---

[9] According to Abdel-Aal's excellent mapping of the changing and mobile forms of ac-cess to land, there are more than 29 possible combinations of land access in a single village in Upper Egypt (Abdel Aal 2002).

ignored this dynamic system of land access that provided farmers with the capacity to use, rent, share, and distribute the land in ways that best suit their families' interest. Furthermore, it imposed an order of vague formality and aimed to restore the land to the original owners. In Ottoman and colonial times, the great-grandfathers of the "original owners" enclosed their fields in an attempt to secure them from repossession by the primary owners. These *original* owners were the great-grandfathers of today's farmers, such as Gamal.

For the farmers of 'Izbet Sabri, this formal measure contributed to the informalization and even militarization of the struggle for land access. In 1997, an "entrepreneur" from Cairo heard the news concerning the free market in real estate. Using his network in the land registry offices, he located the heirs of the original owners of the land, either from 'Izbet Sabri or in its vicinity. Seven families, all residing in Cairo, together owned approximately 130 acres. Those who held the formal title to the land knew that they owned the land, but were not willing to fight to get their property back.

Back in Sharqiyyah, through relatives who had never left 'Izbet Sabri's neighboring village and through land registry documents, the entrepreneur learned that many farmers using the land resided in 'Izbet Sabri. After returning to Cairo, he bought the land from the heirs in its entirety, convincing them that there was no way that "these farmers would give [them] the land." He was right. The heirs were too numerous. "They didn't even know how to find their land. It was a story forty years old," added Gamal as he recounted the story. For a small amount compared to the value of the land, "the man bought our land in *Masr* [the colloquial name for Cairo in rural Egypt], and then came here to ask us for rent."

In a well-planned strategy, the new owner did not inflate the price of the land as much as the other landowners around the village. As a result, one-third of the farmers, whose finances were in better condition, began paying rent to him. This move helped legitimize the new owner's position. He not only collected rent, but also legitimacy. The rest of the village refused to pay any amount of rent, believing that the land belonged to them. The political divide between those who accepted paying the rent and those who resisted grew larger, at times even turning into violent clashes. The resisting farmers sued the "new" landowner in court, arguing that the land that the entrepreneur had bought was not the land he claimed to own. Strategically accepting the possibility of a correspondence between the title and the land, they worked with the ambiguity between the paper that represented ownership and what was represented, the land itself. Farmers also filed complaints against the entrepreneur for hiring intimidating bullies who threatened to beat them if they continued to resist paying rent.

The countryside teems with similar stories, making visible how the land changes hands in Egypt by means of legal and illegal technologies of control. The struggle to survive in the villages starts with trying to keep the land, but it does not end there. To continue growing cotton, farmers like Gamal have to keep struggling on other fronts as well. One location of struggle is financing the growth of cotton.

FINANCING THE PLANT STOCK WITH LIVESTOCK

A family's cotton cultivation is possible only if they grow other plants to sustain themselves. Gamal's family grows vegetables such as tomatoes and eggplants for their own use on a small plot of their land. His wife sells some of these vegetables once a week in the neighboring village to provide the household with petty cash. She sells some of the cheese in the neighboring village market, alongside the eggs that the family's chickens yield. Because the price of a village egg (*baladi*) is double that of a market egg, she sells her own delicious eggs and buys the cheaper ones from the city. The family also grows *berseem* to feed their water buffalo (*gamoosa*), whose milk provides the household with butter, cheese, milk, ghee, and *mish*, a very bitter aged cheese, a small amount of which is enough to add a delicious flavor to the basic staple food of the household, home-made bread.

The life of the family's *gamoosa* began as a joint venture between a richer farmer and Gamal. Forced to sell his previous *gamoosa* to a local trader to finance an expensive medical treatment that his wife had received three years ago and following a bad harvest that cost Gamal his cow, the family was left without any capital in the form of livestock, other than a few chickens. Gamal then made an arrangement to share a *gamoosa* with a richer farmer whom he knew from the neighboring village. They began to look after the animal together. At the right time, the *gamoosa* was brought to the animal market to be mated. Until the buffalo became pregnant, Gamal financed the feeding of the *gamoosa*, but during the pregnancy and the calf's nursing, the owner contributed to the fodder expenses.[10] After the calf was born, Gamal and his partner became the owners of the new livestock. Gamal had to pay the original owner a bit more to claim the calf's entire title for himself. This calf became the *gamoosa* who now provides Gamal's family with milk.

Two different markets connect the life and death of live capital in the Egyptian countryside. Since the cotton plant owes its life partly to this calf, the welfare of Gamal's family is dependent on both plant stock and

[10] This is one of the most common arrangements in the Egyptian countryside.

livestock.[11] Said, the farmer from Kafr Gaffar, had to sell a cow that his wife had reared in the village's famous animal market which brings together farmers and traders every Saturday during summer. Men, children, and sometimes women pull cows, *gamoosa*s, and their calves, as well as donkeys and their foals as they resist making the long walk in the dark to the market. Each type of livestock has a separate location of exchange and a separate site of their reproduction. *Gamoosa*s have the largest space in the market, having two different places of exchange. Mobile food carts circle the marketplace, and are in turn encircled by a fence that the governorate erected to fix its boundaries.

Traders from all over the Nile Delta arrive at the market with piles of cash and usually a guard. Until a decade ago, theft and burglary were almost unheard of in the countryside, but, as I was told, it has increased drastically. Farmers bring their livestock to "liquidate" it and cover their expenses, sometimes accruing from the regular needs of cultivation, and infrequently from unfortunate events such as illness. Farmers also sometimes sell their livestock to marry their sons, but this applies only to richer villagers who do not need the extra *gamoosa* or cow to subsist.

Said had to sell a cow to continue financing the growth of his cotton. In 2001, instead of selling livestock, he borrowed cash from a trader to finance his production. The deal entailed Said exchanging his cotton with the money lender, who fixed the price of the crop in advance, in exchange for the money he lent to Said. Said could have made more if he had not needed to borrow money. Therefore, in 2002, instead of borrowing cash, he chose to sell his cow.

At night, as Said and I discussed the day we had spent in the market, I learned that he had asked his oldest cousin to accompany us because he was more experienced and knew "how to talk to a trader." That morning, we had pulled the nervous cow to the site where other animals of her kind were kept. Merchants and brokers looked at and compared the different animals. A couple of traders approached the tense cow as she angrily swished her tail to get rid of the flies buzzing around her big body. A couple of slaps on her back, a quick weighing of the neck, and a brief look into the mouth were enough for most of the traders to offer a price. After we had spent two hours displaying Said's stock, a trader offered a price that convinced Said's cousin to start the bargaining. Said and his cousin did not want to stay long. As the sun rises, the price of a calf goes down. Calves cannot resist the heat as easily as mature animals. They may get sick quickly and even die in the marketplace. If this happens, not

[11] The word "livestock" first appeared in 1777 in Sheridan's *The School for Scandal* as two separate words. The word took a different form, live-stock, in Henry Fawcett's *Manual of Political Economy* in 1863 (Fawcett and Fawcett 1907; Sheridan and Heath 1984).

only does their price collapse, bringing down the entire investment that the farmers make, but it also affects the market in a bearish way. In such a case, farmers lose, and merchants make money.

After a long bargaining session, they shook hands and exchanged the money and the cow. We had an early lunch of *falafel* and pickles in the market and returned to the village shortly after the noon prayers, leaving the cow to be slaughtered in a few days in Mit Ghamr. The cotton could continue to grow more fiber; the cow lost her life; and Said had secured cash to invest in the plant stock.

The Gamoosa Dies, the Cotton Grows

Back in Kafr Gaffar, Said used some of the money to buy fertilizer from the very trader from whom he chose not to borrow cash. He had already applied some phosphorus fertilizer before the sowing and some nitrogen fertilizer before the thinning; yet the field needed more help as the plants required more nutritional elements as they grew.

Unregulated growth is also a problem, for the main objective of farmers is not to have the tallest and biggest plants, but to have as many healthy fiber bolls as possible on each branch of the cotton tree. To regulate this growth, farmers like Said also apply PIX, or mepiquat chloride, to the growing cotton, aiming for a balanced growth of the plant's reproductive components (bolls and flowers) and vegetative components (stems and leaves).

All the measures that farmers take to provide the cotton with suitable conditions for regulated growth also contribute to other competing species' growth in the same field. Other plants begin growing and "stealing" from the farmers' investment. They have to be uprooted and added back to the soil as fertilizers. This procedure of preventing nonprofitable life forms from growing is crucial for the farmers' income. Weeding also requires money, investment, and labor. Although herbicides are also used, cutting the weeds as the field is hoed is still the most frequent method of weed control in 'Izbet Sabri and Kafr Gaffar.

Not only other plants, but also insects find cotton attractive. Usually likened to war by farmers, scientists, and governments, "insect attacks" have to be resisted to achieve higher yields. Although pesticides are used extensively, this method is not the most effective against "the strongest enemy of farmers," as Ahmad and Gamal from 'Izbet Sabri called the cotton-leaf worm.[12] The life of this enemy is closely monitored not only

---

[12] *Spodoptera littoralis*, also called Egyptian cotton worm or Mediterranean Brocadem, was named by Boisduval in 1833, first appeared in Egypt in 1865, and became a serious

by Egyptian farmers but also by the cotton merchants of Alexandria and abroad.

The "enemy" is a moth whose attack on the fields is the most severe in the Nile Delta. When the humidity drops significantly in the South, the worm migrates to the north. An adult insect leaves around 1,000 to 1,500 eggs under each plant's leaf. The larvae feed at night and spend the day in the shadow. Because of the continuous agricultural activity, the worm always finds a nest for survival in Egypt. Especially during cotton season, it flourishes. The first two generations of moths survive on the crop that precedes the cotton, usually *berseem*, while the third and the fourth generations attack the cotton plant itself.

Thus, the war against the worm has to be waged twice. The soldiers in this war are children as young as seven, the mass labor stock of Egyptian agriculture. Children collect the affected parts of the leaves and then burn them in piles around the field. Labor control is essential in this procedure, because children can harm the plant as they collect the eggs. There is usually no reward for good work, yet mistakes are punished either through defamation, or at times beatings. In the latter case, the gang leader hits the child's hands with a wooden stick which he carries with him at all times. An overseer told me that he was warned by the field's owner not to hit children's hands, but their backs instead if necessary, for the hands are needed the most. "Their delicate hands and the length of their bodies help us get rid of this pest," a large landowner and cotton trader in Alexandria told me. These small hands are perhaps the cheapest and most abundant labor force behind the making of a commodity for the world market.

In late May and early June, each village cooperative recruits gangs of child workers from its vicinity. As a result of declining income, increasing population, and decreasing cotton production, the ranks of these gangs fill fast. The timing and administration of this operation are supervised by agricultural engineers working for the government. The recruited children wake up early in the morning. Bringing their lunch with them, they meet other child workers in the cooperative's local office. Each gang is composed of fifteen to thirty children overseen by a gang leader (*khouly*). The leaders are also recruited by the cooperative. The workday starts at 7:00 a.m. and ends at 6:00 p.m. Around 1:00 p.m., the gangs break for lunch and a short nap until 2:00.

Farmers spray pesticide on their fields before the operation starts. Children then enter the field, usually less than two days after the application, and spend thirteen hours, inhaling and touching the poison. It is

threat in 1881 and 1882 (Abdel Salam 1999), as the country was occupied by the British. For a discussion of the role of these struggles see (Mitchell 2002).

not uncommon for them to experience dizziness, vomiting, and diarrhea. Sick leaves are permitted, but punished by pay cuts. In 2002, the daily wage per child was less than eighty cents per day, slightly more than six cents an hour. In the month when the children collected the cotton-leaf worm eggs, their daily wage was not enough to buy one kilogram of lint cotton. After a working period of forty days, each child can make as much as thirty dollars. The money goes directly to the child's family, who invest it back in agricultural production.[13]

The money that Said's two sons earned was used to finance the family's cotton cultivation. Said and three of his neighbors had used the same water pump for the last three years. Although it was maintained frequently, the continuous usage recently started to create problems. Nothing can be as devastating as a broken pump for a cotton farmer, since a successful yield depends on the availability of irrigation whenever necessary. The pump belonged to a relatively more affluent neighbor who charged farmers like Said around USD 7 per acre for each irrigation round. Having a pump is a sign of affluence in the countryside, and buying a pump of one's own is a sign of take-off.

Said pooled some of the money he received from selling the cow with his sons' wages (a small amount, yet quite important for the sons' pride) and proposed to one of his neighbors a partnership to buy a pump. The neighbor could only contribute twenty-five percent of the total cost. Said nevertheless bought a new Indian-made pump from Mit Ghamr. It arrived in the village with great fanfare, and was installed by a relative of Said's who worked in the city as a mechanic. Other than the original partners, three more farmers were planning to use the pump to water their own fields. Each was to pay a specific amount; I was unable to learn how much exactly, most probably because the payment depended on the specific form of cooperation each farmer maintained with Said. The income from the pump would in the long run finance the pump itself.

It is usually argued that water is a scarce and misused resource in the Egyptian countryside and that its more efficient use can be achieved by making it a market commodity (World Bank 2001). The argument goes that if farmers pay for water, they will economize on their usage. Yet I was struck by how careful the farmers are in using only the necessary amount of water in their fields. First, pumps are operated with diesel engines, and diesel devours the scarcest resource in the countryside, cash. Second, because each farmer is required to work on the field to ensure the regular distribution of water on the soil's surface, the farmers cannot pump water at its maximum capacity. Moreover, pumping more water

[13] While I carried out my research, the official rate for USD 1 was LE 4.61. In the private sector and on the black market thought, the rate could go as high as LE 5.25.

than necessary would decrease the yield. Third, farmers usually share water pumps on a rotating basis. This effectively limits the amount of water they can use.

Egyptian farmers irrigate their cotton more frequently than Turkish farmers. Egyptian cotton requires more water because it stays on the field for a longer time, producing the legendary fiber length and strength. Beginning with sowing, the fields are watered every ten days until the third week of August. These lengthy hours of pump operation add a constant noise to the natural habitat of the countryside. As in Turkey, watering does not mean merely attaching a hose to a pump and waiting for the field to absorb the adequate amount of water. Although the Egyptian Delta is leveled well and resembles a massive open-air greenhouse, individual fields change constantly as a result of the dynamic interaction among plants, snakes, mice, humans, and insects. All farmers operate on the assumption that nature changes constantly. Farmers work nonstop in their fields to ensure that hoses and canals carry the water onto the field and that the soil receives an even distribution of water.

RESEARCH IN THE WILD COUNTRYSIDE

As irrigation becomes more sporadic and eventually stops in August to allow the plant time to dry before picking, discussions in the village about yield, price, and growing methods begin to dominate the conversations among farmers. Like Turkish farmers, Egyptian farmers carry out a heterodox and constant research on cotton by means of individual observation and consultation with agricultural engineers, technicians, traders, cooperative officials, and each other. Yet, there is one important distinction between the two farming people: Egyptians are more skeptical about the way in which the government representatives and agricultural engineers approach them, especially when it comes to cotton, the government crop. One reason for this mistrust is the sheer number of agricultural technicians and engineers in Egypt.

Egypt's towns and villages of the countryside teem with technicians, usually from nonfarming family backgrounds. They work in cooperative societies and the regional branches of the Ministry of Agriculture and Land Reclamation. According to Abdal Aziz, a cotton farmer with a tiny plot of fifteen *qirat* in Kafr Gaffar, these young experts "know nothing." I was sitting with him in front of a make-shift coffeehouse along the irrigation canal that passed through the middle of the village as he explained to me how these agricultural experts are seen: "These technicians live with us, but they don't talk to us." With a gentle move of his head he pointed to a passing young man wearing a white carefully ironed *galabiyya*.

What do you mean?
They don't talk to us. Even in the mosque, farmers have a different place. They come and tell us, do this, don't do that. They are so ignorant, they don't know the difference between *bamya* [okra] and *otn* [cotton]. But when it comes to preaching no one can compete with them.

Abdal Aziz's frustration with these trained technicians is indicative of the way farmers accumulate resentment about the way in which they are treated. As in Turkey, farmers are the first ones to be blamed for backwardness. It is not infrequent for a young technician, even with a rural background and residence, to speak to older farmers in a condescending tone. "It has always been like this. Farmers don't know anything. This is what they say about us. If I give them a sack of [cotton] seeds and a few *qirat* of land, those engineers could not grow cotton. Even if they did grow some, they can't survive with it. We [farmers] know more," Abdal Aziz continued. His father was sitting with us, unhappy about how his fifty-year-old son complained about other Egyptians. "We are a great nation," he interrupted Abdal Aziz with a touch of proud nationalism. "First Turks came here, then the British. We got rid of them and became a strong country again," he continued, later telling me that I was not the only Turk who lived in their village. I felt guilty, for my nationality was associated with the successor state of the Ottoman Empire, Egypt's occupier. "No, I don't mean Ottomans," he said laughingly as I offered him a clumsy apology. It turned out that a Turkish soldier named Gaffar who during World War I had fled from his regiment in the Ottoman army had settled in the village and never left. He had spent his life there, running a coffeehouse until he died in the 1950s.

Coffeehouses, like that of the late Gaffar, and to a certain extent mosques, serve as vibrant discussion forums for farmers. For the cotton farmers of 'Izbet Sabri and Kafr Gaffar, cotton-growing parallels a continuous learning process. Cultivating a plant for commercial use requires an expertise that must be constantly maintained. From irrigation schedules to different ways of planting, farmers always search for new ways to increase the yield. Having a higher yield and being a competent producer brings rewards whose importance extends beyond making a few hundred LE more. Being a skilful farmer is a source of great pride in the Egyptian and Turkish countryside.

Whether one is a trader or a farmer, being good at one's work depends on a number of things, one of the most important of which is research. Both groups carry out *research in the wild* in order to make sense of the world and create tools for interacting. Merchants even employ professional researchers, mostly economists, to domesticate the wild research they carry out in their own trading houses. Farmers with large plots of land sometimes employ researchers with a background in the agricultural sciences to study their fields for them. Small-scale growers carry out their own research, just as they farm the cotton by themselves. However, they operate on assumptions quite different from research experts. The practices of these smaller farms in Egypt and Turkey seem to work well, since they are not only able to sustain the growth of cotton, but also produce considerably higher yields than large landowners in their own countries and in the United States. Egypt's small land-holders have always had better yields than the U.S. cotton-growing companies. In 2002, the difference reached 206 kilograms per hectare in favor of Egyptian growers, which was almost twenty percent more than the yield of U.S. growers.[14]

When considering the way farmers carry out research in the wild, one is struck by their relativism concerning the meaning of nature. Like the merchants in their refusal to impose one single logic of operation onto markets, farmers shy away from defining a static externality. They adjust the timing of their entire work on the field based on their research. Even the content of the main processes of cotton cultivation is altered according to this dynamic universe of which they are a part. A farmer's habitat is always changing; it is not a static entity.

Making sense of this change is governed by two methods of learning in Kafr Gaffar and 'Izbet Sabri: observation and discussion.[15] All farmers carry out incessant study of their fields and habitat. They consult their neighbors to test the validity of their observations. Furthermore, they compare their own conclusions with those of other farmers in an open forum, for example, in the coffeehouses. For two main reasons, this constant research activity in the wild is not immediately visible to those experts who pass by the village. First, the ignorance of experts is fed by the ideological position that locates farmers as naturally backward in the national order of things. Secondly, by and large experts lack a language to translate the farmers' experiences, observations, and conclusions into their own language of science.

These two universes of research do not communicate often. When they do happen, these exchanges lead to surprising results. The right and capacity to speak the language of the other are usually granted to the schooled and cultured expert. Without exception, these experts talk to farmers as if they were not adults and use "simple" words to help them understand the complexity of what the experts know. In one instance, an expert explained the merits of genetically engineered seeds to an Egyptian farmer by telling him that he could grow a type of cotton that would resist

---

[14] USDA Foreign Agricultural Service. In 2002, the U.S. yield was 790 kg/ha, while Egypt's yield was 996 kg/ha.

[15] Note that these are also the two methods formal scientists use every day.

pest attacks. He told the farmer that "some part of the pest was injected into the cottonseed." The lobbying of farmers and Third World governments to accept the BT cotton seed technology has continued for some time now. Only recently has it started to reach the Egyptian countryside, despite the government's resistance. Mohammad, a farmer with a large landholding in Kafr Gaffar, told me that he was amazed to hear that the pest was injected into the seed. "I told him that it is good not to have pests in the field. But you take the pest outside the field and put it in the cotton itself," he added as he told me about the conversation he had with an engineer. Farmers also translate their language when they talk to the experts. They use "simple" words to explain their points; yet, without exception, they fail to communicate their way of seeing things. The very structure of the exchange is skewed toward the way experts perceive issues.

Discussions come to a halt as the harvest starts. The work is so time consuming that, until the cotton is sold and the cash secured, farmers can barely find time to spare to talk in public spaces other than mosques. Even mosque attendance drops during the harvest.

The Harvesting and Marketing of Cotton

The cotton harvest starts in the south as early as in late July and moves gradually northward toward Lower Egypt. In the Delta, cotton-picking begins in late September and terminates in October. All the cotton grown by the approximately 250,000 farmers is sold in the 3,630 cotton marketplaces, the *halaqa*s.[16]

The harvest is carried out by reactivating the networks already shaped and revised during the previous stages of the cotton's growth. Small farmers form cooperatives and pool their labor by bringing together worker gangs. Each family contributes with almost all of its members, as long as they are not too old to spend the entire day in the field. Each labor-pooling group has varying and quite complex ways of reconciling the differences between the distinct levels of contribution that each family makes to the harvest. The difference is usually settled with cash to be paid after the harvest.

Like pest control, the main harvest work is carried out by child workers whose parents control their labor. Both in Kafr Gaffar and 'Izbet Sabri, child workers pick approximately half of the entire harvest. The rest is picked by older workers of both genders. If cotton pickers are unpaid workers who are a part of a labor-pooling arrangement, the gangs are composed of workers of all ages. As soon as the first round of picking is

---

[16] The estimates are from Krenz et al. (2001).

completed in the fields of the contributors to the labor pool, the workers start to pick cotton for money in other farmers' fields.

The daily wages are usually slightly more than USD 1 per day. In 2001, adult male workers in the two villages were earning approximately USD 1.50, whereas adult female workers' daily wage was USD 1.26. Children were paid USD 1.10. These wage differentials do not necessarily reflect the amount of work one performs. Like Turkish female workers, Egyptian women claim to pick as much cotton as men. My observations also support their position. A discussion of whether men and women can pick similar amounts, however, is never entertained by male farmers.

Cotton-picking requires much time and energy. Especially for children, working in the field becomes progressively more difficult as the temperature rises. The overseers usually control a group of twenty to thirty-five children. The labor contractors set work quotas to be met everyday. Unlike in Turkey, the Egyptian daily wage is not dependent on the amount of cotton picked. Workers do not have any incentive to work faster, and children do not have any reason to work at all, other than being forced to. As the days pass, their feet become swollen and their hands riddled with cuts from the spikes of the cotton bolls. Moving around the plants whose giant bodies are larger than their own, the children's hands slowly fill their small bags and eventually empty them into a larger jute sack. The overseer, with the help of other workers, then presses the cotton to decrease its volume so that the sack can be sewn shut. Finally, the presence of the landowner becomes visible, as the cotton is exchanged from the workers' hands into his own. Claiming the cotton, he will sell it in the hope to profit from its yield.

Controlling the children in the fields gets progressively more difficult after the third week of continuous work. After sunset, when the children no longer have the energy to enjoy a celebration, overseers use competitive games to enhance work performance by announcing "the fastest kid of the day." Overseers also make up cotton-related games to entertain the children. For example, in the fields where I worked, the overseer would shout: "Where are your hands?" The children would reply together: "On the cotton." The overseer would then ask: "Where is cotton?" Children would answer the question even louder: "In the sack!" This and many other rhymes would be repeated many times as the slow hours of work passed. Yet, these games, "fun" activities, and rewards are never enough to sustain a long work day. Children begin to play their own games, start wandering around the field, and frequently slow down the work as they become exhausted. Whenever an overseer cannot make children work faster, he resorts to physical punishment, for his own success in meeting quotas depends on the children's discipline.

The labor contractors for whom these overseers work extend credit to workers and their children. Similar to the Kurdish labor contractors of

Turkey, some of them own grocery stores in the village. Workers shop in these stores in exchange for finding work and sharing some of their income with the shopkeeper-labor contractors. These store owners also buy wheat and rice from farmers, storing the produce in order to sell it to back to villagers, farmers, and others, in exchange for either cash or later labor settlement.

The end of the harvest and the selling of the cotton usually happen at the same time. There are even instances of selling the cotton before the harvest. These local forms of forward-trading emerge due to the farmers' financial weakness. Informal local petty traders who operate only in the village and do not carry out large operations organize this type of exchange. Their activity is limited by their storage facilities and financial strength. Moreover, because they are frequently farmers, they do not have the time to forge larger trading networks. These farmer-traders usually buy the villagers' cotton by financing its cultivation by direct means (such as lending money), or by indirect means (such as lending fertilizers or pesticides). After the harvest, the lender pays less for the indebted farmers' cotton than other competing buyers. This first round of exchange is completely invisible in Egypt's national statistics. In 'Izbet Sabri, ten percent of the cotton-growing households sold their cotton in this way. In Kafr Gaffar, I could not locate the exact percentage because of the large population of cotton-growers; however, one can safely assume that the percentage is not less than in 'Izbet Sabri.

After this first round of exchange terminates, the smallest and poorest farmers disappear altogether from the marketing of seed cotton. In the following rounds of trading, private registered traders, public companies and cooperatives become the major buyers of cotton. Almost all of the seed cotton grown in Egypt is brought to the 3,630 *halaqa*s or cotton rings, organized and maintained by the Public Bank for Development and Agricultural Credit (PBDAC). Each *halaqa* is run by a government-appointed ring manager. The manager is assisted by two employees, a secretary who takes care of the paperwork and a person who weighs the cotton. These open-air sites of markets are guarded at night by security personnel, again hired by the PBDAC. In the beginning of the seed cotton marketing year, each *halaqa* is assigned to one buyer, either a cooperative or a trading house. These buyers also send their company representatives to work full-time in the *halaqa*s.

Once a week, a grading expert working for the Cotton Arbitration and Testing General Organization (CATGO) visits the *halaqa* to grade the cotton and calculate the ginning outturn. In the *halaqa* I observed, however, the expert visited twice a week. Two *halaqa*s, one of a cooperative and the other of a private merchant, had decided to pool their resources and form a joint *halaqa* so that they could bring in an expert two days per week. This move decreased the time they needed to price and grade the cotton.

*Halaqa*s operate everyday between 9:00 a.m. and 5:00 p.m., accepting farmers' cotton in exchange for a receipt issued by the *halaqa* secretary. The farmer's name, the crop's weight, and the receipt number are written on the jute sack containing the cotton. Farmers usually leave the *halaqa* and return when an expert arrives to grade the cotton. There are eight grades of each seed cotton type in Egypt. After examining a sample from all of the bales, experts assign a grade and write it on the bale.[17] This is the moment when cotton as a generic term is translated into the language of the market. The very act of translation is the first step of the documentary circulation on which the cotton is going to embark soon in the world market.

Farmers have a right to contest the expert's grading results, and usually they do. It is frequently argued that farmers are not aware of the price differentials between different grades and types of cotton. One of the main reasons for the countryside's underdevelopment is blamed upon the farmers' ignorance about the quality of their crop.[18] But I have yet to meet a farmer who is not aware of grade differences and their effect on the price of seed cotton. This argument which draws on an ideological assumption about the farmer's intellect is an example of trained ignorance that strangely posits that a farmer, whose entire cash income is dependent on his cotton's price, would not know the fact that better grades earn a premium.

Other qualities such as the type and color of cotton being equal, the weight and grade of cotton move the price significantly. This is why the role of the employees who grade and weigh cotton is critical. It is commonsense in the countryside that one kilogram is never the same in two different *halaqa*s. Furthermore, the same cotton can be graded in many different ways, depending on which *halaqa* one visits. This is never a problem of standardization or calibration. In the *halaqa*s allocated to private trading houses, it is common to have heavier "kilograms" than in public company *halaqa*s. Moreover, CATGO graders who visit private trading house *halaqa*s are "visited" in advance by the representatives of these companies.

Khaled was one of these frequent visitors. I met him in a regional branch of a private trading house. He was responsible for overseeing the purchasing of cotton in more than fifteen *halaqa*s. In the two days that I spent with him, we visited nine *halaqa*s in the governorate of Daqahliyyah. Because of the political nature of these market sites, I confirmed in advance that the farmers of Kafr Gaffar, which is located in this governorate, did

---

[17] These grades, from the best to the worst, are the following: X, X̲, XX, X̲X̲, XXX, O, O̲, OO.

[18] See Bank (1993); Krenz, Holtzman et al. (2001).

not sell their produce in any of these *halaqa*s, as I did not want to be present should a clash between company and farmers erupt. Before the harvest, Khaled had been responsible for collecting information, conducting research, and finding ways to communicate the merchants' interests to the farmers. After the harvest, however, his work was to make sure that the trading house acquired the desired amount of cotton, paying no more than what he called the "target price." "What do you mean by target price?" I asked him during a lunch break in a gas station.

> You know we have floor prices in Egypt. We pay farmers less than these prices. Of course, it is business. They sell, we buy. I want to pay as little as possible, the peasants want to get as much as possible. It is natural.
>
> *So the target price is lower than the floor price. Is it legal?*
>
> I don't know. But we pay cash. Yes, government companies and cooperatives pay more, but peasants get only eighty percent of the price. For the rest, they have to wait. When we pay, we pay the whole thing. So although our prices are less, peasants sell to us.
>
> *What about grading and scales? I know that in Turkey, grading can be affected. Or the scales can be fixed before weighing. There are even cases of fixing the ginning machine to produce a smaller outturn.*
>
> It never happens here.

Farmers strongly disagree. The underpaid CATGO graders have no incentive to ignore the traders' interests, which can be simply summarized as buying good-grade cotton for a cheaper price. One way of doing this is "not to like the cotton" and to constantly complain about it to increase the bargaining position. One part of Khaled's job is "not to like the cotton," as he put it. Farmers nervously bring their cotton to *halaqa*s and meet these eternally unhappy people who buy their cotton almost unwillingly. Being a good farmer is one of the most important sources of pride in the countryside, but farmers lose their pride to merchants in the market place. Whether in Turkey or Egypt, as amateur actors in the market theater, farmers are less experienced in deploying technologies of price-making.

Khaled has another important responsibility: he encourages graders to be more pessimistic in their judgment. As I sat and watched them argue, he lobbied a CATGO grader for almost an hour to decrease the grade of a series of bales. The grader told him that he already was "careful" when grading. He could not downgrade an already graded shipment. "They would kill me, are you kidding?" he asked rhetorically and walked away from us. Khaled's main objective was not to change the grader's mind, of course, for he knew that it was almost impossible to change the grade. It was an act of maintaining the grader's pessimistic stance. Along with many other forms of gifts, graders receive constant attention from private

Figure 10   An Egyptian farmer entering a *halaqa*
to sell his cotton.

firms' employees in these sites of exchange and production. The grader's
translation contributes greatly to the production of the very value of the
exchange objects to be circulated in the documentary realm of the world
market (figure 10).

Farmers resist the downgrading of their cotton in three major ways.
First, like traders, they lobby the grader to influence his translation. The
very maintenance of carefully created hierarchies between "ignorant"
farmers and "developed" experts has concrete effects that contribute to
the making of the price on the ground. Farmers deploy political technologies of price-making (such as lobbying, acting, performing, and
bargaining), but always from a less advantageous position, since they belong to a "lower grade" agency. It is easy to observe how farmers feel in
traders' offices in Turkey, or in *halaqa*s in Egypt. They encounter a power

field whose dynamics are maintained and produced to work against their interests. Farmers use different ways to counteract the effects of this mercantile field. A performance of helplessness slightly helps in these engagements, as it aims to directly affect the conscience of the translation agents.

Second, farmers exert pressure by using anger. There is a tacit assumption of those who look down upon farmers that one should avoid the "wrath of the peasant." Since they are considered "irrational and violent actors who follow their emotions," farmers' "emotional" responses seriously limit the traders' choice and acts. "They would kill me," was the response of the grader whom Khaled lobbied to downgrade the cotton. Although many urban bullies and police have killed and wounded hundreds of farmers in the last decade, it is the farmers themselves who are regarded as violent. In both instances, farmers to a certain extent adopt an agency that is produced for them and exploit this subjectivity's ambiguous configuration to strengthen their relatively weaker agency.

Third, farmers may threaten to withdraw their cotton from a certain *halaqa*. This is the most effective, yet the least frequently used method to empower their position vis-à-vis the traders. It cannot be employed often, because moving cotton around takes up much precious time and energy. Still, it does happen. 'Izbet Sabri farmers took thirty percent of the cotton they produced from one *halaqa* to another because the farmers could not win their case in the *halaqa* closest to their village. The earlier consolidation in their standing against the "land entrepreneur" helped them to forge a common stance more easily. Previous forms of labor-pooling also provided them with means to rally more quickly. The farmers hired a truck and moved the entire produce to another *halaqa*, where they had a "better translation" and, as a result, a better price. This price was still lower than the floor price, but it was paid in cash. This option cannot be used frequently, for it is too costly and time consuming. Richer farmers can move from *halaqa* to *halaqa* by investing in a rented truck.

Not all *halaqa*s are the same in the eyes of the farmers. For the cotton-growers of Kafr Gaffar and 'Izbet Sabri, the main difference arises from the "owner" of the *halaqa*. Although these sites of the market cannot be "owned," as they are by definition public spaces, in everyone's imagination they are categorized as public and private. The market is a personal place for Egyptian peasants.

Public *halaqa*s, assigned to government trading companies, are different in that cotton growers have fewer contentious encounters there. Although working for the same CATGO, their graders are neither pessimists nor optimists. Scales seem to work properly. However more desirable these public *halaqa*s appear, their inability to provide farmers with cash immediately after the purchase makes them less competitive. They pay more, but they pay later. After the harvest, almost all farmers find themselves in debt. The only way of disentangling themselves from the webs of indebtedness is to find cash immediately. This is why the same "floor prices" of public and private companies are different when seen from the vantage point of the farmers. In the Egyptian countryside, private floor prices are always lower than public floor prices.

The best price is always the floor price that the government announces. Since the liberalization of the cotton sector, it has become a norm to announce floor prices in accordance with world prices. Yet, as for the merchants of Alexandria, the world price is a mystery to the Egyptian government. One has to make a political choice to locate it somewhere, and the government chooses Alcotexa's season opening export lint cotton price as the price representative of the world market. The translation of the world price into the floor price is carried out in the following way: first, the export price of lint cotton in USD, as announced by Alcotexa, is converted into Egyptian pounds (LE), using the official exchange rate. This automatically transfers the difference between the official and the informal rates to the traders. Second, a fobbing expense is subtracted from the lint price. The price of cotton seed and the cost of extraneous matter are then deduced from the remaining amount. Finally, the international marketing cost is deduced. The remaining amount is announced as the floor price for seed cotton to be used in the *halaqa*s.

These floor prices are prosthetic prices in nature, for the actual prices that farmers receive are usually below the floor price. The floor price aims to keep the actual price above subsistence levels so that farmers do not stop growing cotton in Egypt altogether. Similar to the associate price of Alexandria, the rehearsal price of Izmir, or the futures price of cotton of New York, a floor price is a prosthetic device produced by governments to effect price realization in actual market settings. However, it would be misleading to regard this price form as an example of government intervention to the otherwise naturally working market, primarily because the price from which the Egyptian government derives the floor price is the associate price of Alcotexa, the institution of traders of the "free market." Second, as I have argued in chapters 1, 2, and 3, all forms of market prices are prosthetic in nature. They inform the making of actual market prices through pricing prosthetics. The Egyptian floor price, thus, is no less prosthetic than the original market price from which it derives—that is, the associate price.

Like other prosthetic prices, the floor price is hardly the actual price paid to the farmers. Prosthetic price forms may look very complicated, but there is one simple price for farmers: the actual price, or, in other words, whatever they are paid. The actual price is always less than the floor price announced annually by the Egyptian government. Because of the deals that indebted farmers make with informal petty traders, cotton-growers end up receiving cash settlements against their debt. The price that money-lending traders pay is, without exception, significantly lower than the floor prices.

In addition, the grading of seed cotton in *halaqa*s creates price differentials that become invisible in the way in which the floor prices are deployed. Lint cotton, whose export price is used as a constant in making the floor price, has more intratype grades than seed cotton. The pessimism or optimism of graders, the false scales and bad ginning outturns, and the very mismatch between grading seed and lint cotton all result in depression of the price of seed cotton as its quality increases vis-à-vis lint cotton. Even if one still uses the problematic concept of "government intervention" in markets, its basic form in Egypt helps private merchants make money off the farmers.[19] Lint cotton has thirteen intratype grades whereas seed cotton has only eight. The monetary value of one grade difference in seed cotton is proportionally less than that of lint cotton (Krenz et al. 2001). The very nature of pricing prosthetics in Egypt does not provide farmers with an incentive to produce better-quality cotton. Egyptian traders make more money than farmers when farmers produce better cotton.

CONCLUSION

The processes of cotton exchange and production in the semiurban countryside of Egypt are informed by power dynamics similar to the ones I have discussed in the previous chapter. The making of markets draws on simultaneous processes of the exchange and production of commodities, their translations, research results, and struggles between farmers, children, overseers, graders, traders, pests, and many other agents who want to use the cotton for satisfying their own needs. This chapter has prioritized the vantage point of adult cotton growers in order to approach the creation of a world market of cotton in locales such as the cotton fields of rural Egypt.

From the soil preparation until the sale of the cotton, the farmers of these two sites of the global cotton market, Kafr Gaffar and 'Izbet Sabri, engage in a multitude of struggles. Following the cotton's growth allows

---

[19] Note that even these forms of "intervention" in markets are not solely a government capacity, for the actual prosthetic prices in New York are maintained by formulas (such as that of Black and Scholes), rules (such as the regulation that the futures market cannot move more than 300 points a day), and simultaneous interventions in the market by its multiple agents of making. See chapter 1 for a more detailed analysis of this point.

these engagements to become visible in the context of neoliberal market reforms, which aim at forging a free market in Egypt and connecting this market to an external entity called the global market. The first two sections of the chapter have shown that market reforms have reshaped relations of power in the countryside and, paradoxically, even acted against their own objectives of institutionalizing formalized market rules. From providing a net for illegal trading to increased violence in the countryside, the reforms have resulted in producing a variety of informalities. However, I argue that it is misleading to see these reforms as projects of letting the market work by itself, for they are making the object of their reformation. As they empower traders, the reforms create regimes of exchange and production that may lead to the disappearance of the most important agricultural market commodity of Egypt.

The growth of cotton requires many forms of cooperative living among farmers, animals, plants, and the environment. *Berseem* lives longer in the field, allowing farmers to harvest fodder for their *gamoosas*, whose death may occasionally provide cash for the growth of cotton. Children are forced to work to wage war against the farmer's worst enemy, the cotton worm. The cotton worm is eradicated by the small hands of children. As the cotton grows and nears its final death, farmers forge more coalitions to survive. They use complex mechanisms of labor exchange in their cooperatives, carrying out research to determine the best way to grow cotton, testing their results, and discussing them in such forums as the coffeehouse. These activities are performed at the same time as the farmers wage a political struggle against neoliberal market reforms in order to subsist. Farmers struggle against pests, as well as new entrepreneurs who show up in the village with their bullies. Whether registered under their name or under that of a new entrepreneur, the land becomes weak as the plant stock depletes its nutrients. Farmers use fertilizers to give life back to the soil; yet such activities require cash, a resource that farmers lack. They borrow from traders, who at the end of the growing season claim the farmers' cotton for less money.

The farmers who do not find themselves in debt can make it from the cotton field to the *halaqa*, only to encounter another field of struggle. The cotton has to be translated into the language of the market by graders whose manner of grading changes significantly as one moves from public to private-sector *halaqas*. The invisible hands of the market hit the farmers hardest in the private sector. Moreover, the very experience of performing an exchange, from bargaining to weighing, works against the farmers' interests.

Cotton growers, however, are not entirely helpless in this essentially political field of cotton trade. They forge innovative methods of resisting both the problematic translation of their produce and other technologies that traders use to depress the floor price. The peasants' success is limited, as market reforms essentially work to empower private merchants. Even the formation of floor prices works against the farmers' interests, transferring their wealth to that of the traders in two ways. First, the government's pricing prosthesis, the floor price, is a derivative of the associate price of the merchants of Alexandria, who follow the making of other "global" prosthetic prices as they take shape in Izmir, New York, or Memphis. By letting mercantile interests dictate the actual prices in the *halaqa*s, the government protects merchants, providing them with a tool that they cannot produce together. The floor price makes it possible for farmers to produce the best cotton of the world, only to survive under extremely difficult conditions. Second, as farmers produce better-quality cotton, merchants end up earning more money without a relative increase in the farmers' income because of the very difference between the grades of lint and seed cotton.

This universe of the market, as seen from the experience of Egyptian farmers, cannot be analytically located by imposing boundaries that attach categorically separate logics of economic, scientific, social, or political encounter. Throughout any stage of the cotton's growth, one cannot locate a boundary that demarcates a pure logic of operation. This does not mean that markets take place in cultural contexts, or that they draw on encounters embedded in social relations. The seemingly separate worlds of the cultural, the social, and the economic, and the multiple interstitial spaces that connect them to each other in the form of political culture or social economy are produced not by the interaction of farmers, workers, children, plants, cows, traders, and all other agents of relations of production and exchange, but by the researchers who assume independent spheres of life in the struggle to make a global market. In Egypt's countryside, one can observe neither a separate field of interaction, nor an embedded form of coexistence. The cotton fields and *halaqa*s that dot the Egyptian countryside are fields of power that interact in multiple ways to make a global cotton market.

CONCLUSION

What Is a Global Market?

AT THE BEGINNING OF THE twenty-first century, two hegemonic approaches inform our understanding of markets. The neoclassical perspective argues that it is the almost natural coming together of supply and demand that sets the price and makes the market. Institutionalists bring into the analysis the social context of this interaction and argue that market exchange is embedded in society. Drawing on new directions in the study of markets, *Market Threads* proposes that neither of these approaches can fully capture how markets are made and maintained on the ground.

Markets are neither asocial mechanisms of price setting, nor are they embedded in society. As many traders and farmers suggested during my research, such a magical mechanism would help them save much time spent maintaining the market and growing its commodity. An empirical showing that markets are not asocial mechanisms of exchange does not mean that they are social in nature. Various forms of institutionalist approach have provided social theory with a powerful perspective from which to present claims against the universalizing tendencies of the neoclassical approach. The strength of institutionalism in analyzing the conditions that make markets possible, however, is not reflected in its analysis of concrete market practices and price-making functions.

The findings of this book call for moving beyond both neoclassical and institutionalist analyses of markets. Instead, it makes clear the urgent need to study relations of economization as fields of power made and maintained by various human and nonhuman agents that confront each other on asymmetrical platforms. The study of a market means presentation of a description and critical analysis of a field of economization by opening up three main forms of engagement in market exchange. First, one has to study how markets are used to organize the production and exchange of commodities. Second, markets should be approached as arrangements or *agencements* that bring together market devices, rules and regulations, price realization strategies, discourses, selective deployment of scientific knowledge, and maintenance logistics. Third, markets are areas of confrontation among various human and nonhuman actors. In the absence of economic equality, these areas draw on multiple relations of domination between genders, generations, classes, and human and nonhuman actors. To understand a global market means to make sense of the constitution of such a field of power.

This book has analyzed the three facets of a market field by examining how global, regional, and local actors make a world market on the ground. Focusing on price-making and the circulation of commodities, the first two chapters presented an analysis of the making of a global market from the vantage point of global traders. Through studying the processes that make world prices in multiple forms, from the A Index to NYBOT futures, chapter 1 demonstrated that the world market price of a commodity is a prosthetic price used by traders to make actual prices. In this context, the process of price realization is performed and maintained by constant interventions in markets, through different forms of perception, standardization of the object of exchange, various calculating tools, rumors, and indices. It is also at times formatted with the help of the direct intervention of market boards and formulas, drawing on assumptions about the neoclassical political economy of things. Markets are constantly intervened in and maintained. This is their condition of possibility.

In the world cotton market, realization of the price is a relation of power in itself, for the actual price is not realized in the spatial universe of supply and demand. Yet the acceptance, to a certain extent, of an unmediated relationship of causality between what is called supply and demand and the price is one of the major interventions in the processes of price realization. This intervention is carried out by moves such as embedding Marshall's supply and demand graph in the cotton options market through the Black and Scholes formula. Thus, it is simultaneously correct and incorrect to argue that markets are made by the coming together of the forces of supply and demand.

In order for supply and demand to have any effect on the market, they should be located by market agents. Prices do not move without people acting. And people act usually, but not always, after having decided on specific actions. Market forces have to be perceived and processed by traders. If we have to consider representations and perceptions to better understand markets, then our analyses have to leave the comfortable world of realism and enter the shaky and uncertain universe of the indeterminate power fields.

In all the moments of world price realization, the taking for granted of a correspondence between a representation and "reality" is a technology of market power. Yet even this correspondence is suspended, depending on the moment of exchange, for without taking strategic breaks from these assumptions of correspondence it is not possible to execute successful trading decisions. This is true not only because the indexical nature of world prices makes it tautological to claim a correspondence, but also because such strategic suspensions are ways of relating to a market that trades on perceptions.

The *prosthetic price* is a key concept for understanding how prices are realized in markets. In order for prices to be made in a market field, like that of the global cotton market, prosthetic prices are produced and deployed to equip those who exchange cotton with tools, competencies and resources. The actual price of cotton is made through the deployment of various prosthetic prices, such as the "World Price of Cotton," the "Adjusted World Price," and the "A Index." These prosthetic prices do not set the actual worth of a bale of cotton, but inform in various ways the realization of actual cotton prices.

This book has shown that, without framing the market fields, traders become disabled actors. It is by making and using frames, such as market reports, that traders imagine a unitary temporal topography of exchange in the world. World prices are also realized through these frameworks. The fact that a world price of cotton, such as the A Index, does not set the monetary worth of a bale of cotton means that the world price of cotton is neither real nor fictional. It is a prosthetic price, a tool of engagement with the market field, which enables traders to imagine a market field.

The tools of price realization are developed through various technologies of pricing prosthetics in a market field, where neoclassical assumptions and discourses, institutions such as the New York Board of Trade; architectural, institutional, and formulary designs like trading pits and options pricing techniques; regulations like those of the Commodity Futures Trading Commission; and scientific interventions such as that of the Black and Scholes options pricing formula interact in multiple and heterogeneous ways.

Chapter 1 has shown that price-making in global markets cannot be seen as a mere price-setting mechanism, for a number of reasons. First, price-making cannot be captured by drawing on the analogy of a technical mechanism. It can be understood only by using a dynamic perspective that incorporates an analysis of the deployment of technical devices in price realization. Hence, world cotton market prices are not merely set. They are realized, contested, made, and unmade on a dynamic platform of trade. It is in the price realization moments of the world markets that actual prices are made by allowing them to appear real; they are conceived vividly as real and converted into actual money. To make an actual price, the necessary condition is to realize it within this process. This is why I propose to use "price realization" instead of "price-setting," for the term better captures the processes of price-making. The market price is made possible and visible by pricing prosthetics, not by the coming together of two lines of supply and demand, as depicted first by Cournot and then reproduced by Marshall.

This is why this book concludes that markets are neither embedded in social relations, nor disembedded from them. They are fields of power operating on dynamic and heterogeneous platforms of power relations. The study of markets, then, requires researchers to locate how different market participants engage in and understand the sustenance, production, and contestation of market fields of power. For this, the analyses of markets have to further open the black box of prosthetic and actual price realization processes. It is therefore necessary to discuss the everyday universe of world trade.

The goal of chapter 2 was to do exactly that. There, the argument moved away from the processes of price realization and focused on how commodities circulate in the world. The constellation of relationships makes the price obtained through the deployment of prosthetic technologies—such as indexing, enframing and guesstimating—come together, interact, and resolve in various rounds of exchanging cotton. It is the everyday practice of exchange in world markets that one has to examine more closely in order to see how markets are made in a clearer way. The market activities neither halt when a market price is made, nor terminate when an actual price is made. The commodity has to be exchanged, and at times the execution of trading decisions collapses, bringing down with it both actual and prosthetic prices.

Chapter 2 demonstrated that the execution of contracts in world markets—in other words, the activities that enable the circulation of commodities—is made possible by two simultaneous market activities. First, the actual exchange of cotton is reproduced in a documentary route of circulation, which concurrently provides buyers and sellers with instruments to make possible the actual exchange of cotton. These activities require the introduction of a whole new set of actors to the world of the market. From the point when the cotton bales are gathered, until the time when they are claimed by their new owner abroad, warehouses cut samples from the bales, send them to the USDA; the USDA's human and nonhuman graders classify the bales and then assign permanent identification numbers. Based on these data, cotton bales acquire an electronic warehouse receipt issued by EWR Inc., after which they are made ready to be shipped by traffic departments and freight forwarders. These market agents create a documentary route of circulation, putting together endless paperwork representing everything in the trading relationship from the exchange act to the price of the commodity and the commodity itself.

It is the creation of this documentary circulation that allows for the actual circulation of commodities: yet even this vast parallel world is not enough to ensure the successful execution of a contract. Each step of representation opens up new possibilities of contestation, for the very circulation of commodities relies on a correspondence between the flow of things and their representations. At any point, depending on one's market position or the way in which circulation is carried out, the correspondence could be challenged.

The "jungle of risk," as the president of a forwarding company put it in chapter 2, has to be contained. This requirement introduces the services of controllers and arbitrators, whose job is to ensure that the documentary route of circulation matches the actual route of circulation. Yet their capacity is of a limited nature, for there are always loopholes in these jungles, no matter what one does to contain the correspondence. A perfect match between actual and documentary routes of circulation is not possible, because there are no objective criteria to which one can refer in order to check the level of correspondence. Perfection or imperfection of contracts is not relevant here, because the correspondence to perfection—that is, "the reality"—cannot be guaranteed, since trade contracts never refer to anything exogenous to the worlds they imagine.

Controllers do their best to monitor the actual circulation of things and compare it with their documentary representations. Their reports serve as reference points in arbitration cases. However, if one does not recognize the power of the arbitration board or the power in the sales contract, or does not honor the awards that the arbitral authority issues, the maintenance and thus the making of an actual market no longer function.

This is why it is crucial for merchants and traders to introduce the second set of market practices that enable the circulation of commodities. These create a supporting universe of networks within the two routes of the documentary and the actual circulation of things. Both their capital and its effective deployment are based on traders' knowledge and networks, as the vice-president of an international cotton trading house has described in chapter 2: Knowledge is an instrumental activity used to build the capacity to manage risk, to contain the jungle. For this, the merchant needs a network—"a bunch of people coming together," a "human bridge"—constructed by agents all around the world, who reach customers and "know" them. "[W]ithout a network, without having these human bridges to reach other people, you can have neither capital nor knowledge," as the international merchant put it.

Nothing is as central to a successful trading relationship as networking. Nothing is as effective for networking as learning about and meeting people and exchanging gifts with them. Regularly organized business meetings provide traders with opportunities to establish new relations and renew older ones. Sending e-mails, letters, and cards strengthens already constructed human bridges. It is not only commodities, however, that travel over these bridges. Gifts also circulate during the networking activity among international traders. These gifts maintain the human bridges.

The making and maintenance of world markets in the documentary and actual routes of commodity circulation are thus made possible by a different kind of engagement with the market. It is through constructing these "human bridges"—strange tools of production that are simultaneously human and nonhuman—that it becomes possible to know the market and make it. Gift and commodity exchanges do not exclude each other. Gift exchange is a technology of power for those who exchange commodities.

To summarize, the world cotton market, as seen from the vantage point of international traders, is based on the simultaneous circulation of commodities and their representations. The agents of these routes of circulation, however, are more numerous than the immediate universe of the two market agents of the neoclassical market view. These agents build a platform from the interaction of capital, knowledge, and network in order to relate to and profit from the world market. Yet this handful of global traders needs thousands of local agents to maintain the world market and continue working on bridges of commodities, gifts, and documents.

As a result, a full understanding of the world markets of cotton requires the story of the markets' making to be written from the vantage point of the other side of the bridge as well: from that of local traders and farmers. Global things, like the world price of cotton, are forms of collectives that bring together particularities by indexing them. These global things, such as the A Index, are derivatives of their own local articulations. The practices of their derivation are based on various technologies of indexing, such as the pricing routine of Cotlook Ltd. This is why this book has argued that the global market is a universe of indexical possibility. Such a universe is produced not only by bringing together dyadic encounters of exchange, but also through the making of the very prices of distant yet related regional markets. It is only after rendering visible the making of dyadic actual prices in their local geographies of production that it becomes possible to produce global prosthetic prices. In other words, an analysis of the world market will be incomplete if one does not bring into the discussion its local articulations from the "original" location, where the indexical nature of the market is derived.

BRIDGING THE GLOBAL AND THE REGIONAL

In chapters 3 and 4, I changed the vantage point for approaching global markets from that of international merchants to that of regional traders. The processes of global market-making, from pricing prosthetics to market maintenance, are always articulated in particular regions, whether in Izmir, Turkey, or Alexandria, Egypt. This book, however, has shown that these regional localities are no more original—that is, closer to an authentic locality—than the global things from which they are derived.

The interaction of these different locations of the global market should not be assumed to resemble a trade relationship between a "global" merchant and a "local" sales broker. Such relations between seemingly global agents and local intermediaries are encounters between different agents who have asymmetrical mercantile platforms in terms of capital, knowledge, and network; yet all of them are still local agents. The interaction of the global market and local markets is a relationship of derivation, not encounter.

How, then, are these seemingly more "original" regional prices made? Chapters 3 and 4 focused on the relations of exchange and the various technologies of their production, as deployed by regional and local traders based in Izmir, Turkey, and Alexandria, Egypt. These chapters argued that global processes as derived encounters are made and informed by regional relations of marketing. However, the technologies of creating a regional market price are not categorically different from the indexing of a global price. Both global and regional price realizations rely on concrete practices informed by relations that structure the traders' daily encounters. Chapter 3 demonstrated that the practices of price realization deployed by traders in the Izmir Mercantile Exchange (IME) create an original price form that is neither entirely prosthetic nor actual: the *rehearsal price*. This is perhaps one of the most developed and interesting forms of pricing in world cotton markets.

The institutionalized design that structures the locations where trading practices produce the rehearsal price is made possible by determining the multiple boundaries of the market that belie the artificial binaries of market and nonmarket, public and private, economy and society. Chapter 3 showed that the exchange of cotton in Izmir takes place in a market process where, even in their immediate universe, locations of exchange are demarcated by multiple boundaries. Pit trading at the IME is framed by temporal and geographical limits, bringing together traders for only ten minutes, between 12:20 and 12:30 p.m. every weekday, in a circular structure called *korbey*.

It is in this temporal and spatial framework that the "theater of the market" takes place. In this theater, market agents produce rehearsal prices, a heterodox price form caught in the middle of the process of price realization. This price form assumes both prosthetic and actual character. It is prosthetic because its making is a simultaneous investment for trading, which takes place after traders cross the first boundary of the market in order to engage in postpit trading. However, the rehearsal price is also an actual price, because actual cotton is exchanged after its acceptance. This process of rehearsing the price draws on various trading performances which are affected by many factors, such as the perceived levels of demand and supply of cotton.

Once this first boundary of the market is crossed after leaving the pit at 12:30 p.m. sharp and entering the second location of the market, traders begin to use rehearsal prices as anchors that simultaneously set free and structure the movement of actual prices. Actual prices are realized during postpit trading, when traders are no longer required to trade in the pit. The dyadic encounters from which these scattered prices are made sprinkle the area between the walls of IME and the outer perimeter of the pit. This is where the hand of the market, which traders locate while rehearsing the price in the pit, is made invisible. The encounters are dyadic, and they have to be registered, but traders can make unregistered deals, too, because the market is now located in a unique temporal and spatial site of postpit trading that allows novel forms of visibility and invisibility.

Following the making of the actual prices, traders cross the second boundary of the market later in the day, around 2:00 p.m. These actual prices of postpit trading are scattered and unruly things, floating around the exchange. Another intervention brings order to this wild economy of things, giving birth to the market price of the IME. The Closing Price Committee of the Exchange comes together at the end of the postpit trading and draws another market boundary. Its members decide on the market price, deliberating, talking, discussing, contesting each other, and finally reaching a consensus. The posted market price of cotton in Izmir is this prosthetic price, on which traders living in later time zones will soon come to rely.

Chapter 3 argued that these three boundaries of the market—demarcating the limits between pit trading, postpit trading and price committee meeting—are not the only locations where markets are made. As a trader put it, even "the supply is determined" in strange market locations, like that of the Permanent Working Group on Cotton. The factors that affect the perceived reasons of price change are interpreted and represented by those who have a stake in their making, such as cooperatives and sales agents. It is also in meetings such as those convened by the working group that the perceptions of "what the market will be" are discussed and negotiated, and figures like those of supply or cost are produced.

However, not all traders in the world have the support of trading pits and multiple boundaries of the market; still, the market is made and its prices are nevertheless realized in settings that lack organized exchanges. These trading practices without institutionalized exchange also contribute to the making of global markets as derivative encounters of exchange. One of these mercantile geographies is Alexandria, Egypt.

Chapter 4 discussed the trading practices of Alexandrian merchants, who do not have an exchange building. The analysis of Egyptian cotton markets and the way in which global markets are made in their local sites of encounter in Egypt affirms the arguments of the previous chapters and carries them to another level. On one hand, the chapter demonstrated that the global market is a derivative possibility, not the actual mercantile encounter itself. Its making is derived by bringing together individual acts of trade, whether they take place in Alexandria or Izmir. The site of the global market is not geographical; it is documentary and technological, located in indices, reports, and market pictures.

On the other hand, an understanding of the making, unmaking, and remaking of Egypt's cotton market and the ways in which it has contributed to the making of global markets allows the historical setting of one of the major global experiments of economic restructuring to become visible. It was in Egypt that the world's first cotton futures market was opened in a colonial setting and then connected to other imperial trade regimes. Alexandria never was a periphery of the global market, even though its site emerged in the midst of war and destruction. The market was saved and developed by an imperial occupation force. Nasser's reversal of the colonial rule and his nationalization of the cotton trade brought an end to the influence of Alexandrian merchants vis-à-vis the farmers and the native power elite.

The introduction and institutionalization of neoliberal economic policies under Sadat and Mubarak, forged with the expertise of international financial institutions, aimed at reconstituting Egypt's centrality in world markets, by exploiting its competitive advantage. The reforms started out with agriculture. Their results were devastating, even from the vantage point of trading regimes. Egyptian cotton traders, all public, lost their clients one by one as free market reforms were implemented in the country. The reforms aimed at keeping Egypt's doors open to the world, hence their Egyptian name *infitah*. However, the more the doors were pushed open, the more Egypt lost ground in the world trade in its most competitive commodity, cotton.

The privatization of the cotton sector in 1994 forged a new regime of exchange in Alexandria. Private merchant houses instituted their dominance in trade within a few years and began to use their leverage in the regulatory body of the Egyptian cotton export sector, the Alexandria Cotton Exporters' Association (Alcotexa). Although a cotton exchange was opened, it has never been used. After all, traders know that what makes the price is not an exchange building, but their deliberative practices.

Chapter 4 discussed how the merchants of Alexandria come together every week in order to set the prosthetic price of the Egyptian market; however, they do not take this prosthetic price as an actual price as they govern their trade. This new price form is not rehearsed in a pit, but produced every Sunday by the Managing Committee of Alcotexa. Every week, the committee comes together and determines an index of minimum export prices for each variety and grade of cotton grown in Egypt. This price then becomes the minimum price of cotton for the following week.

The associate price of Alcotexa poses an interesting puzzle in understanding the realization of cotton prices in world markets. Alcotexa is not a government institution, but run by private merchants. The associate price is a tool that these private merchants use in order to empower their trading position in two ways. First, the associate price enables them to intercept the market process. The price is the beginning of trade, not its end result. Second, it provides private merchants with tools to increase their competitiveness vis-à-vis public companies, because public companies have to use the associate price as their minimum actual price. For private merchants it is only a prosthetic device. The status of private traders allows them to use it in a more neoliberal manner. Then, in Egypt, too, we see that cotton trade takes place in a market process where sites of exchange have multiple boundaries of formality and informality. These boundary-setting practices and their institutional sanctioning are technologies of power for those who can or cannot cross them.

After the associate price is realized through deliberations among traders, a new process of market exchange begins. The Egyptian traders' strength draws on the power of their mercantile platforms of capital, knowledge, and network. They need "arms" reaching all the way to the countryside in order to find the best cotton. Their regional offices provide these networks for them. At the same time, they also need to sustain networks abroad in order to be able to hold a rich client portfolio.

Still, this is not enough. Only a handful of people in the Egyptian trading companies can actually trade cotton. To be able to trade, one has to have experience in carrying out research and making the actual price. The trader's background is crucial for making actual prices. Traders should be experienced in bargaining, at all times ready to talk about prices, and in order to be able to accomplish this, they should be informed at all times. Traders also know that informing other traders is a way of affecting the market. One has to be selective and careful, and this requires much attention and everyday market work.

However, this world of cotton trade changes fundamentally as one moves the vantage point to a different location. Once seen from the farmers' perspective, these mercantile platforms undergo a metamorphosis and appear in ways that are invisible if one uses the vantage point of traders. Mercantile prostheses lose their meaning, relevance, and at times even their function. The "price" becomes something else, not easily fitting into the world of farmers. The ways in which relations of exchange and production are enmeshed take on a different form. The remaining two chapters of the book present an account of markets from the vantage point of cotton farmers.

THE RURAL FIELDS OF GLOBAL MARKETS

Chapters 5 and 6 presented an anthropological analysis of markets and their making on the ground, as approached from Turkish and Egyptian farmers' experiences in growing and exchanging cotton. Instead of looking at commodity circulation and price realization in global and local geographies of exchange, the book has chronicled how the cotton seeds started their life in three cotton-growing villages I call Pamukköy, 'Izbet Sabri, and Kafr Gaffar and then were sold at the end of the growing season as seed cotton by those who bring the crop to the market in Izmir, Alexandria and beyond. In other words, instead of following cotton bales and their prices as they circulate in the world, these final chapters of the book followed the stages of the cotton's growth from the field to the harvest, and finally to the buyer's warehouse.

These two chapters addressed the following central question: What is a (world) market as one observes it from the countryside? *Market Threads* has argued that it is from the relations in the countryside that the very condition of possibility for global markets emerges. The object of exchange—whose prosthetic, rehearsal, or actual prices were set among traders and market experts—is grown in villages like Pamukköy and Kafr Gaffar.

Rejecting the two hegemonic ways of approaching the countryside, either as an externality determined by structural forces such as world markets, or as a bounded geography that can only be understood by remaining within the imagined social boundaries of a village, chapters 5 and 6 argued that the growing and exchanging of cotton in villages and their vicinities are also construction sites of a global market field of cotton. These two chapters focused on two main activities that take place within these sites. First, I analyzed the dynamics that shape the growing of cotton until it is sold to merchants. Second, I analyzed the power dynamics that produce the context in which cotton changes hands in the countryside.

Not taking the boundaries of the countryside too seriously has made visible a rather surprising parallel between the farmers' and the merchants' ways of carrying out research in order to be successful in their respective professions. Most accounts of the way in which nonscientists carry out research in governing their activities draw on cases of concrete problem contexts, such as patient support groups. This book has shown that all agents of a world market, from global traders to farmers with small plots of land, depend on constantly carrying out research to increase their income and be successful.

In villages like Kafr Gaffar and Pamukköy, farmers experiment with various cotton-growing techniques and even reserve a few corners of their fields as laboratories. They constantly look for sources of information and test the validity of the information they gather by applying it in their fields. They also discuss the results among themselves and share their findings. As the chapters have made visible, most of the discussions that farmers have in coffee houses is based on this research in the wild. The *kahves* and *ahwas* serve as locations for exchanging information and cultivating expertise in cotton-growing.[1]

Traders and farmers are positioned between economic and natural forces. Their income is directly dependent on their understanding of the way in which natural and economic forces affect their lives. They study and understand these forces in ways different from those of economists and agricultural scientists. Economists and agricultural scientists have much in common. They both have a realist understanding of the object that constitutes their scientific fields. However, the mercantile and agricultural fields of traders and farmers cannot risk putting all of their eggs in the basket of realism. According to traders and farmers, their economic or natural environment is not a context merely engulfing their human agency. Nonhumans such as trees, cotton, insects, boll worms, and weeds have the capacity to affect their lives in various ways. Moreover, farmers and traders take into account different manifestations of agency, such as gossip or reports. When humans and nonhumans with divergent motivations encounter each other, many accidents and contingencies emerge.

According to the peasants of Pamukköy, Kafr Gaffar, and 'Izbet Sabri, the soil, the weather, and the sun change every year. In order to increase the yield, one has to recognize these changes and adapt accordingly. When considering how farmers carry out research in the wild, one is struck by the relativism in their conception of nature. Similarly to the merchants' refusal to impose a single logic of operation on markets, farmers shy away from locating a static externality surrounding them. Farmers adjust the timing of their entire work in the field according to the research they carry out. They even alter the content of the main processes of cotton cultivation according to this dynamic universe of which they are a part. Farmers' habitats are always changing; cotton cultivation is not a static limit surrounding their life.

Two methods of learning are used to make sense of this change: observation and discussion. All farmers carry out an incessant study of their fields and their habitat. They consult neighbors to test the validity of their observations. Furthermore, they compare their own conclusions

---

[1] For an excellent analysis on how farmers attend to the conditions of knowledge about agricultural production, see Aksoy (2005).

with those of other farmers in the open forum of the coffeehouses. For two main reasons, this constant research activity in the wild is not immediately visible to the experts who pass through the village. First, the ignorance of experts is fed by the ideological position manufactured to locate farmers as naturally born backward in the national order of things. Secondly, the experts, by and large, lack a language to translate the farmers' experiences, observations, and conclusions into their own language of science.

These two universes of research do not often communicate in the countryside. The right and capacity to speak the language of the other is usually granted to the schooled and cultured expert. Without exception, these experts talk to farmers as if they are not adults, using "simple" words in order to make them understand the complexity of what experts know. Another factor that explains such a failure of communication is the farmers' performance of the "powerless" and "passive" subjectivity assigned to them, so as to empower their positions vis-à-vis the people with whom they deal. Chapters 5 and 6 discussed examples of encounter where a farmer performs a weakness which he has been assigned, only to become a new person as he leaves the site where the encounter with the expert, trader, or government official has taken place.

Neither farmers nor traders blindly trust scientists. Their resistance, usually informed by everyday experience, leads them to heterogeneous ways of making sense of the conditions surrounding them. This conclusion calls for a radical rethinking of the ways in which scientists and non-scientists produce knowledge, as well as the way in which farmers are conceived as ignorant and undereducated country people who need the guidance of modern agricultural scientists. A cotton farmer needs the help of a modern agricultural scientist only as much as an international trader needs the help of a modern economist.

The Production and Exchange of Cotton

Chapters 5 and 6 discussed how the growth of cotton requires the forging of many forms of cooperative living among farmers, animals, plants, and their environment. *Berseem* and barley live longer in the field, allowing farmers to gain fodder for their cows and water buffalos, whose occasional death provides cash for the growth of cotton. Children are forced to pick cotton or wage a war against the cotton farmer's worst enemy, the cotton worm. As the cotton grows and comes closer to its death, farmers forge more coalitions to survive. They use complex mechanisms of labor exchange in their institutionalized or nonformal cooperatives, carrying out research in order to locate the best ways of growing cotton, testing their results, and discussing them in forums. These activities are performed simultaneously while the farmers wage a political struggle against the market reforms in order to subsist. Farmers struggle against pests, as well as new entrepreneurs who arrive with their bullies. The land, whether registered under their name or that of the new entrepreneur, becomes weak as the cotton plant feeds on the soil's nutrients. Farmers use fertilizers to give life back to the soil, but such activities require cash, a resource that most farmers lack. They borrow from traders who at the end of the growing season buy the cotton for less.

How can we account for the coexistence and mutuality of these two seemingly different worlds of trade and growth, exchange and production? One way is to appreciate the fact that the relations of exchange and production are simultaneous instances of the same relation of economization. The market does not just happen after the cotton is produced. Nor does the production terminate once the cotton is sold. These two moments of the same process continuously inform each other. In the world cotton market, one cannot analytically identify the relations of exchange and production as separate fields of encounter.

There is no moment in global market practices where one can identify a clear distinction between exchange and production. As we have seen in the first four chapters, merchants and traders have to produce an entire series of prices, knowledge, networks, and relations so as to be able to exchange cotton. In order to do so, traders and merchants work just as farmers do. However, the amount of work and the benefits they receive are not justly distributed in the world cotton market. One has to ask a different question: What exactly is the value of the trader's work when compared to that of the farmer? The political consequences of the answer are vast, partly explaining why merchants love to hear that they also create value, but are less willing to discuss whether they deserve to benefit from cotton production and exchange in proportion to their contribution to the processes of cotton's growth and exchange. Farmers are always willing to discuss both questions.

The market, as seen from the experience of cotton farmers, cannot be analytically located by imposing boundaries that attach categorically distinct logics of economic, scientific, social, or political encounter. At any stage of cotton's growth, one cannot locate a boundary that demarcates a pure logic of operation. This means neither that markets take place in cultural contexts, nor that they draw on encounters embedded in social relations. The seemingly separate worlds of culture versus the social or the economic, as well as the multiple interstices that connect them to each other in the form of political culture or social economy, are produced not by the interaction of farmers, workers, children, plants, cows, traders, and all other agents of relations of production and exchange, but by the researchers who assume independent spheres of life in the fields of struggle for a global market.

The patterns of the farmers' engagements defy any predetermined logic of encounter. It is possible to locate these activities neither as capitalist agricultural production, nor as subsistence-oriented cultivation, without privileging a vantage point and then making it the criterion for imposing a predetermined theoretical order of things. The farmers' cash-raising activities present a clear illustrative example of this situation, which locates farmers, much like traders in the new Memphis in Tennessee or the old Memphis in Egypt, in a simultaneous engagement within relations of production and exchange. In these relations, all actors of cotton growth and circulation deploy heterogeneous strategies of money-making or survival by constantly transgressing the invisible boundary between formality and informality.

THE MARKET FIELDS OF POWER

If farmers' and traders' lives cannot be located in mutually exclusive sites of exchange and production, how can we theorize their relationship in a new way? How are the making of prosthetic prices, the maintaining of markets, and the growing of cotton related? What does it mean to talk about the market as a power field? These questions bring us to the second set of conclusions that follow the analysis of the power dynamics that produce the context in which cotton changes hands in the countryside.

Prosthetic prices play a major role in the ways in which cotton is priced in Egypt and Turkey. However, the doors of the sites where these prostheses are manufactured are more open to traders than they are to farmers. Very few farmers in Egypt and Turkey follow the world prosthetic prices or the associate and rehearsal prices of Alexandria and Izmir. For a vast majority of cotton growers, market prostheses such as market prices do not mean much, for a number of reasons.

First, traders and their agents are not trusted in the countryside. They are considered money lenders. This presents an interesting contrast to the way in which regional traders, commissioners, and agents are perceived by international traders and farmers. As we saw in chapter 2, international merchants consider regional traders such as the ones who live in Izmir and Alexandria as their safety belts. Yet for the farmers these regional traders are not worthy of trust. The words "merchant" and "trader" are used in a pejorative manner in the countryside, much in the way in which urban neoliberal economists use the word "peasant" pejoratively in the singular.

In the countryside, traders are frequently thought to protect the yarn producers' and the merchants' interests. Farmers have solid reasons for their skepticism toward merchants' motivations: If the merchants depress the prices, they can buy more cotton and sell for less. Not only does the markup make a difference, but it is a fact that, when the cotton price is depressed, more and more yarn factories switch from cheap, oil-based polyester inputs to cotton—they buy more cotton and thus contribute more to the merchants' income. Finally, as the price decreases in the countryside, merchants need less capital to purchase the commodity; therefore, their carryover increases in real terms. Thus, any price associated with merchant houses or their organizations is regarded with suspicion, as another tool of the merchants to get their hands on the farmer's produce. The price is considered a mercantile tool in the countryside.

Second, whatever the price happens to be (price always "happens" in the countryside), a great majority of the cotton farmers are either locked into relations of debt with merchants, or pledged into selling their cotton to their cooperatives. The price is not "taken" in the countryside; it is accepted as long as it remains above the cost of growing cotton. This does not mean, however, that cotton growers have no effect on the making of prices in their multiple forms. The organized power of farmers under TARİŞ, the only cotton sales cooperative in the Söke Plain in Turkey, provides a force to counter the merchant interests that run against those of the farmers. The cotton price for a farmer is never the prosthetic prices posted by the market boards. As a farmer put it, "the price is what I carry in my pocket after I sell my crop,"

Moreover, market places where farmers sell their crop are hardly neutral sites of encounter. As chapters 5 and 6 have demonstrated, the traits of trading play a crucial formative role in the way in which prosthetic prices are translated into actual prices paid to farmers. Traders know their trade well. They are experienced in buying and selling. This is their occupation. They perform better, not only because they are more skilled, but also because their financial power backs them with a cushion in case they do not win the bargain. This is hardly the case for farmers of Pamukköy, ʿIzbet Sabri, and Kafr Gaffar. They cannot simply wander around the plain or the delta to find a buyer, show their samples, and expect to gain a good bargaining position. The amount of cotton that farmers hope to sell after long months in the field is very little when compared to the amount that traders buy everyday. Farmers are aware of such a discrepancy; yet knowing this does not help them. They have to sell their cotton quickly, for they do not have many options. They cannot have their cotton ginned and wait for the best opportunity to sell their commodity. Farmers enter into these locations of exchange from a location where they must spend all their available time growing cotton, killing insects, occasionally selling their cows to be slaughtered in order to continue growing cotton, hiring or pooling labor in informal cooperatives, hoeing their fields, or picking their cotton. Farmers do not have the time to carry out these two simultaneous forms of production in order to survive. They cannot maintain market platforms and grow cotton at the same time, for market exchange draws on concrete forms of production, performance, and maintenance.

Merchants also empower themselves by constantly complaining about the cotton quality and thus relatively increase their bargaining position. This natural negativity of traders sets the tone of the market place. Farmers bring their cotton to market places usually feeling nervous and meet these eternally unhappy people who buy their cotton almost unwillingly. While being a good farmer is one of the greatest sources of pride in the countryside, even the best farmers lose the war of morale in the market place. They are less experienced in deploying these technologies of making a price, as used by the actors of the market theaters, whether in Turkey or Egypt.

The relatively better-off farmers who do not find themselves entangled in the debt travel from the cotton field to the market place in a more advantageous position, only to encounter another field of struggle. Their cotton has to be translated into the language of the market by graders whose ways of translation change significantly as one moves from the public to the private sector. The invisible hand of the market hits the farmers the hardest in the private sector.

Still, it would be misleading to assume that cotton farmers are marginalized victims in a cruel world of market maintenance. The cotton growers who own land are locked into relations of exclusion also as the ones who exclude, for the child workers who pick their harvest can enjoy neither their hard work nor their childhood. They are the wretched of the cotton markets. Moreover, landless farmers and migrant or nonmigrant adult agricultural workers are categorically like the land-owning farmers of Pamukköy, Kafr Gaffar, and 'Izbet Sabri—locked in negotiations they cannot win.

Farmers strongly resist the downgrading of their cotton and have two means of resistance. Much like traders, they lobby and try to affect the stance of graders. Yet the very maintenance of carefully created hierarchies between "ignorant" farmers and "developed" others has concrete effects that contribute to the making of the price on the ground. Farmers do deploy technologies of price-making—such as lobbying, acting, performing, and bargaining—but always from a less advantageous position, since they belong to a "lower-grade" agency. It is important to consider how the farmers feel in the traders' offices in Turkey, or *halaqas* in Egypt. They encounter a power field the dynamics of which are maintained and produced to work against the interest of the farmers. "Things happen there," as a cotton grower put it in chapter 5. Farmers use three different ways to counteract the effects of this mercantile field. First, they lobby those who translate their produce into the language of the market. A performance of helplessness will slightly affect the conscience of the translation agents.

Second, farmers exert pressure by showing anger. Those who look down upon farmers tacitly assume that one should avoid the "wrath of the peasant." Since they are considered "irrational and violent actors who follow their emotions," the farmers' emotional responses limit the traders' choices and acts. "They would kill me," was the response of a grader mentioned in chapter 6 to the private company representative who wanted him to further downgrade the cotton. In both instances, farmers adopt, to a certain extent, an agency that is produced for them and exploit this subjectivity's ambiguous configuration to strengthen their relatively weaker agency. Third, farmers can threaten to withdraw their cotton from a certain market place. This is the most effective, yet the least frequently employed method to empower their position vis-à-vis the traders. This method cannot be employed often, because the great majority of farmers lack the resources to choose such an option.

Cotton growers also forge other innovative ways of resisting the problematic translation of their produce as well as the other technologies that traders use to push the floor price downward. Their success is limited, as neoliberal market reforms essentially work to empower private merchants. Even the formation of floor prices, as is the case in Egypt, works against the interests of farmers, transferring their wealth to the traders in two ways. First, the government's pricing prosthesis, the floor price, is a derivative of the associate price of the merchants of Alexandria, who follow the making of other prosthetic prices of the world, as they take shape in Izmir, New York, or Memphis. By letting mercantile interests dictate actual prices in *halaqa*s, the government protects merchants and provides them with a tool that they cannot produce together. The floor price makes it possible for farmers to produce the best cotton in the world, yet only survive under extremely difficult conditions of violence and suffering. Traders make more money as farmers produce better cotton. The rate of increase in the traders' income is higher than that of the farmers for every little increment of positive change in quality.

WHAT IS TO BE DONE WITH THE MARKET?

Market Threads opened with a simple question: What is a global market? By examining how the world cotton market is produced and maintained, it has presented a detailed analysis of the arrangements, calculative devices, power relations, and forces drawn on in the circulation and production of cotton. Starting with the question of price, the ultimate object of fascination of any study of market exchange, the book has examined the relations that make it possible to realize global, regional, and local prices. By following the circulation of cotton, I have chronicled the way in which two parallel routes of circulation are forged in the world. This analysis has made visible the invisible agents of markets and the way in which they maintain a global commodity market. Finally, this study has investigated how the object of the market is grown, examining the struggles of humans and nonhumans to control the massive power of a little plant, cotton.

The analysis of price realization in multiple sites of market encounter has demonstrated that "market price" is a deceptively simple term, too narrow to capture the specifics of the relations of power that underwrite the production of markets and their pricing prosthetics. The world market price of a physical commodity is a tool of trading, not the actual worth of the underlying commodity, even if one assumes that markets attach monetary value to actual things. The "market price" is a prosthetic device in all locations of the world's cotton markets. The realization of the price is informed not by anonymous, unmediated forces of supply and demand, but within the inherently political sites of encounter, whether in Izmir or Alexandria. Thus, the nature of the market price changes as its sites of construction change. Yet one crucial group of agents that contribute to the making of global commodities seems to be excluded from the very processes that realize the price: the farmers.

Can farmers contribute to the making of prosthetic prices and the maintenance of global markets? This question is not categorically different from asking whether traders can contribute to the growing of cotton. If every farmer could participate in the cotton market in the way in which cotton traders and merchants trade each day, there would be no farmers to grow cotton. Following and contributing to the price realization processes is a process of production itself. One has to contribute to them every day; attend to their maintenance as an active participant; produce reports; carry out research to locate the ways in which market forces are perceived; affect the perceptions by gossip, market reports, and meetings; and build platforms of knowledge, capital, and network. This is the everyday life of markets in their actual and derivative locations, such as the spots, futures, and options markets. The farmers of Pamukköy, Kafr Gaffar, and 'Izbet Sabri and a vast majority of farmers elsewhere cannot contribute directly to the realization of prosthetic prices and the making of markets around them, as they are maintained by merchants, experts, and the organized power of traders. Market prices belong to the world of the traders, merchants, brokers, and the large landowners who can afford to contribute to their realization. What is to be done with the markets?

The answer should not be to define another limit to these operations, but contribute to their making by, paradoxically, opening up markets a little more, expanding their processes of price realization to include those who are excluded from them, and not assuming that the latter have inherently negative or positive effects on the workings of society.

The first step of such a change in perspective, this book argues, requires a radical break from the prevailing understanding of markets in both political economy and economic sociology. Markets do not merely emerge as a relationship among self-interested buyers and sellers, governed by appropriate economic institutions. Nor are they to be understood as networks embedded in wider social structures. They are relations of power, maintained every day by constant interventions; the production of mercantile tools such as prosthetic, associate and rehearsal prices, and indices; and various forms of struggles among the actors that make a global market possible. In addition to these complex relations of power, each market is also shaped by its primary commodity's specific nature, its production, and agency. Markets are particular configurations of power whose workings cannot be understood by revealing a central logic of operation, for they have none. Thus, proposing free market reforms by setting prices free is not categorically different from proposing free society reforms by setting individuals free. Both of these logics share an absurdity and a level of abstraction hard to find in the workings of actual markets.

There is yet another option. Instead of proposing to help the market reach all domains of society, or searching for boundaries to curb the markets' expansion, researchers and policy-makers can imagine tools for forging novel openings in the ways in which market prostheses are realized. Researchers can contribute to the opening of markets by revealing the dynamics of the specific practices that realize their prices and maintain their routes of exchange. Farmers can contribute to the realization of market prosthetics through the deployment of the very mechanisms that are used by merchants and traders every day. This can be done only if an organized movement of farmers claims the worth of their crop by contributing to the struggles of market-making, not by staying away from them. For the very practice of trying to locate a boundary between society and market will work to strengthen specific market agents, such as international merchant houses.

Markets are the only fields of power in the world that simultaneously claim to be transparent and invisible. They will remain invisible and transparent if their study continues to be informed by various forms of realism that aim to maintain a correspondence between truths and realities. Yet, as *Market Threads* has shown, realism is not a *sine qua non* technology of power in the production of markets. A realist merchant is doomed to go bankrupt. We should leave the comfortable waters of realism, diligently protected by various scientific fields, and engage in new possibilities of encounter for imagining a better future, not only because traders, merchants, capitalists, and market experts have already left it, but also because a better future should be different from anything we have today.

 Glossary

THIS GLOSSARY CONTAINS THE main concepts and terms I refer to in the book. I drew on the glossary of MacKenzie (2006) for most of the definitions of financial terms. His definitions are marked with an asterisk. I thank him for allowing me to use them.

Actual price	The actual amount of money representing a set quantity of an actual physical commodity. It is also referred to as transaction price in a rather misleading way, because for any price to be an actual price it had to be transacted, but transaction may fail in international trade.
Associate price	A price form invented and performed by the Alexandria Cotton Exporters' Association (Alcotexa). It is simultaneously prosthetic and actual, for it is used by public companies as a tool to price actual commodities. It is also prosthetic because private companies use it as a tool to make other actual prices.
Bear*	A market in which prices fall; an investor who expects them to fall.
Black-Scholes formula*	The canonical option pricing model, based upon the assumption that the underlying stock price follows a log-normal random walk.
Broker*	A market participant who executes customer orders.
Bull*	A market in which prices rise; an investor who expects them to rise.
Call*	An option to buy.
Derivative*	A contract or security (such as a forward, future, option, or swap), the value of which depends upon the price of another "underlying" asset, or on the level of an index or interest rate.
Documentary circulation	The world of paperwork created and circulated for anything in the actual circulation

of commodities, from the price to the commodity itself.

Expiration*

The point in time when a derivatives contract such as an option ceases to be valid.

Future*

A standardized contract traded on an organized exchange in which one party undertakes to buy, and the other to sell, a set quantity of an asset of a particular type at a set price at a given point in time in the future. The term is also used for contracts which are equivalent economically to such future purchases and sales but which are settled by cash payments.

Hedge*

To eliminate or minimize a risk by entering into transactions that offset it, usually by reversing the position one takes in spot and reflecting in onto futures.

Korbey

Trading pit in Izmir Mercantile Exchange.

Long position*

A portfolio of an asset and/or derivative of that asset that will rise in value if the price of the asset rises.

Margin*

The deposit, normally adjusted daily, that a broker or clearinghouse requires from those who have bought or sold contracts (such as futures) traded on an exchange.

Agencement

The world of sociotechnical arrangements and their capacity to act and to give meaning to action.

Market price

A general price form that is prosthetic by nature unless it is prescribed as the actual worth of a physical commodity.

Maturity*

The date at which a bond's principal must be repaid; the date at which a derivative contract expires.

Open outcry*

A system of face-to-face trading within a fixed arena such as a pit, in which both buyers and sellers shout or hand-signal the prices (and quantities) at which they will buy or sell.

Option*

A contract the purchaser of which gains the right, but is not obliged, to buy (call) or to sell (put) an asset at a given price (the strike price or exercise price) on, or up to, a given future date (the expiration). The seller (or writer) of the option is obliged to fulfill his/her part of the contract if so demanded.

Pit*

The physical location (normally shaped as an amphitheater with stepped sides) of open-outcry trading.

Postpit trading

A temporal and spatial location of the cotton market in Izmir Mercantile Exchange market that is used after pit trading and before the end of the trading day.

Pricing prosthetics

A set of institutionally and scientifically authorized technologies and activities that produce tools of pricing.

Prosthetic price

A price form that does not represent the actual worth of an actual commodity, yet is used as a tool to attach a monetary value to an underlying commodity. Prosthetic prices are produced in the market, but not directly deployed by either buyer or seller in the actual exchange of commodities. All world prices of agricultural commodities, such as NYBOT cotton prices or Cotlook indices are prosthetic in nature.

Put*

An option to sell.

Rehearsal price

A price form invented and performed everyday at Izmir Mercantile Exchange. It is simultaneously prosthetic and actual, for it is both used as a tool to price actual commodities in postpit trading and taken as the actual price during the open-outcry trading in the pit.

Security*

A tradable financial instrument or asset, such as a stock, bond, future, or option.

Short position*

A portfolio of an asset and/or derivative of that asset that will rise in value if the price of the asset falls. A short position can, for example, be constructed by short-selling an asset.

Short selling*

A process in which a trader sells a security he or she does not yet own, or owns only temporarily. Short selling is often accomplished by finding an owner of the security who is prepared, for what is in effect a fee, to "lend" it to the trader: in other words to transfer ownership of it to the trader, who in turn undertakes to replace it. The trader who short sells may, for example, expect that the price of the security will have fallen by the time he or she has to replace it, so he or she can keep the difference in price (minus the fee).

Spot market

The market where the immediate ownership of physical commodities (such as cotton, oil, pork belly) is exchanged.

Strike price*

See option.

References

Abdel Aal, M. 2002. Agrarian Reform and Tenancy in Upper Egypt. In *Counter Revolution in Egypt's Countryside*, ed. R. Bush, 138–58. London and New York: Zed Books.

Abdel Aal, M., and S. Reem. 1999. *New Egyptian Land Reform*. Cairo: The American University in Cairo Press.

Abdel Salam, M. E. 1999. *The Egyptian Cotton: Production, Quality and Marketing*. Cairo: Cotton Research Institute.

Abou-Zeid, M.A.M. 1997. *Structural Adjustment and the Egyptian Farmer: Towards Increasing Rural Differentiation?* Cairo: American University in Cairo Press.

Aksoy, Z., (2005) *Conservation of Crop Genetic Diversity in Turkey: An Analysis of Linkages between Local, National and International Levels*. Amherst: University of Massachusetts Press.

Alexander, J., and P. Alexander. 1991. What Is in a Fair Price? Price Setting and Trading Partnership in Javanese Markets. *Man* 26:493–512.

Anonymous. 2002. *Cotton Outlook*.

Appadurai, A. 1986. *The Social Life of Things: Commodities in Cultural Perspective*. New York: Cambridge University Press.

Arensberg, C. 1957. Anthropology as History. In *Trade and Markets in the Early Empires: Economies in History and Theory*, ed. K. Polanyi, C. Arensberg, and H. W. Pearson, 97–113. New York: Free Press.

Aspers, P. 2005. *Markets in Fashion: A Phenomenological Approach*. New York: Routledge.

Austin, J. L. 1962. *How to Do Things with Words*. Cambridge: Harvard University Press.

Aydın, Z. 1986. *Underdevelopment and Rural Structures in Southeastern Turkey: The Household Economy in Gisgis and Kalhana*. London: Published for the Centre for Middle Eastern & Islamic Studies, University of Durham, by Ithaca Press.

Baffes, J. 2004a. *History of Cotton Futures Exchanges*. Washington DC: International Cotton Advisory Committee.

———. 2004b. *The History of Cotton Trade: From Origin to the Nineteenth Century*. Washington DC: The World Bank.

———. 2004c. *Cotton: Market Setting, Trade Policies, and Issues*. Washington DC: The World Bank Development Prospects Group.

Baffes, J., and I. Kaltsas. 2004. Cotton Futures Exchanges: Their Past, Their Present and Their Future. *Quarterly Journal of International Agriculture* 43:24.

Balassa, B. A. 1986. *Toward Renewed Economic Growth in Latin America*. Washington DC: Institute for International Economics.

Bank, T. W. 1993. *The Arab Republic of Egypt: An Agricultural Strategy for the 1990s*. Washington DC: World Bank.

Bank, W. 1988. *Adjustment Lending*. Washington DC: Country Economics Department.

Barry, A., T. Osborne, and N. Rose. 1993. Liberalism, Neoliberalism and Governmentality: Introduction. *Economy and Society* 22:265–66.

Bates, R. H. 1981. *Markets and States in Tropical Africa: The Political Basis of Agricultural Policies*. Berkeley: University of California Press.

Becker, G. S. 1976. *The Economic Approach to Human Behavior*. Chicago: University of Chicago Press.

Belshaw, C. S. 1965. *Traditional Exchange and Modern Markets*. Englewood Cliffs, NJ: Prentice-Hall.

Bernstein, H. 1977. *Capital and Peasantry in the Epoch of Imperialism*. [Dar es Salaam]: Economic Research Bureau, University of Dar es Salaam.

Bernstein, H., T. Brass, and T. J. Byres. 1994. *The Journal of Peasant Studies: A Twenty Volume Index, 1973–1993*. Ilford, Portland: F. Cass.

Beunza, D., and D. Stark. 2004. Tools of the Trade: The Socio-Technology of Arbitrage in a Wall Street Trading Room. *Industrial and Corporate Change* 13:369–401.

Bohannan, P., and G. Dalton. 1962. *Markets in Africa*. [Evanston, IL]: Northwestern University Press.

———. 1965. *Markets in Africa: Eight Subsistence Economies in Transition, A New Selection*. Garden City: Anchor Books.

Brigg, M. 2001. Empowering NGOs: The Microcredit Movement through Foucault's Notion of Dispositif. *Alternatives* 26:26.

Bromley, S., and R. Bush. 1994. Adjustment in Egypt? The Political Economy of Reform. *Review of African Political Economy* 60:201–13.

Burling, R. 1968. Maximization Theories and the Study of Economic Anthropology. In *Economic Anthropology: Readings in Theory and Analysis*, ed. E. E. LeClair and H. K. Schneider, 168–87. New York: Rinehart and Winston.

Bush, R. 1999. *Economic Crisis and the Politics of Reform in Egypt*. Boulder, CO: Westview Press.

Bush R., ed. 2002. *Counter-Revolution in Egypt's Countryside: Land and Farmers in the Era of Economic Reform*. London, New York: Zed Books.

Çalışkan, K. 2003. Price Realization in World Markets: The Prosthetic and Actual Worth of a Bale of Cotton. Paper presented at Economies at Large Conference, 14–15 November, New York University.

———. 2005. *Making a Global Commodity: The Production of Markets and Cotton in Egypt, Turkey, and the United States*. New York: New York University Press.

Çalışkan, K., and M. Callon. 2005. New and Old Directions in the Anthropology of Markets. Paper presented at New Directions in the Anthropology of Markets Workshop, 9 April 2005, Wenner-Gren Foundation for Anthropological Research, New York City.

———. 2009. Economization, Part 1: Shifting Attention from the Economy towards Processes of Economization, *Economy and Society*, 38:369–98.

Callon, M. 2002. No Innovating Markets without Innovating Social Policies: From Prosthetic Policies to Habilitation Policies. *Innovating Markets*. London: London School of Economics.

———. 2003. The Increasing Involvement of Concerned Groups in R&D Policies: What Lessons for Public Powers? In *Science and Innovation: Rethinking the Rationales for Funding and Governance*, ed. A. Geuna, A. J. Salter, and W. E. Steinmueller, 30–68. Northampton, UK: Edward Elgar.

Callon, M., ed. 1998. *The Laws of the Markets*. London: Blackwell.

Callon, M., P. Lascoumes, and Y. Barthe 2001. *Agir dans un monde incertain: Essai sur la démocratie technique*. Paris: Le Seuil.

Callon, M., and F. Muniesa. 2003. Economic Markets as Collective Calculating Devices. *Reseaux* 21:189–233.

Callon, M., and V. Rabeharisoa. 2003. Research in the Wild and the Shaping of New Social Identities. *Technology in Society* 25:193–204.

Callon, M., Y. Millo, and F. Muniesa 2007. *Market Devices*. Malden, UK: Blackwell Publishers.

Cancian, F. 1968. Maximization as a Norm, Strategy, and Theory. In *Economic Anthropology: Readings in Theory and Analysis*, ed. E. E. LeClair and H. K. Schneider, 228–33. New York: Rinehart and Winston.

Carruthers, B. G., and A. L. Stinchcombe. 1999. The Social Structure of Liquidity: Flexibility, Markets, and States. *Theory and Society* 28:353–382.

Chaudhry, K. A. 1993. The Myth of the Market and the Common History of Late Development. *Politics and Society* 21:245–74.

Chayanov, A. V. 1966. *The Theory of Peasant Economy*. Homewood: Published for the American Economic Association by R. D. Irwin.

Chiffoleau, Y., and C. Laporte. 2004. La formation des prix: Le marché des vins en Bourgogne. *Revue Française de Sociologie* 45:653–80.

Clifford, J., and G. E. Marcus, eds. 1986. *Writing Culture: The Poetics and Politics of Ethnography: A School of American Research Advanced Seminar*. Berkeley: University of California Press.

Coase, R. 1937. The Nature of the Firm. *Economica* 4:386–405.

Cochoy, F., ed. 2004. *La Captation Des Publics: C'est Pour Mieux Te Séduire Mon Client*. Toulouse: Presses Universitaires du Mirail.

Cook, S. 1968. The Obsolete Anti-Market Mentality: A Critique of the Substantive Approach to Economic Anthropology. In *Economic Anthropology: Readings in Theory and Analysis*, ed. E. E. LeClair and H. K. Schneider. New York, Rinehart and Winston.

Cournot, A. A. 1897. *Researches into the Mathematical Principles of the Theory of Wealth*. New York: Macmillan.

Cox, A. W. 2002. *Supply Chains, Markets and Power: Mapping Buyer and Supplier Power Regimes*. London, New York: Routledge.

Dalton, G. 1971. *Studies in Economic Anthropology*. Washington: American Anthropological Association.

Dana, L. P. 2000. *Economies of the Eastern Mediterranean Region: Economic Miracles in the Making*. Singapore, River Edge, NJ: World Scientific.

Daviron, B., and P. Gibbon, eds. 2002. A Special Issue: Global Commodity Chains and African Export Agriculture. *Journal of Agrarian Change* 2.

Derman, E. 2004. *My Life as a Quant: Reflections on Physics and Finance*. New York: Wiley, John & Sons.

De Soto, H. 1989. *The Other Path: The Invisible Revolution in the Third World.* New York: Harper & Row.

Desrosieres, A. 2001. How Real Are Statistics? *Social Research* 68:339–55.

Dilley, R. 1992. *Contesting Markets: Analyses of Ideology, Discourse and Practice.* Edinburgh: Edinburgh University Press.

DiMaggio, P., and H. Louch. 1998. Socially Embedded Consumer Transactions: For What Kinds of Purchases Do People Most Often Use Networks. *American Sociological Review* 63:619–37.

Dobbin, F., ed. 2004. *The Sociology of the Economy.* New York: Russell Sage.

Duina, F. 2004. Regional Market Building as a Social Process: An Analysis of Cognitive Strategies in NAFTA, the European Union and Mercosur. *Economy and Society* 33:359–89.

Elyachar, J. 1999. *Egyptian Workshop, Global Enterprise: Visions of Economy and Urban Life in Cairo, 1900–1996.* Cambridge: Harvard University Press.

———. 2003. Mappings of Power: The State, NGOs, and International Organizations in the Informal Economy of Cairo. *Comparative Studies in Society and History* 45:571–605.

Ensminger, J. 1992. *Making a Market: The Institutional Transformation of an African Society.* Cambridge, New York: Cambridge University Press.

Epstein, T. S. 1968. *Capitalism, Primitive and Modern: Some Aspects of Tolai Economic Growth.* [East Lansing]: Michigan State University Press.

Farnie, D. A. 2004. The Role of Merchants as Prime Movers in the Expansion of the Cotton Industry: 1760–1990. In *The Fibre That Changed the World: The Cotton Industry in International Perspective, 1600–1990s*, ed. D. A. Farnie and D. J. Jeremy, 15–55. Oxford: Oxford University Press.

Farnie, D. A., and D. J. Jeremy, eds. 2004. *The Fibre That Changed the World: The Cotton Industry in International Perspective, 1600–1990s.* Oxford: Oxford University Press.

Fawcett, H., and M.M.H.F. Fawcett. 1907. *Manual of Political Economy.* London, New York: Macmillan.

Fergany, M. 2002. Poverty and Unemployment in Rural Egypt. In *Counter Revolution in Egypt's Countryside*, ed. R. Bush, 211–32. London, New York: Zed Books.

Ferguson, J. 1988. Cultural Exchange: New Developments in the Anthropology of Commodities. *Cultural Anthropology* 3:488–513.

Fine, B. 2002. *The World of Consumption: The Material and Cultural Revisited.* London, New York: Routledge.

Fine, B., and E. Leopold. 1993. *The World of Consumption.* London, New York: Routledge.

Firth, R. W. 1929. *Primitive Economics of the New Zealand Maori.* New York: E. P. Dutton and Company.

———. 1939. *Primitive Polynesian Economy.* London: G. Routledge & Sons.

Fligstein, N. 1996. Markets as Politics: A Political-Cultural Approach to Market Institutions. *American Sociological Review* 61:18.

Foucault, M., and C. Gordon. 1980. *Power/Knowledge: Selected Interviews and Other Writings, 1972–1977.* New York: Pantheon Books.

Friedland, R., and A. F. Robertson. 1990. *Beyond the Marketplace: Rethinking Economy and Society.* New York: Aldine de Gruyter.

Garside, A. H. 1935. *Cotton Goes to Market: A Graphic Description of a Great Industry.* New York: Frederick A. Stokes Company.

Geismar, H. 2001. What's in a Price? An Ethnography of Tribal Art at Auction. *Journal of Material Culture* 6:25–47.

Gereffi, G., and M. Korzeniewicz. 1994. *Commodity Chains and Global Capitalism.* Westport, CT: Greenwood Press.

Gibson-Graham, J. K. 1996. *The End of Capitalism (As We Knew It): A Feminist Critique of Political Economy.* Cambridge, Oxford: Blackwell Publishers.

Goldberg, J. 1988. *Anatomy of a Scientific Discovery.* New York: Bentham Books.

Grandclément, C. 2004. Bundles of Prices: Marketing and Pricing in French Supermarkets. Paper presented at the 4S-EASST Conference, August 25–28, 2004, Paris.

Granovetter, M. 1985. Economic-Action and Social-Structure: The Problem of Embeddedness. *American Journal of Sociology* 91:481–510.

Granovetter, M., and P. McGuire. 1998. The Making of an Industry: Electricity in the United States. In *The Laws of the Markets*, ed. M. Callon, 147–73. Oxford: Blackwell Publishers.

Gudeman, S. 1986. *Economics as Culture: Models and Metaphors of Livelihood.* London, Boston: Routledge & K. Paul.

Guyer, J. I. 2004. *Marginal Gains: Monetary Transactions in Atlantic Africa.* Chicago: University of Chicago Press.

Haddad, L., and A. Ahmed. 2000. *Avoiding Chronic and Transitory Poverty: Evidence from Egypt, 1997–1999.* Washington DC: International Food Policy Research Institute.

Halperin, R. H., and J. Dow. 1977. *Peasant Livelihood: Studies in Economic Anthropology and Cultural Ecology.* New York: St. Martin's Press.

Haraway, D. J. 1991. *Simians, Cyborgs, and Women: The Reinvention of Nature.* New York: Routledge.

Harriss-White, B. 2008. *Rural Commercial Capital: Agricultural Markets in West Bengal.* New Delhi: Oxford University Press.

von Hayek, F. A. 1986. The Moral Imperative of the Market. In *The Unfinished Agenda: Essays on the Political Economy of Government Policy in Honour of Arthur Seldon*, ed. M. J. Anderson, 143–49. London: The Institute of Economic Affairs.

Hicks, J. R. 1939. *Value and Capital: An Inquiry into Some Fundamental Principles of Economic Theory.* Oxford: Clarendon Press.

Hobsbawm, E. J. 1975. *The Age of Capital, 1848–1875.* New York: Scribner.

Hugill, P. J. 1999. *Global Communications since 1844: Geopolitics and Technology.* Baltimore: Johns Hopkins University Press.

IMF. 1998. *Egypt: Beyond Stabilization, Towards a Dynamic Market Economy.* Washington DC: International Monetary Fund.

ITB. [n.d.]. *Ticaret Borsaları ve İzmir Ticaret Borsası.* İzmir: İzmir Ticaret Borsası.

———. 1996. *İzmir Ticaret Borsası Albümü.* İzmir: İzmir Ticaret Borsası.

Johnson, L. L. 1960. The Theory of Hedging and Speculation in Commodity Futures. *Review of Economic Studies* 27:139–51.

Kaplan, D. 1968. The Formal-Substantivist Controversy in Economic Anthropology: Some Reflections on Its Wider Implications. *Southwestern Journal of Anthropology* 24:228–47.

Keane, W. 2001. Money Is No Object: Materiality, Desire, and Modernity in an Indonesian Society. In *The Empire of Things: Regimes of Values and Material Cultures*, ed. F. R. Myers, 65–90. Oxford: SAR Press.

Keynes, J. M. 1936. *The General Theory of Employment, Interest and Money.* New York: Harcourt Brace and Company.

Knorr Cetina, K., and U. Brugger. 2002. Traders' Engagement with Markets: A Postsocial Relationship. *Theory, Culture & Society* 19:161–85.

Koptiuch, K. 1999. *A Poetics of Political Economy in Egypt.* Minneapolis: University of Minnesota Press.

Krenz, R., and J. Holtzman, 2001. *Policy Lessons from the 2000–2001 Cotton Marketing Season in Egypt.* Cairo: Government of Egypt, Ministry of Agriculture and Land Reclamation, USAID.

Lapavitsas, C. 2004. Commodities and Gifts: Why Commodities Represent More Than Market Relations. *Science & Society* 68:33–56.

Latour, B. 1999. *Pandora's Hope: Essays on the Reality of Science Studies.* Cambridge: Harvard University Press.

LCHR. 2002. Farmer Struggles against Law 96 of 1992, Land Center for Human Rights. In *Counter Revolution in Egypt's Countryside*, ed. R. Bush, 126–38. London, New York: Zed Books.

———. 2005. *Women, Land and Violence in the Egyptian Countryside.* Cairo: Land Center for Human Rights.

Le Velly, R. 2002. "Embeddedness": A Sociological Theory of Market Transactions. *Sociologie du travail* 44:37–53.

LeClair, E. E., and H. K. Schneider, 1968. *Economic Anthropology: Readings in Theory and Analysis.* New York: Holt.

Lee, B., and E. LiPuma. 2002. Cultures of Circulation: The Imaginations of Modernity. *Public Culture* 14:191–213.

Lepinay, V.-A. 2003. *Les formules du marche: Ethnoeconomie d'une innovation financiere: Les produits a capital garanti.* Paris: Ecole des Mines de Paris.

Levin, P. 2004. *Engendering Markets: Technology and Institutional Change in Financial Futures Trading.* Evanston, IL: Northwestern University.

Leys, C. 1996. *The Rise & Fall of Development Theory.* Bloomington: Indiana University Press.

Lie, J. 1997. Sociology of Markets. *Annual Review of Sociology* 23:20.

MacKenzie, D. 2004. The Big, Bad Wolf and the Rational Market: Portfolio Insurance, the 1987 Crash and the Performativity of Economics. *Economy and Society* 33:303–34.

———. 2006. *An Engine, Not a Camera: Financial Models Shape Markets.* Cambridge: MIT Press.

MacKenzie, D. A., F. Muniesa, and L. Siu 2007. *Do Economists Make Markets? On the Performativity of Economics.* Princeton, NJ: Princeton University Press.

MacKinnon, D. 2000. Managerialism, Governmentality and the State: A Neo-Foucauldian Approach to Local Economic Governance. *Political Geography* 19:293–314.

Malinowski, B. 1922. *Argonauts of the Western Pacific*. London: G. Routledge & Sons.

Marcus, G. E. 1998. *Ethnography through Thick and Thin*. Princeton, NJ: Princeton University Press.

Marshall, A. 1982. *Principles of Economics: An Introductory Volume*. Philadelphia: Porcupine Press.

Martin, E. 1994. *Flexible Bodies: Tracking Immunity in American Culture from the Days of Polio to the Age of Aids*. Boston: Beacon Press.

Marx, K. 1995. *Capital: An Abridged Edition*. Oxford, New York: Oxford University Press.

Maurer, B. 2002. Repressed Futures: Financial Derivatives' Theological Unconscious. *Economy and Society* 31:15–36.

Mauss, M. 1954. *The Gift: Forms and Functions of Exchange in Archaic Societies*. Glencoe, IL: Free Press.

Miller, D. 2001. Alienable Gifts and Inalienable Commodities. In *The Empire of Things: Regimes of Values and Material Cultures*, ed. F. R. Myers, 91–115. Oxford: SAR Press.

Mintz, S. W. 1985. *Sweetness and Power: The Place of Sugar in Modern History*. New York: Viking.

Mitchell, T. 1990. The Invention and Reinvention of the Egyptian Peasant. *International Journal of Middle East Studies* 22:129–50.

———. 1998. Fixing the Economy. *Cultural Studies* 12:82–101.

———. 2002. *Rule of Experts: Egypt, Techno-Politics, Modernity*. Berkeley: University of California Press.

Muniesa, F. 2000. Performing Prices: The Case of Price Discovery Automation in the Financial Markets. In *Oekonomie und Gesellschaft*, ed. H. Kalthoff, R. Rottenburg, and H.-J. Wagener, 289–312. Marburg: Metropolis.

———. 2003. *Des marches comme algorithmes: Sociologie de la cotation electronique a la bourse de Paris*. Paris: Ecole des Mines.

Munn, N. 1986. *The Fame of Gawa: A Symbolic Study of Value Transformation*. Cambridge: Cambridge University Press.

Myers, F. 1992. Representing Culture: The Production of Discourse(s) for Aboriginal Acrylic Paintings. In *Rereading Cultural Anthropology*, ed. G. Marcus, 319–55. Durham, NC: Duke University Press.

Myers, F., ed. 2001. *The Empire of Things: Regimes of Values and Material Cultures*. Oxford: SAR Press.

North, D. 1977. Markets and Other Allocation Systems in History: The Challenge of Karl Polanyi. *Journal of European Economic History* 6:703–16.

Odirici, V., and R. Corrado. 2004. Between Supply and Demand: Intermediaries, Social Networks and the Construction of Quality in the Italian Wine Industry. *Journal of Management and Governance* 8:149–71.

Öniş, Z. 1998. *State and Market: Political Economy of Turkey*. Istanbul: Boğaziçi University Press.

Osborne, T., and N. Rose. 1999. Do the Social Sciences Create Phenomena? The Example of Public Opinion Research. *British Journal of Sociology* 50:367–96.

Owen, R. 1969. *Cotton and the Egyptian Economy, 1820–1914: A Study in Trade and Development*. Oxford: Clarendon Press.

Özüdoğru, T. 2006. *Pamuk Durum ve Tahmin 2006–2007*. Ankara: Tarımsal Ekonomi Araştırma Enstitüsü.

Pietrobelli, C., and A. Sverrisson. 2003. *Linking Local and Global Economies: The Ties That Bind*. New York: Routledge.

Podolny, J. M. 2001. Networks as the Pipes and Prisms of the Market. *The American Journal of Sociology* 107:28.

Polanyi, K. 1944. *The Great Transformation*. New York, Toronto: Farrar & Rinehart.

———. 1957. *Trade and Market in the Early Empires: Economies in History and Theory*. Glencoe: Free Press.

Raikes, P., M. F. Jensen, and S. Ponte.2000. Global Commodity Chain Analysis and the French Filiere Approach: Comparison and Critique. *Economy and Society* 29:390–417.

Richards, A. 1995. Economic Pressures for Accountable Governance in the Middle East. In *Civil Society in the Middle East*, ed. A. R. Norton, 55–78. Leiden, New York: E. J. Brill.

Robinson, J. 1980. *Collected Economic Papers*. Cambridge: MIT Press.

Rose, N. 2000. Government and Control. *British Journal of Criminology* 40:321–39.

———. 2001. The Politics of Life Itself. *Theory, Culture & Society* 18:1–30.

Saad, R. 2002. Egyptian Politics and Tenancy Reform. In *Counter-Revolution in Egypt's Countryside: Land and Farmers in the Era of Economic Reform*, ed. R. Bush, 103–25. London, New York: Zed Books.

Sahlins, M. D. 1972. *Stone Age Economics*. Chicago: Aldine-Atherton.

Salisbury, R. F. 1962. *From Stone to Steel: Economic Consequences of a Technological Change in New Guinea*. [Victoria]: Melbourne University Press on behalf of the Australian National University.

Schneider, H. K. 1974. *Economic Man: The Anthropology of Economics*. New York: Free Press.

Seligman, C. G., and F. R. Barton. 1910. *The Melanesians of British New Guinea*. Cambridge: The University Press.

Sheridan, R. B., and R. B. Heath. 1984. *The School for Scandal*. Harlow, UK: Longman.

Simmel, G. 1978. *The Philosophy of Money*. London, Boston: Routledge & Kegan Paul.

Sirman, N. A. 1988. Peasants and Family Farms: The Position of Households in Cotton Production in a Village of Western Turkey. Dissertation, Department of Anthropolgy, University College, London, 419.

Skov, L. 2005. The Return of the Fur Coat: A Commodity Chain Perspective. *Current Sociology* 53:9–32.

Smith, C. W. 1981. *The Mind of the Market: A Study of Stock Market Philosophies, Their Uses, and Their Implications*. Totowa, NJ: Rowman and Littlefield.

Smith, C. W., and J. T. Cothren. 1999. *Cotton: Origin, History, Technology, and Production*. New York: John Wiley.

Stern, S. 2004. Memoirs of a Physicist in Wall Street. *Financial Times*, 18 November 2004.

Strathern, M. 1988. *The Gender of the Gift: Problems with Women and Problems with Society in Melanesia*. Berkeley: University of California Press.

Swedberg, R. 1990. International Financial Networks and Institutions. *Current Sociology* 38:259–81.

———. 1997. New Economic Sociology: What Has Been Accomplished, What Is Ahead? *Acta Sociologica* 40:161–82.

Swetnam, J. 1973. Oligopolistic Prices in a Free Market: Antugua Guatemala. *American Anthropologist* 75:1504–10.

Telser, L. G. 1958. Futures Trading and the Storage of Cotton and Wheat. *The Journal of Political Economy* 66:233–55.

Thomas, N. 1991. *Entangled Objects: Exchange, Material Culture, and Colonialism in the Pacific*. Cambridge: Harvard University Press.

Thompson, G. 1991. *Markets, Hierarchies, and Networks: The Coordination of Social Life*. London, Newbury Park: Sage Publications.

Toth, J. 1999. *Rural Labor Movements in Egypt and Their Impact on the State, 1961–1992*. Gainesville: University Press of Florida.

Toth, J., and J. Elyachar. 2001. Book Reviews: Rural Labor Movements in Egypt and Their Impact on the State, 1961–1992. *American Ethnologist* 28:1.

Tribe, K. 1981. *Genealogies of Capitalism*. Atlantic Highlands, NJ: Humanities Press.

Uzzi, B. 1996. The Sources and Consequences of Embeddedness for the Economic Performance of Organizations: The Network Effect. *American Sociological Review* 61:25.

Uzzi, B., and R. Lancaster. 2004. Embeddedness and Price Formation in the Corporate Law Market. *American Sociological Review* 69:26.

Varian, H. R. 2002. *Intermediate Economics: A Modern Approach*. New York: W.W. Norton and Company.

Velthuis, O. 2003. Symbolic Meanings of Prices: Constructing the Value of Contemporary Art in Amsterdam and New York Galleries. *Theory and Society* 32:181–215.

Wade, R. 1988. *Village Republics: Economic Conditions for Collective Action in South India*. Cambridge, New York: Cambridge University Press.

Wallerstein, I., and T. Hopkins. 2000. Commodity Chains in the World Economy Prior to 1800. In *The Essential Wallerstein*, 221–33. New York: The New Press.

Weiner, A. 1992. *Inalienable Possessions: The Paradox of Keeping-While-Giving*. Los Angeles: University of California Press.

Wells, M. J. 1996. *Strawberry Fields: Politics, Class, and Work in California Agriculture*. Ithaca, NY: Cornell University Press.

Williams, J. 1986. *The Economic Function of Futures Markets*. Cambridge, New York: Cambridge University Press.

Williamson, O. E. 1975. *Markets and Hierarchies, Analysis and Antitrust Implications: A Study in the Economics of Internal Organization*. New York: Free Press.

Working, H. 1949. The Theory of Price Storage. *The American Economic Review* 39:1254–62.

World Bank. 2001. *The Arab Republic of Egypt: Toward Agricultural Competitiveness in the 21st Century, An Agricultural Export-Oriented Strategy*. Washington DC: World Bank.

Zajac, E. J., and J. D. Westphal. 2004. The Social Construction of Market Value: Institutionalization and Learning Perspectives on Stock Market Reactions. *American Sociological Review* 69:433–57.

Zaloom, C. 2003. Resources and Their Ambiguities—Ambiguous Numbers: Trading Technologies and Interpretation in Financial Markets. *American Ethnologist* 30:15.

Zelizer, V.A.R. 1994. *The Social Meaning of Money*. New York: Basic Books.

Index